Speaking Our Selves

Speaking Our Selves

New Plays by African Women

Edited by Asiimwe Deborah Kawe and Robert H. Vorlicky

Foreword by Esi Sutherland-Addy

University of Michigan Press ANN ARBOR

Copyright © 2025 by Asiimwe Deborah Kawe and Robert H. Vorlicky
Some rights reserved

This work is licensed under a Creative Commons Attribution-NonCommercial-NoDerivatives 4.0 International License. *Note to users:* A Creative Commons license is only valid when it is applied by the person or entity that holds rights to the licensed work. Works may contain components (e.g., photographs, illustrations, or quotations) to which the rightsholder in the work cannot apply the license. It is ultimately your responsibility to independently evaluate the copyright status of any work or component part of a work you use, in light of your intended use. To view a copy of this license, visit http://creativecommons.org/licenses/by-nc-nd/4.0/

For questions or permissions, please contact um.press.perms@umich.edu

Published in the United States of America by the
University of Michigan Press
First published March 2025

A CIP catalog record for this book is available from the British Library.

Library of Congress Cataloging-in-Publication data has been applied for.

ISBN 978-0-472-07721-2 (hardcover : alk. paper)
ISBN 978-0-472-05721-4 (paper : alk. paper)
ISBN 978-0-472-90483-9 (open access ebook)

DOI: https://doi.org/10.3998/mpub.12827650

The University of Michigan Press's open access publishing program is made possible thanks to additional funding from the University of Michigan Office of the Provost and the generous support of contributing libraries.

The publication of the open access edition of this book was made possible with support from The Herbert A. and Bessie W. Kenyon Dramatic Library.

Authorized Representative: Easy Access System Europe, Mustamäe tee 50, 10621 Tallinn, Estonia, gpsr.requests@easproject.com

Cover art:
Liberal Women Protest March (Part 2)
Nike Davies-Okundaye, born 1951, Nigeria
Mixed media finished with acrylic on canvas
H x W: 147.3 x 228.6 cm (58 x 90 in.)
2012-14-1
© 1995 Nike Davies-Okundaye
Gift of Ambassador Robin Renee Sanders in honor of the artist Chief Nike Okundaye
Photograph by Franko Khoury
National Museum of African Art
Smithsonian Institution

Contents

Editors' Note — vii

Foreword by Esi Sutherland-Addy (Ghana) — xvii

PLAYS

Us, Too, We're People by Celma Costa (Mozambique) — 3

Tafé Fanga: Le pouvoir du pagne? by Jeanne Diama (Mali),
translated from the French by Judith G. Miller (USA) as *Tafé Fanga:
The Power of the Wrapper?* — 15

Cooking Oil by Asiimwe Deborah Kawe (Uganda) — 43

Nguzo Mama by Penina Muhando (Tanzania), translated from the
Kiswahili by Joshua Williams (USA) as *The Pillar of Motherhood* — 95

Le Roi Est Mort, Vive la Reine by Claudia Munyengabe (Burundi),
translated from the French and the Kirundi by Rivardo Niyónīzígiye
(Burundi) as *The King Is Dead, Long Live the Queen* — 143

Green Chilli by Alaa Taha (Sudan) — 167

Desperate to Fight by Meaza Worku (Ethiopia) — 207

Course Aux Noces by Nathalie Hounvo Yekpe (Benin),
translated from the French by Judith G. Miller (USA)
as *The Race to Get Married* — 225

Other Contributors — 257

Acknowledgments — 263

Digital materials related to this title can be found on the Fulcrum platform
via the following citable URL: https://doi.org/10.3998/mpub.12827650.

Editors' Note

The origin of this anthology resides in Uganda, November 2015. At the time, I, Asiimwe, was (and remain) the Artistic Director of the Kampala International Theatre Festival (KITF). And I, Robert, was attending the Ugandan festival with students in my "African Women Playwrights" course at New York University Abu Dhabi (NYUAD); it would be my first of several future trips to the festival. No one could have imagined that from shared moments among global theater practitioners at KITF and a global student body from NYUAD, a professional collaboration between us would arise to address the paucity of representation of African women playwrights in print. This scarcity was distinguished by the large number of African countries with very few, and in some cases, no women playwrights in print, and, as we'd discover, their absence in English-language anthologies.

After several years of curating and producing (Asiimwe) and watching plays, listening to readings of plays by international writers, many of whom were women (Robert), both of us teaching and talking among students, artists, local patrons, and attending and participating on panels with practitioners from all over the world—many of whom were from Africa—a refrain arose that we wanted to address more comprehensively and pro-actively: What happens to plays by African women after they've been workshopped, read before the public (rarely in their entirety), and occasionally performed? In this case, for instance, what becomes the life of the play after a festival? Why is it so difficult for women's (and some men's) plays to reach broader audiences through future productions, let alone in print publications, particularly if their home base is not in the African diaspora?

Prior to the devastating Covid-19 pandemic, we undertook a grassroots effort to identify women playwrights, living in Africa, from countries that were underrepresented amid the nascent, yet encouraging, pioneering English-language anthologies of plays by African women.[1] Responses to our personal outreach were truly encouraging, as letter campaigns, phone calls, meet-and-greet at festivals, and recommendations through word-of-mouth brought women artists from across the continent to our attention. Our desire to read a diversity of plays by women writers across Africa was transpiring as was the possibility for creating this anthology.

Out of necessity, priorities shifted globally—personally and professionally—with the onslaught of Covid-19 in early 2020. While many theater-makers turned to virtual platforms to continue to make art, others were unable to work creatively or chose not to in response to the crisis. Our grassroots efforts with this anthology were put on hold during Covid-19, as the two of us found ourselves in isolation with conflicting responsibilities, including long stretches of time not in our home countries. This book project was revitalized during Summer 2022. With its renewal, the initial plays identified to pursue for publication were still of interest, along with several new titles that arose from the post-pandemic re-emergence of theater festivals and the ever-productive channels of word-of-mouth. As editors, we have benefitted greatly from collective grassroots efforts since our initial conversations in 2015. Theater practitioners, scholars, audiences, and friends had not forgotten our project, reaching out to us with evermore texts to consider and artists with whom to connect.[2]

Speaking Our Selves includes a foreword by the distinguished Ghanaian professor, scholar, and activist Esi Sutherland-Addy of the University of Ghana, Legon. Professor Sutherland-Addy is also the daughter of acclaimed Ghanaian playwright Efua Sutherland, who is considered, along with Ghana's Ama Ata Aidoo, a generational mother of African drama. Likewise, renowned playwrights Zulu Sofola (Nigeria), Rose Mbowa (Uganda), and Penina Muhando (Tanzania), were also advocates of bringing African art forms into the mainstream (including experimental works), as well as creating spaces at higher institutions of learning to serve as training and mentoring centers in performing arts.

Inspired by the legacies of the African playwright foremothers, our collective English-language anthology presents the plays of eight women: seven women are from countries that have not been represented by women playwrights in previously published English-language women-centric anthologies. While all writers were born (or raised) on the continent, seven continue to live in Africa, while one lives in the diaspora. Half of the plays required complete translations (one from Kiswahili, two from French, and one from Kirundi and French). The majority of plays include portions in an author's preferred African language(s), with English translations alongside. Kirundi, Kiswahili, Runyankore, Luganda, Lusoga, Mina, Fon, and Bambara are among the languages present throughout the anthology. The inclusion of mother-tongues in her published script honors an author's intention not to privilege English over a language of origin when the latter captures definitively the author's intent linguistically in what otherwise feels "untranslatable."[3]

All the writers represented in this anthology come from countries where language was used as a colonial and racial tool to dominate and subjugate indigenous peoples and cultures, be it English, French, Portuguese, Arabic, Italian, or German.[4] Historically, in the asymmetric world order where some languages are indeed languages of power through geographically dispersed usage, English is one such language. Our hope is that the plays will be accessible to more people than they would have had they neither been written in nor translated into English. In this way, the anthology gives all the African women playwrights published here a larger platform for their ideas, aesthetics, and theatrical art forms to be engaged with a wider audience. In turn, it preserves the integrity of their texts' forms, contents, and, in most cases, trans-linguistic flexibilities.

The choice to keep portions of some texts in the African indigenous languages in which they were conceived and written not only fulfills the author's wish for the text's authenticity but also captures the complexity and different dimensions that inform the writer's creative process. It also reflects her complex self as an artist from a colonial nation-state. The presence of these languages demonstrates a nuanced approach to the crafting of the stories shared in this anthology. It also exemplifies the linguistic multiplexity of the continent. To illuminate this feature, the playwrights have utilized footnotes to explain further, and in some cases, to phonetically write the untranslatable.

As one gets into the texts themselves, some may appear long and repetitive. Pay attention to this dramaturgical characteristic. It is a unique element that is present in many of Africa's oratorical techniques. The length of a text along with its usage of repetition could be for emphasis, for tension, for reflection, for collapsing time, place, and space, all of which are among the techniques conveyed from oral traditions. The plays in the anthology that incorporate these practices, one can argue, privilege pre-colonial existing African storytelling traditions as they exert their influence on modern theater and storytelling, as well as the craft of story-making.

Several of the texts have song, dance, and movement that are crucial to plot development. In many of the playwrights' diverse storytelling cultures, song, dance, and story are inseparable. They co-exist as an invitation to a live audience to participate in a public engagement by joining together to question, to challenge, and to experience the story as a community—that is, for audience members to participate in nature among other humans in communal, theatrical moments.

The selected plays in this anthology tackle a range of themes and ideas, be it women's demands for freedom of speech, women's deliberate and intentional counterculture choices to change the course and prevailing narratives for themselves and other women, women's challenges to the status quo and patriarchy, women's recuperation of their basic human rights and dignity, women's interrogation of democratization and the rule of law in their countries, and women's reclamations of socio-political and economic agency. Significantly, whether explicitly or implicitly, many of the plays also present women speaking boldly, graphically, and unapologetically about sex and sexuality, and their accompanying bodily pleasures or violations. "Speaking our selves," some for the first time, the women come into an individual and collective understanding of power dynamics they can grasp and activate. Previously, they had captured such potential, if at all, only in their imaginations.

Although these themes may be specific to the communities where the playwrights live, their resonance to women's experiences globally is undeniable.

Each author also provides a brief comment prior to her cast of characters, offering prefatory remarks she'd like to share with the reader to contextualize her play, encouraging readers to enter the world of her play with just enough knowledge to come to their own ideas about the play itself upon reading it. We've chosen to present the plays in a manner that doesn't suggest how the reader is to approach the play, other than to provide a writer's brief remarks. This is our effort to preserve the reader's experience of encountering the script for the first time on their own terms, rather than engaging with the text initially through a scholar's and/or practitioner's (other than the playwright's) own interpretation and vision of the play. We hope this approach encourages more varied readings of the plays in classrooms and diverse stage productions.

In their own words, the contributors to this volume—playwrights, translators, essayist, and editors—have written interviews available on the Fulcrum platform at the University of Michigan Press. One can access the interviews at https://doi.org/10.3998/mpub.12827650. In conducting these interviews, the editors sought to illuminate the individual works and the translation process while focusing on broader themes in contemporary African women's playwriting. The interviews thus provide critical, artistic, and personal frameworks within which to situate each play, as well as the collection overall.

Throughout the anthology, African women subjects in each of the plays stand on the edge of a range of possibilities for a better life, existence, and survival in a society that presses and pushes them toward accepting things as they have always been. The playwrights are making a statement that their characters are women who will not surrender and who will live their lives, in life or death, reaching for their dignity.

What is also noteworthy in *Speaking Our Selves: New Plays by African*

Women is that the women writers cut across different generations. This offers space for women's intergenerational artistry to be in conversation with one another through the eyes of the readers. What has changed for women since Penina Muhando[5] wrote her play (originally written in Kiswahili in 1983 and here, considered a "new play" for English-language readers and speakers), and when Alaa Taha, Celma Costa, and Nathalie Hounvo Yekpe wrote theirs? Are there threads among all the writers as well as pronounced distinctions? Are the conditions of a woman's place, a woman's body, a woman's thinking—at the time the writers created their plays—evident in the writings of Meaza Worku, Asiimwe Deborah Kawe, Claudia Munyengabe, and Jeanne Diama (whose play has an all-women's cast of characters)? Have the tensions, the struggles, the conflicts, and paradoxes of patriarchy held their own in society from one generation to the other? Or have the dynamic forces of other women's writing over the decades laid a solid ground for younger women to amplify their voices?

We hope that the parallels and intersections in these plays written by cross-generational women will stimulate heightened consciousness for the reader's and audience's generation and the generations to come. We hope that by connecting threads in form and content, appreciating the experimentation in language usage and presentation, and visualizing their embodiment, the plays will ignite the theaters not only of the readers' imaginations but the theaters of live performance for those seeking to produce, direct, and act these plays. This anthology provides the opportunity for producers, professional and amateur groups, teachers, students, and scholars to access the plays. This is the best way for us to get these works circulating globally so they can be read in classrooms, for instance, and seen in live productions.

It is our honor to bring plays by these women writers from countries (to the best of our knowledge) that have yet to be published in an English-language anthology (in alphabetical order, which is also the order of their works in this collection): Celma Costa (Mozambique), Jeanne Diama (Mali), Penina Muhando Mlama (Tanzania), Claudia Munyengabe (Burundi), Alaa Taha (Sudan), Meaza Worku (Ethiopia), and Nathalie Hounvo Yekpe (Benin). Asiimwe Deborah Kawe (Uganda) joins a small group of her nation's women in print, albeit elsewhere. With this publication, our hope is to contribute to the already growing reality of African women playwrights' work reaching publication, if, in fact, this is any given writer's wish. We hope you share our dream when each of the fifty-four countries comprising the African continent has not just one, but many of their women playwrights in their own voices, in print . . . so they can be read, discussed, and produced locally and globally—and everywhere in between.[6]

On behalf of our contributors, welcome to the theatrical worlds within *Speaking Our Selves: New Plays by African Women*. As the book's editors, we take full responsibility for any unintentional errors in this anthology. They are our own.

Asiimwe Deborah Kawe   Robert Vorlicky
Kampala, Uganda   New York City, USA
November 15, 2024   November 15, 2024

Notes

1. Discussions of foundational publications featuring the writings of African women in English-language texts often begin with the enormous contribution of the four-volume series, *Women Writing Africa* (New York: Feminist Press). The series includes women's writings from the 13th century to the early 2000s, in a myriad of genre, first focusing on writings from *The Southern Region* of the continent (Vol. I, 2003), then *West Africa and the Sahel* (Vol. 2, 2005), *The Eastern Region* (Vol. 3, 2007), and finally, *The Northern Region* (Vol. 4, 2008). Notably, only Volume II of the series (Eds. Esi Sutherland-Addy and Aminata Diaw) includes slight excerpts of two plays: Ghana's Efua Sutherland's *Foriwa* (1962) and Cameroon's Werewere Liking's *Singuè Mura* (1990). While playwrights are included throughout the series, they are nearly always represented, not by their dramatic writings, but rather by their fiction, non-fiction, or poetry. And not without historical and theatrical significance, nineteen years after its excerpt appeared in Volume II of the *Women Writing Africa* series, Liking's *Singuè Mura: Given That a Woman . . .* , translated by Judith G. Miller, was published in its entirety in a ground-breaking English-language anthology of African women and men playwrights, *Contemporary Francophone African Plays: An Anthology* (Ed. Judith G. Miller with Sylvie Chalaye, Lewisburg, PA, Bucknell University Press, 2024).

What is obvious across the continent, however, is the historical documentation of women's contributions to ritual and ceremonial practices. Such practices were characterized not only through their performative features (singing, dancing, clapping, stomping, and gestural movements) and musical accompaniment (percussion, horns), but through their form of oral, lyrical poetry (such as recitations, chants, call and response, and improvisations performed by solo or collective voices). These theatrical devices were at the service of women's writing meant for audible performances of "songs" during weddings, funerals, baptisms, marriages, festivals, lullabies, elegies, and praise ceremonies. Often, the poetry (the lyric song) had a dialogic quality to it: question and answer, followed by elaboration of the subject matter. Depending upon the regional location and dating of the poetry's composition, it was written in either an African or Western European language. All non-English writings are translated into English in the multi-volume, English-language series, *Women Writing Africa*.

A break-through English-language drama anthology that focused solely on African women's experiences is Kathy A. Perkins's *Black South African Women: An Anthology of Plays* (Routledge, 1998). Nine works in this volume are written by women. A decade later, Perkins included, as well as looked beyond, South Africa, in her highly influential anthology, *African Women Playwrights* (University of Illinois Press, 2009). This text presents plays by women from countries not previously anthologized: Ghana, Uganda, Zimbabwe, Cameroon, Kenya, and Nigeria. Perkins's anthology, which includes only women writers, is noteworthy for the range of writers' national origins, irrespective of whether or not the playwrights lived in Africa or in the diaspora. The fields of compilation and translations of African women's plays in the English language owe an enormous debt of gratitude to Kathy Perkins's scholarship and editorship.

In 2019, editors Yvette Hutchison and Amy Jephta extended the boundaries of continental representation in their English-language anthology, *Contemporary Plays by African Women* (London: Methuen), by including a writer of Egyptian origin. A significant partner in creating the Hutchison and Jephta anthology is the African Women Playwrights Network (AWPN), founded and originally funded by, and now in collaboration with the University of Warwick (1915–present). In Fall 2022, AWPN held its first festival of new plays at the University of Ghana, Legon. Ten plays (publicized as 10 minutes in length) were selected for performances during the festival. These plays were subsequently anthologized in *Gendering Taboos: 10 Short Plays by African Women,* edited by Yvette Hutchison, 'Tosin Kooshima Tume, and Ekua Ekumah (Methuen, 2023). One writer is from a country—Botswana—yet to be represented in an English-language anthology of African women playwrights. Thus, in the four English-language anthologies referenced here, there are 35 women writers who come from 9 of Africa's 54 countries.

While this book's focus is on English-language anthologies of African women's playwriting, it is revealing to note that, historically, in English-language anthologies that include complete works of African men and women playwrights, the women writers are in a glaring minority in terms of their inclusion. Furthermore, they are nearly always from one or more of the nine countries previously identified. A notable exception, for instance, is the inclusion of plays by Tunisia's Jalīlah Bakkār and Algeria's Fatima Gallaire in *Four Plays from North Africa*, ed. Marvin Carlson (New York: Martin E. Segal Theatre Center Publications, 2008). Carlson's expansive commitment to English translations of North African plays, whether written originally in French or Arabic, has contributed greatly to the increased scholarly and practical interest in women playwrights from North Africa for English-language users.

In 2023, Methuen/Bloomsbury published *Ancient, Indigenous and Modern Plays from Africa and the Diaspora* (eds. Simon Gikandi and R.N.Sandberg), as part of their Global Theatre Anthologies series—which, in turn, will be part of the press's "The Global Play Collection," launching in February 2025. Of the 10 plays in Gikandi and Sandberg's book, two are written by women whose countries are already represented in English-language anthologies featuring only women writers.

Prior to the publication of *Speaking Our Selves: New Plays by African Women*, 45 countries are unrepresented by a woman playwright in an English-language anthology of African women playwrights With the addition of our text to the growing field of published works by African women playwrights, 7 new countries are now represented. This leaves 38 African countries that are part of a 54-nation continent without the voice of a woman (or women) playwright(s) of their citizenry in an English-language single-sex authored anthology. Two-thirds of African countries, to the best of our knowledge, do not have a woman playwright living on the continent published in an

English-language anthology of plays by African women. Very few African women's plays are published in anthologies alongside African men's plays. More women playwrights are published in journals, magazines, online platforms, and in self-published blogs; quite frequently only excerpts of their work are in print rather than in their entirety. What is illuminated here, however, is the paucity of English-language texts dedicated to the representation of African women's lives written by African women playwrights. This rarity is most evident when identifying what countries have yet to be represented in non-short play anthologies, where the editorial focus is solely on African women playwrights.

2. As an editor of this volume, Kawe drew from her wide range of connections throughout the continent to identify unpublished plays written by African women—whether as co-director of the Sundance Institute Theatre Program–East African Initiative, a producer and artistic director of the Kampala International International Theatre Festival, or as an invited guest to festivals in Kenya, Burundi, Mali, and Rwanda, to name only a few. Asiimwe, as curator of this collection, identified the plays considered for publication from grassroot suggestions, theater professionals' recommendations, and her own audience viewing experiences. Through his scholarly and practical research, Vorlicky was able to identify women writers across the continent, whenever possible, who were—as well as were not—in English-language anthologies. While teaching at NYUAD, his travels to Uganda, Ghana, South Africa, and Egypt provided invaluable resources for this volume's focus, especially through conversations occurring at professional conferences, university talks, community and professional theater venues. The editors thank Judith G. Miller for recommending (and then translating) Nathalie Hounvo Yekpe's play for this anthology after having heard the play read at France's Avignon Festival in 2022. And, after Vorlicky's years of teaching Penina Muhando Mlama's foundational essay arguing for the usage of African languages in African writing ("Creating in the Mother-Tongue: The Challenges to the African Writer Today," *Research in African Literatures* 21, no. 4 [Winter 1990]: 5–14)—and with students in New York and Abu Dhabi frustrated at being unable to read a play of hers in English (since none of us read Kiswahili)—Muhando Mlama graciously accepted the editors' invitation for Joshua Williams to translate into English, for the first time, a play of hers. The selected play, *Nguzo Mama*, is in this anthology.

3. For the historical context within which African authors debated whether or not African authors should write in their African languages of origin—rather than Euro-centric languages—see Sutherland-Addy's Foreword in this anthology (Endnote 12). According to Sutherland-Addy, the debate focuses on exchanges characterized by and captured between Chinua Achebe, who encouraged the publication of African writing in non-African languages (*Morning Yet on Creation Day: Essays* [Garden City, NY: Anchor Press, 1979]), and Ngũgĩ wa Thiong'o, who early on championed the preservation of writing in one's language of origin (*Decolonising the Mind: The Politics of Language in African Literature* [Portsmouth, NH: James Currey: Heinemann, 1986]). Throughout the latter half of the 20th century, note that it was not uncommon among men writers to question one another as to the variety of efficacies of writing in—let alone publishing in—mother-tongues, second languages, or translations. But Sutherland-Addy importantly cites Penina Muhando's inclusion of a woman's voice in this contentious debate regarding the value of preserving indige-

nous African languages in works written by Africans. See Penina Muhando Mlama, "Creating in the Mother-Tongue."

4. This list of languages does not account for Ethiopia's linguistic heritage, which is Amharic. Amharic, the working (not official) language in Ethiopia, is rooted in Ge'ez, a semitic language. Ethiopian Meaza Worku, whose play is included here, is situated within a different historical linguistic paradigm than the other works in this anthology.

5. Please note that the author's last name appears as Mlama after her marriage. However, she is known as Penina Muhando on all her creative works, including her play in this anthology, as well as on her pre-marital academic work.

6. At the near-quarter mark of the 21st century, Declan Walsh writes that "[b]y 2050, one in four people on the planet will be African, a seismic change that's already starting to register" ("The World is Becoming More African," *New York Times*, 28 Oct 2023). Certainly, one of these changes, as witnessed by the editors while creating this anthology, is the striking increase in women from across the continent who are writing plays. https://www.nytimes.com/interactive/2023/10/28/world/africa/africa -youth-population.html.

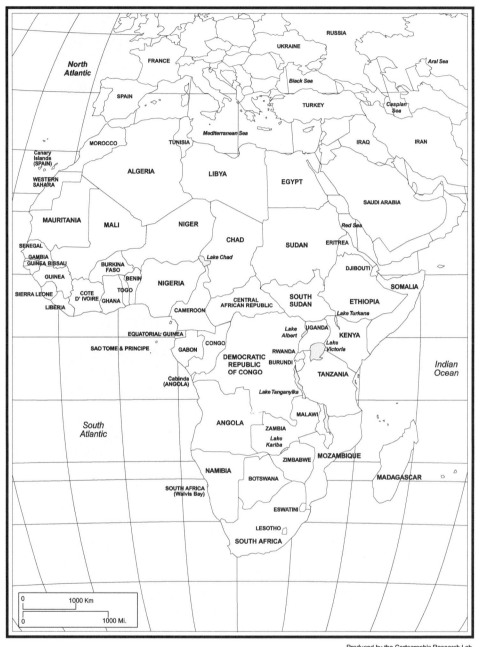

The fifty-four countries of the African continent.

Foreword

Esi Sutherland-Addy

It is a privilege to have had the experience of researching the creative dynamism which continues to emanate from the works of African writers and performers. The scholar finds themselves being stimulated to pursue the plethora of angles from which this body of works may be explored. I find this especially true when I attempt to develop courses which will assist me to inspirit my students with the thrilling sense of discovery that I have often felt on stepping into the imaginative world of the literary artist or being drawn toward their profound reflections of our lived experience and the nature of the human condition. If the range of subject matter addressed through the literary arts itself provides a harvest for intellectual reflection, the balance among flights of fancy, aesthetic sensibility, individual risk taking, and conformity to artistic conventions set the scholar in hot pursuit and development of plausible, analytical frameworks that will hopefully contribute to a body of discourse on African literary arts.

I have found my commitment to engaging the African continent in its diversity in any courses which I dare to call "African" challenged by my inability to access works which represent this diversity. This is especially true of theater, the making of which brings text, enactment, and society into a dynamic relationship. If one goes on further to create an interface between theater and the role of women in its creation and practice, the evidence of women's participation appears to be rather subdued. I will discuss further on in this thought piece several factors that could have contributed to the relative dearth of theatrical works by women. These factors justify the need for just the kind of platform which Bob Vorlicky and Asiimwe Deborah Kawe have committed themselves to designing in order to project and amplify the voices and works of women in African theater. The organizing principles for this anthology begin to challenge the excuses we may have been giving ourselves for not reaching across apparent geographical, linguistic, or generational barriers.

I thought I might take the opportunity so graciously granted me by the editors of this anthology to share ways in which it evokes for me, personally, thoughts about examples of the pioneering vision and work women have contributed to establishing a distinctive post-independence African Theater. The question arises for me as to whether 60-odd years after independence we should be speaking of pioneers in the making of African Theater. Struck by the recurrence of certain perceptions, I shall be reflecting on ways in which women playwrights and theater-makers break through and reinvent conventions in order to set new trends.

The notion of "experimental theater" gives the impression of the immediate and the future, but in my personal experience it evokes memories of a past whose legacy animates the present and the future.

In the early years of independence in Ghana (1957–1966), for example, Efua T. Sutherland (my mother) became "the undisputed matriarch of contemporary Ghanaian theater." One of her most remarkable skills was spotting and nurturing talent for the new theater movement. She dedicated much of her adult life to all aspects of theater development in Ghana with a Pan Africanist vision.[1] The centenary of her birth (1924–2024) is an opportunity to recall her pioneering role in modelling the framework for a new African theater grounded in the continent's heritage with the capacity to embody and perform African stories. Her encouragement of emerging artists and her creation of experimental models of African theater made her practice decidedly intergenerational. Perhaps the words of Margaret Busby, a publisher of African women's literature and a mentee of Sutherland, testify to this intergenerational energy:

The map is not uncharted where you have gone.
The page is not blank where you have written
We hear you
telling our story
to the rhythm of a heartbeat,
to the rhythm of a heartbeat[2]

However, as I write this Foreword in the middle of the year 2023, I must not succumb to the grief welling up at the passing of arguably the most internationally renowned African woman writer of the past half century: Ama Ata Aidoo. What may not be so well known is that Ama Ata Aidoo considers Efua Sutherland as having been her greatest support in launching her into her writing career, from 1964 when she became Sutherland's assistant at the Institute of African Studies, University of Ghana for a short while, and her literary foremother for all time. For Ama Ata Aidoo, this is a glimpse of what Sutherland meant to her:

Ow-w-w,
how you had mothered us:
with that [maddening] formidable [self-] assurance,
those humorously luminous and luminously humorous eyes that
sought out our inner weaknesses
in hopes of setting us straight
not just someday
    but right away,
. . . .
You never gave up on us:
not for a minute.
   knowing as you did
      that given half the chance,
      we could, and still can soar
      high above our normal human frailties and
      make a glowing glittering something of ourselves and our world
. . . .
Encouraging
Supporting
Affirming.
So what did You think we were going to do without you,
Dear Dr. Mrs. Efua Theodora Sutherland?
Not much: [3]

I am struck once again by the need to somehow situate the approaching centenary of Sutherland's birth and the symbolic passing of an era in the loss of Ama Ata Aidoo within the context of their work and how it had contributed toward the establishment of a firm imprint of African playmaking on the local and global scene.

An institution etched in the history of Contemporary African Theater is the Ghana Drama Studio. It was a physical embodiment of the results of the eager search Sutherland had undertaken for living theater and performance traditions in the indigenous communities of Ghana. Conscious of the alienating Western education which she had been subjected to, she went on a journey of self -discovery and was privileged to be let into the world of the dramatic heritage of her people. Her response was to engage with it and re-appropriate it as the foundation for the creation of a post-independence theatrical expression. The Ghana Drama Studio was to be a theater which physically reminded its users and audience of the open air flexible "auditorium" and primacy of multiple stages, including a nod to the proscenium stage opening onto an arena for theater in the round and a raised stage toward the back wall.

As I will show later, in as much as the Ghana Drama Studio was a piece of architecture full of symbolism in homage to African theater, it became the home of vibrant experimentation with dramatic form and content. In a gesture representing her commitment to the establishment of African Theater as a field of enquiry and a basis for formal learning, she turned over the Ghana Drama Studio to the University of Ghana to support the establishment of the nascent School of Music and Drama (now, School of Performing Arts). The famous scholar of African Theater, Biodun Jeyifo, evokes the importance of this building and the program that thrived in it.

The program of experimental theater, which Efua Sutherland began in Accra between 1958 and 1961, and the Ghana Drama Studio, which she built to house her experimental work, are two of the most important "happenings" in the creation of modern drama, not only in West Africa but in the entirety of the African continent. [4]

In its first phase from circa 1960 to 1984, the studio was a bubbling crucible where ingredients of the dramatic heritage and experiences of African theater came together to create an alchemy of theatrical experiences. Creatives were invited into the space, from the owners of indigenous performance traditions, to the irrepressible popular itinerant theater practitioners to amateur theater players and emerging playwrights producing plays in the various dramatic modes seeping into the African consciousness through Western education (including Joe de Graft, Ama Ata Aidoo, Mohammed ben Abdallah, Kofi Anyidoho).[5] It became a place of inspiration and support for many creatives who reached out to the studio from other African countries and the African diaspora. Featuring in person in that space were, to name a few of the symbolic, Duro Ladipo (the great proponent of the Yoruba Travelling Theatre), Ngũgĩ wa Thiong'o (Kenyan writer, academic, and activist), Wole Soyinka (now doyen of African Theater), as well as Félix Morisseau-Leroy of Haiti and Maya Angelou of the USA, representing the African diaspora.

Having been razed to the ground to make way for a state-built national theater (whereby hangs a tale), a replica of this building was constructed on the grounds of the School of Performing Arts at the University of Ghana and is used intensely by staff and students.

As I have sat in workshops at the Studio, a literary scholar and cultural activist of a certain age, seeking to be admitted into the world of the inspired, passionate, fearless, and talented young African millennials, my mind has floated back to my childhood. I would sit quietly in a corner of my mother's studio absorbed in rehearsals of new plays, improvisation sessions of popular theater, and recording sessions of traditional storytelling.

Looking back, even further, I could see how much African theater in the 21st century could take for granted, because of the efforts of the pioneers, to change the mindset about women who took to the stage.

It may be recalled that drama within the well-drawn parameters of social drama in the context of traditional ceremonies and festivals involved women in prominent roles. Ironically, women's participation in the emerging "modern" theater was often seen as placing them outside the control of their societies. This could easily be viewed as paradoxical; these ceremonies placed women in highly visible roles that had embedded in them the requirement to be an accomplished performer. However, regarding the theatrical forms that were embedded in Western acculturation, girls could only take part in school plays which formed part of the colonization project. The Ethiopian experience documented succinctly by Aboneh Ashagrie shows this clearly in discussing the strategies of Senedu Gebru, an educationist and lover of theater, who became one of the leading proponents of the modern theater movement of Ethiopia.[6] There was so much stigma surrounding women taking to the stage that even women working in bars shied away from it. Seeing that males were continuously playing female roles, she passionately promoted drama in the Empress Menen Girl's Boarding School where she taught for many years. This effort is acknowledged to have played a major role in making acting by educated women a reputable activity. She is also reputed to have been a prolific playwright. Meaza Worku, whose play *Desperate to Fight* takes its place in this anthology, corroborates the above account, and makes a further point:

> The late 50s and early 60s were considered a golden time for Ethiopian theatre in which different well-written, produced and read plays by well-educated male playwrights became prominent. No women playwrights have been discovered in theatre history that can be mentioned as role models even in this 21st century, however, there were those few mentioned above who did write plays in the theatre history but never were encouraged or acknowledged by historians. In recent times, women have started to emerge in Ethiopian theatre as playwrights and directors. But after a hundred years life course of theatre, each is treated as a "first" in the field.[7]

Not much seems to have changed between the 1950s and the 2020s. The above comment confirms the absence of women from certain emancipated spaces accompanied by the lack of recognition of their achievements. Even icons of the arts such as Ama Ata Aidoo have had to express outrage at this state of affairs:

> What we are saying though, is that it is especially pathetic to keep on writing without having any consistent, active, critical intelligence that is interested in you as an artist (or creator). Therefore, it is precisely from this point that the African writing women's reality begins to differ somewhat from that of the male writer.[8]

At the same time and without contradiction, Efua Sutherland (discussed above), Rose Mbowa of Uganda, Zulu Sofola of Nigeria, Ama Ata Aidoo of Ghana, Werewere Liking of Cameroon, and Penina Muhando Mlama of Tanzania are recognized among the makers of post-independence African theater who have critically engaged with form and content from other realms and times to create dramas with a distinctly African texture. In this process their experimental work has sought to nullify the tendency to create a hierarchy of theatrical practice privileging those produced through the mode of written scripts over those steeped in the techniques of orality such as improvisation and joint play making.

Emphasizing the validity of drama as a living, functional cultural tool, Sutherland has, for example, promoted the pan-African agenda not only by opening the Ghana Drama Studio up to several African thespians but also by championing drama as a medium for addressing fractured social systems such as the impact of the trans-Atlantic Slave Trade and Colonialism on African communities on the continent and in the African diaspora. It is with this conviction in mind, and based on the healing potential of catharsis, that she championed a Pan-African Historical Theatre Festival to be staged in the proximity of the two European edifices in which the most enslaved West Africans were imprisoned and shipped off to Europe and the Americas.

From my own exposure to the field of theater, I consider it important to explore the idea that playwrights are often also dynamic dramatists who are active in the making of a new theatrical tradition in their respective countries. Thus, one of my observations about the contributors to this anthology is the fact that they are theater practitioners in the broadest sense. Their writing plays blends in with a wide range of preoccupations aimed at asserting the power of their voices in various processes of social and political transformation, experimenting with the craft and aesthetic of drama, and growing the arts scene in their countries through experimentation and the projection of emerging works, for example, through workshops, festivals, and critical works.

The above discussion begins to demonstrate the sheer scope of the theater in projects such as those of nation building, social transformation, psycho-social development, the establishment of the artistic practice, and so on. It is noteworthy that women not only played a significant role determining what Judith G. Miller has called the "African stage textuality," but also firmly manifested the agency in determining "matter and manner" of engagement with cultural continuity and change.[9] Miller's choice of Zulu Sofola, for example, was to deploy the tools offered by drama in refracting the feminine experience of her Igbo culture. Through the prism of tragedy in *Wedlock of the Gods*, Sofola leaves no doubt about her own view that some of the customary practices affecting women cannot be sustained into the post-independence state. African women playwrights working in the 1960s and 70s created outright rebellious heroines to carry the message of the need for social change. In *Wedlock of the Gods* by Sofola and *Anowa* by Ama Ata Aidoo, the women characters balk against the strictures of obtuse traditions and pay the ultimate price for their defiance.[10] Clearly, this current anthology demonstrates that for women making theater in the 21st century, the strictures of these traditions remain a focus. The trope of the defiant female protagonist on a sometimes-suicidal mission to overthrow systems oppressive to women, for instance, finds its place in the plays selected for the anthology.

The editors of this anthology have also taken a decisive stand on the vexed matter of the language of literary production by defying the paralysis that appears to have plagued accessibility of publications. First of all, apart from the fact that published dramatic texts are relatively fewer than other genres, it is notoriously difficult to gain access to a pan-continental body of works. Their solution is to have included texts originally written in English and French as well as Kirundi and Kiswahili. In addition, care has been taken to engage with the nuances of African language deployment in playwriting. For example, Penina Muhando Mlama has made her mark by making Kiswahili the language of her oeuvre. Thus, her play *Nguzo Mama*, included in the anthology—and also her first play to be published in English translation—was originally written in this African lingua franca spoken in Eastern and Central Africa. Furthermore, it is very interesting to observe the ways in which the playwrights featured in the anthology have made their own multilingualism a natural instrument for voicing their message and aesthetic. Care has been taken by the editors to keep faith with the commitment of several playwrights to reflect the flavor of African language idioms and cadences in their text.

One also appreciates the organizing principle of this anthology, which is to expand the range of countries whose playwrights are in circulation internationally outside the limits of the linguistic communities to which they originally belong. It is easy to slip into accepting the vestiges and aftermath of the fracturing of the African continent according to colonial interests as inevitable consequences that must be reckoned into the future shape of polities of the continent. Political boundaries, however, have not been allowed to interfere with the formation of community that perpetuates the hegemony of a colonial/imperial center in Europe and its periphery, creating silos which are difficult to breach.

Equally, imperial culture has long been recognized as a colonizing tool which has a vice-like grip on the mind of the colonized. As Frantz Fanon states in the following brief extract from *Black Skin, White Masks,* "To speak means to be in a position to use a certain syntax to grasp the morphology of this or that Language but it means above all to assume a culture, to support the weight of a civilization."[11] One of the direct manifestations of this process is the relegation of African language culture to the realm of informality during colonialism leading to the eliding of African language (oral and written where it existed) from the formal space. Official legislative, judicial, and executive business were and continue to be conducted in the relevant European language with a few exceptions given to such areas as local government, early primary education, and civic education. To the extent that the literary arts are language based, their written form has been the source of endless debate, especially regarding the languages in which they should be primarily expressed.

The discourse which has been generated around this matter is several decades long and is still a live question. The much-cited debate between Chinua Achebe and Ngũgĩ wa Thiong'o on this question will not be rehearsed here but suffice it to say that playwrights have made their thoughts known on this matter over the course of the past 40 years or so.[12] Mlama, for example, published a forthright paper in 1990, "Creating in the Mother-Tongue: The Challenges to the African Writer Today."[13] In this essay she strongly advocates writing in the mother-tongue but enumerates the role of the geo-politics and capitalism in condemning mother-tongue writing to near obscurity. While accepting that Tanzania is one of the few countries on the continent which was founded consciously on having an African language as its official language and establishing a socialist model of government, Mlama spares no African government, including that of her own country, in her observations about national policy prevarication and capitulation to control by external interests.[14] However, her conviction in the vital importance of writing and producing work in African languages remains strong for a number of reasons. For example, she refers to "[t]he 1987 Organisation of African Unity language plan of action for Africa [which] states:

Language is at the heart of a people's culture and . . . the cultural advancement of the African peoples and the acceleration of their economic and social development will not be possible without harnessing in a practical manner indigenous African languages in that advancement and development."[15]

Mlama concludes, "It is difficult to imagine the African writer today making a significant contribution to asserting the African people's cultural identity without having recourse to African indigenous languages. In fact, language is the only feature that presently gives African societies their cultural identity."[16]

Cultural identity is not the only factor of African life that must be salvaged. Mlama belongs to the school of thought that writers and their works must be committed to the establishment of a people-centered development model. Her long years as a practitioner of Theatre for Development (TfD) which brings theater to the heart of grassroots development also led to experimentation with the craft. For example, with her deep commitment to the well-being of the African girl, she and her colleague Amandina Lihamba developed the school based TfD known as TUSEME (Let Us Speak Out) Girls Education for Gender Equality Model, which is now being deployed in over 30 countries throughout Africa.[17]

At the beginning of this Foreword, I evoked the preoccupations of African women playwrights inspired by the attainment of political independence to establish the role of theater in the process of nation building and the rehabilitation of the image of Africa. The works they created are bold assertions of perspectives of the world from a female standpoint. They are also filled with a palpable excitement generated from a rediscovery of the indigenous heritage of performance and a revalidation of stories waiting to be told.

Speaking Our Selves: New Plays by African Women indeed includes work by Penina Muhando Mlama who, as noted, continues to carry the ethos of theater arts and its practitioners as cultural workers in the service of the development and edification of society. Her presence in this intergenerational anthology evokes, among other things, an era in which the nation was writ large for artistic minds. Additionally, there was a palpable front of complexity as indigenous cultures grappled with the impositions of coloniality and the demands of post-independence self-actualization. Again, theater artists have sought to carve a role for themselves in this process. A question that arises for me is this: As one approaches the work of the late 1990s and the 2000s, is one to anticipate an abrupt transition in thematic preoccupation and style?

Lindsey Green-Simms, citing Achille Mbembe, suggests,

> [R]ather than conceiving of the twenty-first century as a distinct or complete break from the past, we seek to understand it as part of a *longue durée*, a time whose overlapping multiplicities and complexities we are just beginning to discern. Achille Mbembe, in his monumental *On the Postcolony*, has famously described the postcolony itself as a *longue durée*, an entanglement of contradictory phenomena and temporalities that co-exist in a given age. . . . For Mbembe the goal of theorizing the African postcolony is to "account for *time as lived*, not synchronically or diachronically, but in its multiplicity and simultaneities, its presences and absences, beyond the lazy categories of permanence and change."[18]

Although most of the works in the anthology cover "time as lived" in the 21st century (Costa, Kawe, Worku, Diama, Taha, Yekpe), they do engage with the past and mythic time, raising perennial issues as well as a re-envisioned future (Munyengabe, Mlama). Looking at the body of works from the nuanced approach suggested above should assist in a deeper understanding of its significance.

Having said this, there are certainly some signs of the times which bring one into the world of the young African in the 21st century. To ignore these is to ignore the reality of millennial experience which nourishes the work of these creatives. I will take up a few of these. The first is the impact of the creeping disillusionment with the state of the post-colonial African state. While it may be said that the literature of disillusionment was already being produced in the 1970s and 80s, it appears to have taken a different turn in the new millennium. There is a palpable disconnect between the nation writ large and the pixilated picture of the individual experiences of the aggravations of globalization and mismanaged nation states. What are the new communities and support systems available for young persons who are unfamiliar with or detached from socio-cultural traditions? Indeed, questions arise where young people are no longer willing to countenance the dissonances embedded in these traditions. I discovered an intriguing online magazine called the *Open Country Mag*. Its founder, Otosirieze Obi-Young, wrote a revealing thought-piece for the April 8, 2022 copy, "The Next Generation of African Literature," an "In-Depth Special Issue on Contemporary African Literature." The piece piqued my interest regarding his description of African millennials' state of being:

> Most of us were living in the continent, younger millennials, all of us politically tired, many of us economically deprived, every one of us culturally thirsty. We were tired of being tired, which meant we were tired of being

afraid, of not aiming for tall dreams—Our generation, in Africa, came of age in lack, a sense that we had been failed, that not enough was left for us, and our frustrations have over the years taken different shapes. And so, we have been given different names. In 2018, I wrote a literary anthology introduction titled "The Confessional Generation." It struck me, even then, how emotive and outspoken, how daring, how open to change we are, and, much later, how we have the most accessible power at our disposal to effect change. By 2020, it was no longer in doubt, and in the broader, worsening political context of Nigeria [read Africa], we had become the Soro Soke Generation.[19] Speak louder, we push, speak louder. . . .[20]

For women writers this has partly translated into the need to defy the demure posture, the indirection and politeness of speaking and the injunction placed on subjects concerning women. For example, I borrow the theme "Tackling Taboo Topics in African Female Writing,"[21] which stands out in this anthology not only in terms of subject matter but equally in terms of the passion and vehemence of the language in which issues are addressed. This gives a clear enough indication of a certain determination that experiences of women and the state of their minds and bodies can no longer be relegated into chambers of silent whispers. The violence and violation perpetuated in sexual, physical, and emotional abuse, for instance, are thus to be addressed with militancy, yet the different perspectives lie in twists in the plot revealing the brink to which women can be brought that could make them, as one option, shift from the pathology of victimhood to that of the perpetrator. On the other hand, the implication that patriarchy could break the spirit of both men and women is an interesting way of seeking to reconceptualize a world without its domination. Feminist invocations of alternative male responses form part of the pushback against patriarchal entitlement.

I do not wish, however, to impose a homogeneity on this collection of plays, for it is delightfully eclectic. While not suggesting the absence of clever humor in plays written by African women generally, for example, it would be true to state that comedy is seldom the chosen form for African women playwrights. However, this anthology affords readers with the opportunity to experience the works of professed writers of comedy (Worku, Diama, Taha). As stated above, I also recognize experimentation with myth making and form firmly situated within the body of this anthology, in which paragons of leadership are created in appreciation of the triumph of the human spirit. Indeed, the stories of the contributors to this anthology themselves should also be a focus for arriving at an understanding of the full story of life lived in the 21st century. The work of the foremothers may have eased the way, but it is important to recall the roles which the contributors have played by undertaking initiatives for the development and sustenance of a thriving theatrical culture on the African continent. One need only follow their careers to discover a thread running through decades of women creatives operating as practitioners in multiple fields of the arts and at the forefront, building creative institutions to support the flourishing of an inclusive African theater which is proudly feminist.

Notes

1. Useful references for understanding the scope of Sutherland's vision include Awo Mana Asiedu et al., eds., *The Performing Arts in Africa—Ghanaian Perspectives* (Bansbury, U.K.: Ayebia Clarke Publishing Limited, 2014), 4; Anne V. Adams and Esi Sutherland-Addy, eds., Introduction, *The Legacy of Efua Sutherland: Pan-African Cultural Activism* (Bansbury, U.K.: Ayebia Clarke Publishing, 2007), 6–16.

2. Margaret Busby, "The Pathfinder (For Aunt Efua at Araba Mansa)" in *The Legacy of Efua Sutherland*, 363.

3. Ama Ata Aidoo, "An Interrogation of an Academic Kind: An Essay," in *The Legacy of Efua Sutherland*, 230–33.

4. Biodun Jeyifo, "When Anansegoro Begins to Grow: Reading Efua Sutherland Three Decades On," in *The Legacy of Efua Sutherland*, 67.

5. These renowned literary personalities worked with and were highly influenced by Efua Sutherland's vision.

6. Aboneh Ashagrie, "The Role of Women on the Ethiopian Stage," *Journal of African Cultural Studies* 24, no.1 (2012): 1–8.

7. Meaza Worku, "Women and Ethiopian Theatre," *Seasons: Africa Edition,* The International Centre for Women Playwrights (May 2011): 9. https://seasons.women playwrights.org/2011/05/25/women-and-ethiopian-theatre-meaza-worku-ethiopia/

8. Ama Ata Aidoo, "To Be an African Woman Writer—An Overview and a Detail," *Criticism and Ideology*, ed. K. H. Petersen (Uppsala: Scandinavian Institute of African Studies, 1988), 158.

9. Judith G. Miller, "Is There a Specifically Francophone African Stage Textuality?" *Yale French Studies* 112 (2007): 131–44.

10. Ama Ata Aidoo, *Anowa* (London: Longman Drumbeat, 1985) and Zulu Sofola, *Wedlock of the Gods* (London: Evans Bros., 1973).

11. Frantz Fanon, *Black Skin, White Masks*, trans. C. Markmann, (New York: Grove Press, 1967), 17.

12. The works frequently referred to regarding this debate are Chinua Achebe, *Morning Yet on Creation Day: Essays* (Garden City, NY: Anchor Press, 1979) and Ngũgĩ wa Thiong'o, *Decolonising the Mind: The Politics of Language in African Literature* (Portsmouth, NH: James Currey: Heinemann, 1986).

13. Penina Muhando Mlama, "Creating in the Mother-Tongue: The Challenges to the African Writer Today," *Research in African Literatures* 21, no. 4 (Winter 1990): 5–14.

14. Mlama, "Creating the Mother-Tongue," 11–13.

15. Mlama, "Creating the Mother-Tongue," 13. Quote from Organization of Afri-

can Unity, *The Language Plan of Action for Africa*. Council of Ministers Forty-Sixth Ordinary Session, Res. CM/Pes 1123 (XLVI) Addis Ababa, 1987.

16. Mlama, "Creating in the Mother-Tongue," 13.

17. Further perspectives on Theatre for Development may be gleaned from Vicensia Shule, "African Women and Theatre for Development," Olajumoke Yacob-Haliso and Toyin Falola, eds., *The Palgrave Handbook of African Women's Studies* (London: Palgrave Macmillan, 2019), 1–18.

18. Lindsey Green-Simms, "'What's New in Africa?': African Writing in the Twenty-First Century," *Journal of Postcolonial and Commonwealth Studies* 1, no. 1 (Spring 2013): 3–12.

19. The term Soro Soke means "Speak up" in Yoruba. It was adopted for use by the 2020 #EndSARS Movement in Lagos, Nigeria, which involved youth protesting physically and online against mismanagement and impunity of political and security forces. The Special Anti-Robbery Squad (SARS) was first organized by the Nigerian police in Lagos in 1992.

20. Otosirieze, "The Next Generation of African Literature," an "In-Depth Special Issue on Contemporary African Literature," *Open Country Mag* (April 8, 2022). The author's pen name is Otosirieze; his last name is Obi-Young. https://opencountrym ag.com/the-next-generation-covers-open-country-mag-our-in-depth-special-issue -on-contemporary-african-literature/

21. This was the theme of the maiden conference of the African Women Playwrights Network (AWPN), held in the Efua Sutherland Drama Studio, University of Ghana, Legon, in September 2022.

Plays

Mozambican playwright Celma Costa, author of *Us, Too, We're People*.

Us, Too, We're People

Celma Costa

Celma Costa is a Mozambican-born playwright and cultural producer, born in Maputo city in 1994. Her theater practice includes stages in South Africa, Congo, and the UAE.

Her staged plays include *No Joke* (2013), *Death of an African Man* (2014), *Chairs* (2014), *Darkness Is against Us* (2014), and *Bricks* (2015), with an additional excerpt reading of "Us, Too, We're People" (2018).

Costa's plays delve into the intricate ways in which people navigate common events within specific socio-economic contexts. This often includes a racialized lens, often silent and sometimes even erased from the stage. By juxtaposing ordinary situations with complex characters of color, she fearlessly confronts the caricatures often employed in art. In challenging the notion that "*emotion is black (as) reason is Greek*" (Léopold Senghor), Costa breathes life into her characters, endowing them with rich inner worlds revealed through poignant dialogues and intricate monologues. Through these artistic devices, the logic and message of her plays gradually unfold, captivating the audience's attention.

Beyond her role as a playwright, Celma Costa actively engages in arts organization, using artistic methodologies like Subjective Mapping and Forum Theatre to foster dialogue on complex issues. Notably, she has mobilized diverse groups in Congo-Brazzaville and the UAE (2018), harnessing the power of the arts during workshops to ignite meaningful conversations.

Us, Too, We're People was first completed in 2016 and has since evolved into a revised text, featured in this anthology, finalized in 2023. The play was additionally selected as a class reading for students at New York Abu Dhabi University in 2018. Through its narrative, Costa invites the audience to contemplate the intricate interplay among gender, race, and forgiveness in the lives of seemingly ordinary individuals.

While theater holds a central place in Costa's creative pursuits, her interests extend to the realms of gender and international advocacy. With a fervent dedication to social progress, she continues to explore the nuanced intersections of identity, race, and gender through her artistic endeavors. Costa's work serves as a catalyst for introspection and dialogue, inviting audiences to question preconceived notions and broaden their understanding of the human experience.

An interview with Celma Costa is available at https://doi.org/10.3998/mpub.12827650.cmp.4.

CELMA COSTA ON *US, TOO, WE'RE PEOPLE*:

In 2016, during my early 20s and final year at university, I wrote "Us, Too, We're People." It was a time when the "Fees Must Fall" student protests were just beginning to sweep South African universities. Living in South Africa was never easy, especially as a Mozambican. As a target of xenophobia, my circle of friends consisted mainly of other "foreigners." The tension and violence stemming from the country's violent history felt overwhelming.

We could always feel the rage even when there was hope. When emotions have no outlet, one turns to the arts. During my teenage years, I delved into *Tshepang: The Third Testament*, a South African play by Lara Foot. This raw depiction of infant rape and its socio-economic context provided a stark portrayal of post-apartheid South Africa. It was my first glimpse into how history can shape a nation and how violence perpetuates itself. The image of a broomstick penetrating a loaf of bread until it crumbled remained etched in my memory.

Although I pursued politics, I knew that theater was my true calling. It was the platform where genuine change, even of a political nature, could occur. Theater allowed us to bring forth real, unfiltered stories to the forefront. *Us, Too, We're People* now appears as a revised text in this publication. The first was lengthier, had more characters, and mirrored my mindset of creating theater within a student space. It was an angry play, graphic in its depiction. I wanted readers and audiences to experience the same horror, shock, and indignation I faced daily in South Africa. I needed them to feel the frustration of a rising climax with little resolution. That remains the state of our nation today. Problems persist, promises go unfulfilled, and survivors of sexual assault and abuse, especially women and girls, continue to suffer.

A crucial aspect of this play, one I have always defended, is the presence of a motionless woman's body on stage for most scenes. The actress does not speak but represents the violated human being lying before us. In discussions about the proverbial elephant in the room, I urge you to replace that image with this violated body. Too often, our belief systems, policies, and laws allow us to disregard such bodies and move on. I implore you not to overlook it. Allow this body to choke your senses, to demand attention.

The revised edition maintains the story, logic, and message while feeling significantly different. It is considerably shorter, a change that has left me somewhat uncertain. However, it was a necessary adjustment. Eight years have passed since I first wrote the play. My work now revolves around gender issues, providing me with a deeper understanding of the complexities involved. I am acquainted with policies and the various efforts made by civil society stakeholders. In a world plagued by dehumanization, I have become acutely sensitive to images of violence. Consequently, I have dialed back on the horror. The invitation to reflect remains, but this will not be a spectacle of terror or gratuitous sensationalism.

I invite you to read it slowly, to allow the words to settle and the scenes to unfold at their own pace.

Us, Too, We're People
Celma Costa

CHARACTERS
(Anele) Saul: Male, early 20s.
Betty: Female, between 17 and 18.
Fatima: Female, Betty's mother, in her 50s.
Jeremiah: Male, Saul's father, in his 40s.
Frida: Female, Saul's mother, Jeremiah's exhausted wife, in her 30s.
Teresa: Female, in her 30s.
Ilda: Female, hairdresser, in her 20s.
Joel: Male, janitor, in his 40s.
Tomo: Male, experienced Police Officer, in his 50s.
Doc: Male, Tomo's co-worker, in his 30s.

SETTING
A small community, where everyone knows each other's business.

SCENE 1
(Stage is completely dark. The noise of an old rocking chair, placed on the far left of the stage, is audible. On it, sits FATIMA, pensive. BETTY in the center of the stage, lying down, immovable, dead. [And so remains unless indicated otherwise.] On the far right, SAUL stands, if possible naked or nude, hands tightly grip his groin.)
(Spotlight on FATIMA.)

FATIMA: There is too much silence here.
My daughter?
(Lights a cigarette.)
Where do I start?
(Smokes.)
She's-
SAUL: *(Spotlight on him, interrupting.)*
My angel!
FATIMA: *(Morbidly.)*
Dead.

(A permanent spotlight on BETTY, and a dim light that alternates between SAUL and FATIMA as they speak.)

FATIMA: *(Reminiscing.)*

Betty. That's her name. Was. I gave her a pretty name.

(Smiles.)

And a pretty education!

But she couldn't *help* herself.

SAUL: I couldn't help myself.

Her lips gave birth to me.

(Steps forward.)

I felt love. I felt unafraid.

(Breathes.)

Love and things made sense.

FATIMA: I see.

(Smokes.)

So *now* you're asking me?

SAUL: *(Agitated, tries to speak with his hands but realizes he can't let go of his groin.)*

I said I could not help myself!

FATIMA: I knew it when I saw him.

(Smokes.)

That devil boy Anele!

SAUL: It was love, and it was real, because she *saw* me.

FATIMA: But they will say it was me. Bad mother.

That it was me who failed her.

SAUL: She looked spent. She looked tired.

Please don't blame men for everything!

She even looked satisfied!

FATIMA: Mothers bury their children.

SCENE 2

(Onstage, BETTY on the floor and TERESA, walking into a salon. She sits on a chair and behind her stands ILDA, a salon worker who begins combing TERESA. Sweeping the salon, JOEL.)

TERESA: *(Empathetic.)*

Eish, I feel bad.

ILDA: For what, for who? Did this Betty not go out with her own two feet? With her own two legs? And even with other things on show?

TERESA: People still think like that?

ILDA: A great deal of us do!

TERESA: I just feel bad for her!

ILDA: *So* many feelings!

TERESA: The girl got raped! And killed!

ILDA: If you tease does a dog not bite?

TERESA: *(Incredulous, breathes, then continues.)*

It's rough on the family.

ILDA: That project of a mother? No wonder Betty kept running from her!

TERESA: People like you are honestly the problem!

ILDA: *Ah!* So, the problem is me? Another raped, it's me. Climate change, it's also me?

TERESA: *(To Joel.)*

Please tell me you think differently.

JOEL: *(Still sweeping.)*

About?

TERESA: Betty.

JOEL: I don't know what to think of her. I didn't know her.

TERESA: Not what you think of her. What *happened* to her.

ILDA: So you don't ask me but you ask a man about his opinion on another man? *Eh!*

TERESA: Joel is not like them.

ILDA: Joel is not a man?

(To JOEL.)

Joel, are you not a man?!

TERESA: *(Ignoring.)*

Joel.

(Stands up, walks toward him.)

Tell me, what do you think? Don't tell me you also blame her?

JOEL: What exactly happened?

ILDA: We know what happened, we saw it! She was drinking with Anele! What else must you see?

JOEL: But were *you* there?

ILDA: Must I also be in the bedroom with them?

(Laughs.)

JOEL: Where is the boy now?

TERESA: He's been taken.

ILDA: He went himself.

TERESA: He turned himself in?

JOEL: Maybe he's religious.

ILDA: Between the Police and God judging him, it's better if it's Police.

US, TOO, WE'RE PEOPLE   **9**

JOEL: So maybe he'll be punished.
ILDA: *(To TERESA.)*
TERESA: This I don't believe.

SCENE 3
(Two chairs, facing each other, on an otherwise empty stage. On them, sit
SAUL and TOMO.)

TOMO: *(Disgusted.)*
So it's finally you.
SAUL: *(Calm.)*
Excuse me?
TOMO: *(Looking at SAUL'S papers.)*
It didn't take long for you to show up here.
SAUL: You were expecting me?
TOMO: I've seen a lot of them like you, so I'm not surprised.
SAUL: *(Silent.)*
TOMO: Do you admit to it?
SAUL: *(Silent.)*
TOMO: Did you force yourself on that girl?
SAUL: *(Silent.)*
TOMO: *(Impatient.)*
Why would *you* of all people do this?
SAUL: *(Silent.)*
TOMO: If this is not a confession, please tell me why you came.
SAUL: *(Silent.)*
TOMO: Anele, listen, you can't just come and then not speak.
SAUL: Saul.
TOMO: Eh?
SAUL: *(Dissociating, looking away.)*
It's my Christian name.
TOMO: *(Perplexed.)*
SAUL: Saul!
(Agitated.)
My father called me Saul when I looked away.
(Mumbles.)
That's when I stopped being Anele.
TOMO: Okay, well, do you admit to what you did?
SAUL: Who will admit to what they did to me?
TOMO: You had no right. You know that. You—we watched her grow up. I

watched *you* grow up! You are forcing me to, to sign on this thing.
Again, I will put a man like you behind bars. Every day the same. Anele,
why?

SAUL: Please, sir, Saul.

(Enters DOC, giving papers to TOMO.)

TOMO: *(Stands up, and motions for DOC to follow him.)*

(TOMO and DOC approach BETTY'S body.)

DOC: *(Looking down at BETTY.)*

She was a prostitute.

Those girls do anything for a new underwear, hair, the works.

Her mother is old and bitter. Doesn't even cry. Just smokes.

TOMO: Every day the same.

Another girl dead. Another man locked.

DOC: But we can't just blame him.

TOMO: *(Pointing at BETTY.)*

How can we blame her if she's dead!

SCENE 4

(Onstage, BETTY as usual, and a chair, where TOMO sits. SAUL stands, walking around, shackled, aimless.)

TOMO: *(Impatient.)*

Boy, it's been two hours. I have a home to go to!

SAUL: *(Sarcastic.)*

Are you the only one? With a home to go to?

TOMO: *(Silent.)*

SAUL: It must make you very afraid to experience something nice in all this
misery.

TOMO: You seem more sober now than when we started.

(Leans closer.)

But I'd like to understand what exactly happened. And if this was the only
time. Because Anele, if it was your first time, maybe you didn't—maybe
you didn't realize what was happening. It happens sometimes. We, men,
we just kind of forget we're there. Is this what happened?

SAUL: Wrong name!

TOMO: *(Calmly.)*

Saul.

Did you intend to violate this girl?

SAUL: You speak about love as if there's no violence in it.

TOMO: I'm not talking about love.

SAUL: You're talking about me and Betty, and what we had was love.

TOMO: I just need you to tell me your side of the story. It won't count for much, but it can count for something. *This* conversation can count for something.

SAUL: *(Agitated.)*

I told you before, and I will repeat: Betty was the one who showed me love. I could have been born of her. She never ever looked away. Even that night, even as she went, as I watched her go, her gaze stayed with me.

TOMO: I know things are difficult, confusing, especially for *us*. But I need you to tell me what you did.

SAUL: I don't know what happened.

TOMO: Tell me what you *did*.

SAUL: I wasn't there.

TOMO: But you came here.

SAUL: *(Silent.)*

TOMO: That girl is now dead. You killed her.

SAUL: Someone once killed me too!

SCENE 5

(Lights on, SAUL, this time, lying on the floor instead of BETTY, asleep. There is a mattress on the side, where JEREMIAH lies, relaxed and satisfied, while FRIDA wraps herself in a capulana cloth while sitting on it, preparing to leave.)

JEREMIAH: Where are you going with all this hurry?

FRIDA: *(Shaking with fear, quietly, almost whispering.)*

I'd like to get some warm water for you. May I?

JEREMIAH: So go! Don't just stand there! Hurry yourself, I am not done!

FRIDA: *(Exits the stage and shortly returns with a bowl with warm water, and a towel, which she places on JEREMIAH'S groin. JEREMIAH relaxes further. FRIDA looks away, looks down.)*

JEREMIAH: *(Notices FRIDA'S distant look.)*

Look at me!

FRIDA: *(Takes a deep breath and faces him, reluctantly.)*

I am looking.

JEREMIAH: I hate it when you run away like that, with your eyes.

FRIDA: But you have me every night.

JEREMIAH: If not by force, then how?

FRIDA: *(Silent, resentful.)*

JEREMIAH: I want you to stop doing that. Your son is now doing the same.

FRIDA: *(Agitated.)*

What do you mean? Anele—Saul, what is it he's doing?

JEREMIAH: Looking away, pretending he's not there.

And stop it with this name! We gave him a good name. Like me, a good
Christian name.

FRIDA: *(Agitated.)*

Jere-mi-ah, you're not . . . you're not *making* him run from you, are you?

JEREMIAH: Don't have crazy ideas.

(Removes the warm towel from his groin.)

Go and call him.

FRIDA: But he's sleeping.

JEREMIAH: Wake him up.

FRIDA: Please, I beg you.

JEREMIAH: You're making me upset!

FRIDA: But you can have me, I'm right here! I'm not looking away, I'm
sorry!

JEREMIAH: *(Stands up and leaves the mattress, walks hastily towards SAUL'S
body.)*

Saul! Wake up!

Go into the room!

*(SAUL, fearful and agitated, looks at his mother for protection, but FRIDA,
despite the pain, and for self-preservation, denies him the look and turns
away.)*

SCENE 6

*(FATIMA is rocking on her old chair, alone and quiet. A finished cigarette in
hand. BETTY on the floor, in front of her.)*

FATIMA: Forgiveness belongs to God, and I don't have much of it in me.
This life has robbed me of it.

All of them are dirty, that family. Father, mother and son, the whole of
them. I look at them, I see what they do in those rooms, what they made
my Betty do.

Others look and say the same about me, that they knew what happened in
these rooms, in my house.

I hate them most because we are alike. Our roofs were separate, but we
heard each other's cries. You grow up eating up a kind of love that is
always cooked with violence, seasoned with force, served in misery,
swallowed in silence.

This space is filled with silence.

(In a ritualistic way, she stands from her rocking chair, goes offstage and emerges back on with a cloth with which she covers BETTY'S body.)
Someone is still looking away.

THE END

The author reserves all translation, serialization, and dramatization rights. Requests for any of these rights should be addressed to Celma Cainara Manjate da Costa at celmaccosta@gmail.com.

Malian playwright Jeanne Diama, author of *Tafé Fanga: Le pouvoir du pagne?*

Tafé Fanga: Le pouvoir du pagne?

Jeanne Diama

Jeanne Diama is a Malian writer, director, and actor, having trained at the Conservatory of Multimedia Arts and Crafts Balla Fasséké Kouyaté in Bamako. In Bamako, she has also taught theater at a school for the hearing impaired. From quite early on in her studies, she became interested in writing. Somewhat later, she began directing and acting for the stage, performing not only plays, but also adaptations of novels and essays. Her texts, some of which include *Chroniques d'une prostituée* [*Chronicles of a Prostitute*], *Le Pouvoir du pagne?* [*The Power of the Wrapper?*], *Du bout de mes entrailles* [*From the Bottom of my Guts*], *Absolem* [*Absolom*], and *Coups humains* [*Human Blows*], query what it means to be a Malian woman today, examining her rights and her demands.

During 2017–2018, Diama participated in the experimental writing lab "Elan" at the festival, Les Récréâtrales, in Ouagadougou, Burkina Faso. And in November 2018, she acted there, benefiting from a "Visas for Creation" fellowship from the French Institute in Paris. As author, actor, and director, she also took part for three consecutive years in the arts festival Les Praticables in Bamako (2017–2019).

In June 2019, at the invitation of the program "Writing for the Stage" at The International Festival of Francophonies in Limoges, she participated in the first writing residency for Francophone women writers, staying at the festival's Writers House. This was followed in 2020 by a second residency spent between Limoges and The International City of the Arts in Paris. She also won in 2020 the "From Text to Stage" prize from the French Institute for her play, *Cousu-main* [*Sewn by Hand*]. In 2020, Diama also participated in Paris's Africa Season, acting in a play by the Congolese writer Sinzo Aanza, staged by the director of the Récréâtrales Festival, Aristide Tarnagda. Performed at the Odéon Théâtre in Paris, this work toured to Caen and Nantes.

In 2021, the Nova Villa Association invited Diama to a colloquium in Reims, France, to speak on "What we can learn from Africa." She also benefitted from a writer's residency in Reims, where she visited high schools and led writing workshops. The following year, her project on Covid, *Mon Coronovirus 2.0* [*My Coronavirus 2.0*] was funded by the African Culture Fund, and her *Embargo* proposal won a residency in Lille where, thanks to the International Commission for Francophone Theater and the Association Sel-Ba, she was able to develop her project with a Malian actor, an Ivorian writer, and a Belgian set designer. In 2022, her play, *Tafé Fanga: le pouvoir du pagne?* [*Tafé Fanga: The Power of the Wrapper?*] was performed at Limoges at the Festival of Francophonies, where she interpreted the role of Ella. The play later toured to the festival Casamance on Stage in Senegal. In 2023, her project *Nos étoiles filantes* [*Our Shooting Stars*] was selected by the International Cultural Center John Smith as the basis for a residency in Ouidah, Benin.

As director, she staged in 2016 Georges Bernay's play *Aux confins des âmes perdues* [*At the Frontier of Lost Souls*]; and in 2018, she directed a staged reading of *Femme Iset* [*The Woman Iset*] by the Cameroonian writer Hermine Yollo. She also directed a reading of *Hashtagmetoo* by Ivorian writer Yolande Pehe at the 2018 Praticables Festival; and for the third edition of the festival in 2019, she staged a first version of her own text *Cousu-Main,* a play about women's plight in the north of the Sahel, in which she decries how rape is used as a weapon during periods of war. In 2022, she brought this production to two festivals in France. *Cousu-Main*, which excoriates violent sexual abuse, was also read at the 2023 Avignon Theater Festival.

Diama has acted in both film and television (2012–2023), performing in the series "Bamako la ville aux trois caimans" [Bamako, the City of Three Crocodiles], written by Aïda Mady Diallo and produced by Afribone. She can also be seen in *Bamako, Capitales Africaines* [*Bamako, African Capitals*], a series by Jean-Noel Bah. And she acted in the series *Un Dimanche à Bamako* [*One Sunday in Bamako*], produced by Banco Productions. For Banco Productions, she also performed in Toumani Sangaré's film *Nogochi*. She has, in addition, held roles in several short films: *Chambre Noire* (nominated for a prize at FESPACO); *Contraception* by Eliasaph Diassana; the animated film *Souroukouba and Zonzaniba* by Gaoussou Bassékou Tangara; and Policikè by Toumani Keita (produced by Vortex).

An interview with Jeanne Diama is available at https://doi.org/10.3998/mpub.12827650.cmp.7.

JEANNE DIAMA ON *TAFÉ FANGA*:

Like every Sunday, Ella is hanging out with her chosen family. And, like every Sunday, the discussion centers on men, marriage, and how old Ella is getting. She dares, nonetheless, to criticize society and skewer how women see themselves. And she offers her vision of what a woman is.

The other guests dare as well.
They are . . .
Young women who've succeeded professionally,
Who reflect a society that hounds young women,
Women who pick themselves back up when they fall,
Women who want to love, but whom?
Women who want to speak, but don't know how,
Women who hurt, but keep on going,
Women who want to talk, but are afraid.
Their lives are often a routine of false smiles, false happiness, and false ambitions.
But they make fun of their fears and their wounds,
Their pain that has lasted too long,
Their hidden fed-up-ness,
Their long-camouflaged tears.

Because now they want to speak. At last.

18 SPEAKING OUR SELVES

Tafé Fanga: Le pouvoir du pagne?

Jeanne Diama

Translated from the French by Judith G. Miller as *Tafé Fanga: The Power of the Wrapper?*[1]

CHARACTERS

Ella: 25 years old
Aunt Madeleine: 50 years old
Aunt Coumba: 50 years old
Aunt Ami: 50 years old
The Praise-Singer/Griotte: 40 years old
Evelyne: 27 years old
Mariam: 30 years old
Aissata: 30 years old
Assan: 30 years old
Oumou: 30 years old
The Hairdresser: 30 years old

SCENE 1

(We're at a gathering of family and close women friends. Like every Sunday, ELLA spends her day visiting her AUNT MADELEINE, and, like every weekend, AUNT MADELEINE gathers together women friends of her neighborhood for sharing food, drink, and gossip. [The younger women gather alone later to participate in the tontine.[2]] As is the custom and in hopes of collecting a little money, a PRAISE-SINGER, also known as a GRIOTTE, stops by at the beginning of the gathering to offer songs honoring those gathered and to proffer some marital advice to the younger women, ELLA and EVELYNE. The GRIOTTE leaves after performing.[3])

1. Translator's Note: *Tafé Fanga* is the Bambara expression for a woman's sexual power, which Diama has translated as "The Power of the Wrapper." She adds a question mark to the translation in order to query the efficacy of such power.

2. Translator's Note: The tontine, a central theme in this play, is, as the author tells us, an unofficial savings plan. Every other week, or once a month, a group of women meet to contribute a certain sum of money to a communal pot. Each member of the group will receive all of the money from one of the meetings when her turn comes. In the play, the tontine is a central theme whose meaning changes as the play comes to a close

3. Translator's Note: Many of the characters, here the griotte, speak from time to time in Bambara, one of the languages of Mali. The author thus suggests the multilingualism of Malians and, also, their linguistic code-switching, depending on the nature of the discussion. The author has translated these Bambara lines into French and placed the French after the Bambara in her text. The transliteration of the Bambara

THE PRAISE-SINGER: *Wise words teach us that we, women, must be strong. Wise words teach us that we, women, must accept what is handed out to us and be resilient, so that our children will be blessed and protected. Wise words of wise men teach us that we, women, are the pillars of the home, and if we do not behave, things fall apart. Wise words teach us that it is the role of women to bring the children up properly. If the child misbehaves, if the family and the home fall apart, we, women, are to blame.*[4]

(All at once, the aunties and EVELYNE rush on stage. AUNT MADELEINE, her friends COUMBA and AMI, her daughter EVELYNE, tighten their wrappers. Other women move off and on, except for ELLA who is seated, glued to her phone. She is wearing a very short white dress made of damask (or bazin).[5] *A HAIRDRESSER braids her hair. She raises her eyes from time to time to take in what's happening. After a few moments, everyone on stage approaches ELLA and sits down around her. They are speaking all at once and the ensuing confusion makes it hard to hear what's being said. EVELYNE takes a picture of the gathering. MADELEINE speaks to ELLA.)*

AUNT MADELEINE: Ella?

ELLA: What is it, Auntie?

AUNT MADELEINE: You know, daughter, Mahamane is ready to bring the cola nuts for Evy. It's absolutely sure this time, *as God is my witness,*[6] so you really need to think about participating in the tontine for the engagement and the wedding. That way, you won't have to worry about buying the cloth and the dress.

ELLA: All right, I will—but when the time comes, I'll pay.

AUNT MADELEINE: But you do know if you don't have the money, there's no problem. We can make sure you have some . . . and that's why you have to hang on to Mohamed. He's a really good boy. He'll buy you anything you want; you only have to ask.

---

is somewhat approximate. We have chosen to translate the French lines into English; and have placed the corresponding transliterated Bambara in the footnotes. The author would expect the play to be performed entirely in English in a production in an Anglophone country. The lines in italics in the dialogue correspond to the Bambara phrases. When there is a long exchange in Bambara, there will be only one footnote for the whole exchange.

4. Anw ka ma kôrôbakoumadô ko kanwmoussow, kanw kan mougnou ka sabali. Anw ka ma kôrôbakoumadô fana bafô ko ni mousso, i mougnou na, i dén bé bari ka. Anw ka ma kôrôbakoumaw ko, kanwmousso dé yéfourou sin sinbagawyé, ko nanwfililadron, ko dién bé gnagami. Anw ka ma kôrôbakoumadôw ko, kanwmoussow dé yédoutiguiwyé, ko anw dé bé denw la don. N'ga ni déntchien na, ko moussow, ni dougnaga mira, ko moussow, ni fourou ma ta gnèkanwmoussow.

5. Translator's Note: Bazin (a kind of damask), wax (a technique for putting patterns on cloth and, also, a name for the cloth), and bogolan (a brown and black died woven fabric) are part of the repertory of what is often thought of as "traditional" African cloth. Many wrappers (large swaths of cloth tied around the waist) are made of patterned bazin or wax.

6. Translator's Note: Mali is a majority Muslim country. The characters in this play are both Muslim and Christian. All references to God ("Allah" in Arabic) will be translated as "God" in this version. Here the expression "walaye" corresponds to "*as God is my witness.*"

ELLA: That's not how it works. I'm the one who buys everything I want.

AUNT COUMBA: The car, your clothes, everything?

ELLA: Car, clothes, everything, everything, everything.

AUNT MADELEINE: Then what's he good for?

AUNT COUMBA: And what good does he do you? *Listen to what I'm telling you,*[7] sweetheart, when you catch a juicy man, I'm telling you, a man full of juice like that one, you have to squeeze him, squeeze him good. That way, if he leaves you, you'll have emptied him out. *You should squeeze him so hard, there won't be a drop left.*[8]

AUNT MADELEINE: *And, please, take pity on us, I tell you this every time, wear a wrapper when you come to these gatherings. You're not a child anymore. You're a woman now, just look at how full your breasts are. Please, when you come to my house, wear wax or bazin wrappers. It's our tradition, Ella.*[9] As God is my witness, Ella, I can't understand how Mohamed—with his name and his looks—lets you leave the house like that. He's from Algeria, right? That's certainly not how women dress over there, is it? *All those women are covered from head to foot.*[10]

AUNT AMI: So, *tell me,*[11] what do you wear when you go to his family?

ELLA: He doesn't have a family.

AUNT MADELEINE: *My God,*[12] you mean you won't have parents-in-law? It's not possible. *Ella, no, no you can't possibly do that!!!*[13]

AUNT AMI: *How do we know he didn't kill his family?*

AUNT COUMBA: *Dear God, have pity on us, I beg you, don't say such a thing!*

AUNT MADELEINE: *ELLA, where did you find this Mohamed? Tell us!*

ELLA: *Calm down; we were at school together.*[14] He didn't kill his family. He was here when they died. It was an accident. OK?

AUNT MADELEINE: *Praise God. I panicked, I thought you'd just made yourself unmarriageable.*[15] Do you have your period?

ELLA: No.

AUNT MADELEINE: Are you sure? Because if you do, you better not go into the kitchen.

ELLA: And why not?

---

7. Bé na min fô i yé, a lamèdè.

8. i babissi dé koye, ka na foye to a kono.

9. Ani m'mafo i yeki ka ta fésiri ni bé na doubakônôsaaaa, i té dèmisèniyétougounikoye, i yémousso-falénba dé yé, i sin bara la djè, to ka waxi don, ou bien ikabazin don, o dé yandanbékoye.

10. ou faribè da tougoulén do, hannn!

11. Né ko.

12. Allah na Kira!

13. Ka na kèèdèèèè.

14. Môgôba don na lé dé ya somôgôfagawa? /Astafouroulah, ka na fôdè. /I YE MOHAMED NI BO MIN? I ti koumawa! / An yé école dé kègnongonfè.

15. Alhamdoulilah, i bé nan djatiguè, i toun bi ni ka fourou ko guèlè ya doni.

TAFÉ FANGA: LE POUVOIR DU PAGNE? 21

AUNT MADELEINE: Well, Ella, how many times do I have to tell you? You'll spoil the food; and you know I told you not to wear white when you're not pure. Everybody can see what's going on, if by chance . . . Hmmm . . .

ELLA: I don't have my period. I'm not impure, and I'm wearing white because you asked me to.

AUNT MADELEINE: I told you to wear an outfit made of bazin and what do you go and do? A little dress that shows every one of your curves and makes it look like you're not eating enough. Yeah! *You're so skinny you look like your little cousin Fantani's pencil. When it comes time for your wedding, you better gain some weight. Otherwise, they'll say your father didn't give you enough to eat. We'll wash you with fresh milk. We'll massage you with shea butter. That way you'll shine like a star before entering into the prison of happiness.*[16]

ELLA: *You know, I don't need any of that, including the prison of happiness, no need to get me ready before my marriage.*[17] In any case, I'm not a virgin anymore.

AUNT COUMBA: *God have pity on us, Ella. God, have mercy. You don't just yell it out—and why the devil did you do that?*[18]

ELLA: I don't know.

AUNT MADELEINE: *Ella, for God's sake, you're going to kill me. Was it Mohamed?*

ELLA: *No, it's Soul.*

AUNT AMI: *Lord in Heaven, who is this Soul, anyway?*

ELLA: *We were in tenth grade together.*

AUNT MADELEINE: *But Ella, in tenth grade, you were only 14 years old. And just look at Evy, she's still a virgin.*[19]

ELLA: Hurray for her! I take my hat off to you, Evy!

EVY: You're not even wearing a hat.

ELLA: It's just an expression.

AUNT MADELEINE: *Please shut up. Is it so difficult to understand you should cover yourself when you're outside? That's the way you get respect when you're a girl.*[20]

(AUNT MADELEINE dismisses everybody.)

---

16. I djalén i ko fantani ka dessin crayon. Ni la fourousérafo i ka farikolodônisôrô nô tè ou bafôki fa ti balodè. An bi ko nônôkènèdji dé la, kimoun ni fènè. Ya ni ka bôkasssoblônkono, fô i bé mènèmènè.

17. Mè né mako té sékassoblôn ma, awniaw ma né farifaga.

18. Astafouroulah Ella, ka na to mogowere ka ni mai dai, mounyibilala?

19. Eh Ella, é bé né faga n'Allah na Kira dé tchè, Mohamed dé yi ka bogotigui ya kè? / Soul dé ya ta./ Eh Allah Soul fana yédjònyésaaa?/ Anwyé 10ème dé kègnôgonfè. / Allah na kira Ella, ko ké to 10 ème é té toun bé santaninani dé la. A filai Evybanôna.

20. I nè mine! Fini do min bi farid'àtougou, kouma nana? Bognabé o dé la.

Let's go see how the meat's coming along. (To ELLA.) But I haven't finished with you yet![21]

SCENE 2

(All the aunties leave. ELLA is alone with the HAIRDRESSER. She sums up the conversation she's just had with AUNT COUMBA and AUNT MADELEINE.)

ELLA *(To the HAIRDRESSER.)*: So, in a nutshell, I start by believing my man will leave me one day and by anticipating my revenge. Is this some kind of a joke?

And am I dreaming or did she just say that wax and damask cloth are *our* tradition? And am I dreaming or did she prefer to pretend that I'm not wearing bazin just because I had a dress made that stops at my knees?

Today, we're discussing Evelyne's marriage, and next Sunday it will be my turn. She really wants me to get married. They all want me to get married. You'd think I was the only 25-year-old woman in Mali who wasn't married. All the days that God made, and if it's not my aunties, it's people I've never met, or my colleagues, the fruit vendor, even the neighborhood mechanic . . .

You know how that makes you feel when the mechanic or the fruit vendor, who know nothing of your life, ask you if you're married and you say no and they feel they have the right to tell you you're turning into an old maid?

And the worst is—they have no idea it's none of their business.

So, I smile and wish them a good day.

I've smiled so much I don't even have to pretend anymore.

My face freezes into a smile as soon as I see certain people or hear certain remarks like "how come men don't want to marry you?" Do I need to tell them I'm the one who doesn't want that frigging thing to happen to my life? Of course, the answer is no, because we all know that no one would believe me—every woman obviously wants to get married. It's become a universal truth in Mali, a fact proved by Malian science; and if it happens you don't want to get married right away, it's obviously because no man wants anything to do with you. No man wants to marry you—or somebody has put a spell on you.

My aunt thinks it's the embroidery vendor who cast a spell on me, because they quarreled six months ago. It's the only way she can understand that

---

21. An ga ta sogo ko. M'be ni soro, ounkono.

Mohamed and I aren't engaged, even though we've been going together
for four years.

And this kind of family reunion is the worst. If you ever make the mistake
of letting them see even one of your men friends, it's enough for them to
decide he's the one who's going to marry you.

Don't ever do that . . .

The mechanic or the fruit vendor, knowing nothing of your life, asks if
you're married and then thinks it's OK to tell you you're turning into an
old maid. *What a joke!*[22]

Then it's your mother, and after her, your father. Even if they don't say so
directly, it's in the way they hold themselves. The looks. The gestures . . .

But when you don't want to get married . . . How do you say that? How?

What do you do when you're a prisoner of your feelings?

When you have to choose between your family and yourself?

It's easy enough to say, choose your happiness. But you wouldn't be on this
earth without those people; so, what do you do? You choose your
happiness over theirs. Is that it?

(The HAIRDRESSER holds out her hand and ELLA hands her a braid.)

Especially when you see what's happened to the marriage of the person
who wants so furiously for you to get married. *(Whispering.)* Aunt
Madeleine—her guy is a major asshole who cheated on her with the
housekeeper—who he later married and had kids with. And he's an
alcoholic who doesn't work, who lives in a house without paying a dime
for it, while the women, well, the women have to work their tails off to
keep him in style ever since he lost his job because he showed up at
work completely drunk and exposed his little prick to everybody before
yelling "Allah Akbar!" And this aunt used to say all the time that as a
Christian she'd never accept a co-wife. "Never, it's in the Bible, if ever my
husband takes a second wife and even if he dares cheat on me, I'll pack
my bags and go home to my parents."

Well, it looks like she's changed her mind because every year at Christmas
she welcomes the co-wife into her own home. But you'd better not say
that out loud. You have to make do with a little smile—and that's it.

And my cousin Evelyne. For God's sake, she abandoned her studies and a
fellowship to a university in Canada to grab onto a promise of marriage
that after seven years is still only a promise. Like a blast of
wind—wooosh.

Men can be incredibly ungrateful and egotistical.

---

22. a ma ban sa wa.

And women usually take the prize for stupidity.

(She shakes her head and bends down to open another packet of extensions. She starts to cut the braid and then stops.)

But how can I make them understand that marriage can't be an end in itself and that I don't want anything to do with it? I can't say it, no I can't. I have to do what a good daughter does. Participate in endless family gatherings whose subject is always your future marriage.

I'm a very smart woman. I'm 25 years old, and I have a salary that's well over the average. I was the only woman of my generation to earn a diploma and I never got less than an A. I'm a woman who fights every day to prove I'm a winner. I'm a woman who knows what she wants; and today what I want is not what they want. Why is that so hard to understand?

(She hands a braid to the HAIRDRESSER.)

I've always asked myself what's the big deal about marriage? Especially when you know that more and more people are getting divorced. In the last century I can understand how, in those days, sure, it was the only way to have a sexual relationship. But today, it's crazy what people are capable of doing in order to get married. Those poor sheep, those poor cows, and those poor little sacrificial chickens . . . and people get married for every reason imaginable and even unimaginable . . . God help us!!! You'll see, in a few minutes Evelyne's childhood friends will come and start to talk about marriage and babies, but never about financial independence. That's how the tontine works in all its glory. And you know why? Because society finds it abnormal. That's something we should talk about! How is it that in 2020 everybody finds it abnormal for a woman to want to work and earn her own money, for her not to want children or not to want to get married? How is it possible to think that's not normal? In this family, in any case, I'm the only one who finds it normal and that's why I've always refused to participate in the tontine. But today I'm being forced to, or my auntie will kick me out of the family.

(Noises from outside.)

Poor little sheep. I really don't understand these Sunday gatherings. I'm not saying that family isn't important, but come on, we're already living on top of each other during the rest of the year. Give me at least my Sundays.

(We hear AUNT MADELEINE'S voice.)

AUNT MADELEINE: Ella. Ella. Ella.

ELLA: Shush. I have no intention of going to help them, none at all. I have something a lot more important to do here: stay and get braided!

(She hands another braid to the HAIRDRESSER.)

She speaks of *our* tradition, *our* culture. In our culture, women didn't used to bother themselves with so much clothing. We always went around with bits of cloth that covered our breasts and our behinds. There never was a problem until those people came to tell us it was indecent, and give our men the idea they needed to control us better. I suppose we could say that even if the men let themselves be fooled so easily, on some level it suited them. Right?

I haven't said anything because I'll never have any peace. But Mohamed just asked me to marry him. So, mums the word.

HAIRDRESSER: If Aunt Madeleine hears that, she'll freak out. Don't you think?

ELLA: I know. Oh! *(Laughter.)* Are you married?

HAIRDRESSER: No, I'm divorced. I left my husband and my job, and I started working for myself.

ELLA: Why?

HAIRDRESSER: I'd had enough.

ELLA: That's all?

HAIRDRESSER: I was the only woman working in the salon—so you can imagine what a hell it was. My colleagues were idiots.

ELLA: And what do you think mine are? They're so incredibly sexist, misogynist, and stupid, I feel like I'm working at the Ministry of Sexism.

But, as a matter of fact, the worst aren't really those big asinine macho men who think they're so brilliant. Those guys have mush in the place of brains. I mean, they're really two-neuron terrorists.

The worst are the ones who think they're super-feminists.

(She imitates the voices of her colleagues.)

"You know, Ella, you should dress exactly as you want. Besides, I'm sure the boss likes it. I'm sure you can get everything you want from him. That's all he's waiting for—and be sure to talk to him about our raises."

"Ella, you know it's your right to dress like a whore. That's nobody's business but your own. In any case, as far as I'm concerned, it doesn't bother me in the least."

Thanks a lot!

"Ella, thankfully, you're making this office bearable. Your make-up is always so perfect, maybe a little too much, but, really, it's no big deal. Why don't the other girls make us think they're beautiful? A little make-up doesn't hurt anybody."

"Ella, shit, you're so beautiful, I could rape you."

Well, thanks . . .

And, you know, the best are the "intellectual" discussions I have with the real brains of the office. You have to hear it.

"Ella, you're beautiful and intelligent. You don't need all that other stuff. Why do it? A woman is life, A woman is image."

I always wondered what he meant by that.

(*The HAIRDRESSER begins to laugh.*)

"You know, I get you. You want people to know you're independent, but independence is really in the head and the heart. Take me, for example, I'm very independent, and yet so simple. Listen, when God created woman, He created her for a very specific reason. You see, when Eve bit into the apple, she condemned all the men on this planet; yes, all the men! And given that, you have to make up for it and stop pushing us towards temptation. You—well, in my case, you don't really tempt me, but that woman on the fourth floor . . . Can you imagine if I weren't so strong, but I meditate, so I'm able to stay focused, right, on my wife and on her alone, on her and not all those low-life Kim Kardashians. But you shouldn't let your boyfriend make you wear so much make-up, all the same. I think you're beautiful, but that red is really a little too much. You should try a simple gloss. OK? Be strong!"

Why do those guys think they should spend so much time counselling us about how we dress and look?

HAIRDRESSER: It's not them. It's society. Society decided that women should wear wrappers, wear clothes made of wax prints or bazin. It's the culture, the tradition.

ELLA: Oh *that* tradition! Wax, bazin—What a load of bull! (*Earnestly, her fist in the air.*) For your information, and for society, and for everybody, wax and bazin do not come from here. We don't even make them. And it's not because we dye them, that they're ours.

HAIRDRESSER: Yeah, and we're the ones who're accused of being assimilated because we'd rather wear jeans than a wrapper! *Come on, hand me another braid!*[23]

(*ELLA hands her an extension.*)

ELLA: Let's take this subject by the balls. It's pretty heavy, (*Laughs.*) as you know. First off, I don't like it when they call my vagina a pussy. I really really don't like it when they do that, but all the young guys say it all the time, everywhere, and now I can't get it out of my head. You know what

---

23. Fitinidiyanwala!

that means? Those young guys are just spoiled little cocks who think they possess all the chicks. And that's how they're brought up.

And let's be realistic about this. If my vagina resembled a pussy, I'd be scared out of my mind.

Can you imagine if it were always crying "meow, meow." I'd feel like hitting it all the time, but I'm the one who'd get pots thrown at me.

Do you ever feel, like I do, that you want to bash in somebody's balls? I sure do, especially the balls of those young guys who like to lurk outside my house, grinning, and repeating "pussy" every second phrase. That really makes me want to smash their balls, those guys who think they're the kings of the universe.

HAIRDRESSER *(Laughing.)*: *Stop!*[24] I bet that would really hurt! I should try it on my former colleagues.

(Laughter.)

ELLA: And they never stop saying we're the lucky ones, we, the women. How truthful is that?! Right!!! I mean, in addition to the fact of losing blood every month for 3, 4, 5, or 7 days, maybe even two weeks—accompanied by atrocious cramping, or the fact of bringing an 8 or 10 pound baby into the world out of a little hole, or the fact of having your clitoris cut when you're just a kid, or the fact of having a little bit of flesh that, when it gets torn during your first sexual encounter, makes you cry all the tears in the world, or the fact that after every sexual encounter your vagina can be sore for days, or the fact you can be pummeled and ridden for hours on end and never arrive at anything. Zero pleasure. Because, no, it isn't enough to have Your Thing in My Thing to make an explosion. And if, besides all that, you had your clit cut when you were little . . . But besides all that, we're doing fine. Really fine.

HAIRDRESSER: Yeah . . . *(Ironic.)* really fine . . . because with all that, you have to consider you can cry every tear in your body the first time you have sex, suffer through a monthly period, get no pleasure out of how many times you get poked, and still, at the point when you really want a baby . . . nothing. Zero. Out of luck. Nature can be a real shit.

ELLA: Afterwards, the men say, "but it's not our fault." But does anybody ever say that about us? Of course not.

And I don't understand why they say guys lose their virginity; in fact, they don't lose a thing. Unless it's their sense of direction, *(Both laughing.)* if you know what I mean.

HAIRDRESSER: It's exactly what happened to me. He had no idea where to

---

24. Sabali!

go with it—up high, down low, to the right, to the left? *(They laugh.)* If you need a GPS to figure it out, you should ask for it. Ask for it, it's your right. You have every right *(Wink)*.

ELLA: It's a situation I don't get, because . . . you can't say you're not in a good position when you connect. You've got the right axis. Your vision field is really . . . clear. So why doesn't it work? What's the problem here? It's really an existential question I'm asking.

(Laughter.)

Last Wednesday on television I saw the Phallocrats in action. Get this: according to the explanations of the sexologist on the show, I have to stop crying because that's what impacts negatively my man's libido. So, when I happen to be unhappy for whatever reason, I have to control myself because it's absolutely necessary that the god who rules my body be able to ejaculate. Hallelujah!

HAIRDRESSER: When it comes to being idiotic . . .

ELLA: Where does this thirst for power over everything and everybody come from? Why the need to be superior? Why line up against us when we fight for our rights? Our rights to have sanitary napkins free of chemicals. Why are you so upset by our wanting to have the same salary you do for the same job? Why are you so upset that we want the same positions you have because we have the same diplomas and the same qualifications? Why are you so upset because we want to work as you do and not just stay at home with the children? Why are you so upset when we have the same number of sexual partners as you do? *(She opens another packet of braids.)* All of a sudden, we're whores, frustrated, hysterical because we want the same thing as you. What's going on? Could it possibly be you're afraid of us? But we don't bite. That is, if you're not asking for it.

(Laughter.)

I know perfectly well I'm not responsible for the sick way society looks at women. So why am *I* afraid? Why this fear of speaking, of confronting, of recounting. My fear of everything.

SCENE 3

(We hear noise, footsteps, laughter. EVELYNE'S friends arrive for the Sunday tontine. They enter chatting.)

AISSATA: *How? Well, put a little garlic in the ginger juice, let it sit for a while, add a dash of hot pepper, and your man won't be able to get enough of it.*[25]

---

25. N'gui kana fô, ni yé l'ail donikè i ka djinibéré la, a to l'ail gnaga ka digue gnamakoudjikôrô, fonrontodonifara o kan, na yo min, a nèguè dé bé da, a té da abada.

ASSAN: *How's it going, Ella?*[26]

ELLA: It's going fine. Thank God.

(The women take their places on the stools and the floor mats while they keep on chatting.)

AISSATA: *I use blessings to purify my whole house. If you don't chase away the evil spirits, they're capable of slipping into your own sister's body, and she'll end up becoming your husband's mistress and, finally, your co-wife.*

ASSAN: *Yeah, you abandon your father's house; you abandon your mother; you do all that for an ungrateful man who won't recognize your true value, a man who steals your dignity.*

AISSATA: *It doesn't matter whether you're related or not. You must never leave your husband alone with another woman.*

OUMOU: *Ella, listen to me good. Don't let Mohamed get away from you. OK? You should go see Madou for that. He'll throw the cauris for you. He knows what to do.*[27]

ELLA: Madou? *Isn't he the one*[28] who predicted my cousin's marriage, who told her she'd find her happiness in her fiancée and not in studying medicine—so she gave up her studies? That's him, right?

EVELYNE: Don't start.

ELLA: *What did I say?*

MARIAM: *Ella, you'd better hold on tight to Mohamed. That kind of man is rare on our planet.*

AISSATA: *In any case, he's handsome; he's respectful, and—this is the best—he has a bank account full of French money.*[29]

MARIAM: Yeah, that's the most important thing.

ASSAN: Anyhow, you can't eat handsome, so even if your man is ugly, well, my dears, you have to reason with your heart, close your eyes, give yourself to God and enjoy—enjoy the money. Your beauty will make up for anything he's missing.

(Laughter.)

AISSATA: *You can say that again! We aren't short of ugly men in Mali! Either it's their noses that look like two bicycle tires, or their mouths that look like the back of a public bus. Even if God steps in to help us, those men . . . Well, forget it. Nobody could want them.*

---

26. Kowkagni?

27. N'gasôgôna na bèkassayé baraka té, ni ma to ka djinèdjougouguèn ka bô i kasso, a bé son ka dôn i wolowolodôgôni na, o la ban na kitchèsougourounyé, ni ka la laban ka kè i sinamousso. /I bi fa fili wali soyé, kibafili wali soyé, fitiri walé bé kla ka ni dambébèbô i la. /Somô ko té ola dè, kana son kitchèkélén ni mosso si to ou lélén na ko tôyésomôgô ya yé, kanakèdè. / Ella n'békelenfô i yé, ni ta fè Mohamed ka bolikè, ta Madou kolini fila la feye, a bé sé dé.

28. Madou kolini fila la

29. Ma foyefo. /Ella Mohamed minèdè, hummm, ni tchèsougouni té sôrôbilendè./ En tout cas dè, a tchèkagni, a bé môgôbogna, mais surtout, a bakoundé sa, n'gabakoun dé.

ASSAN: *If you ever make the mistake of sniffing their underclothes, God protect you. Because the germs will kill you.*

AISSATA: *I'm telling you, sometimes I feel like telling him to wash his own underwear.*

OUMOU: *And just think, these are the same men who stretch out next to you to make love.*

AISSATA: *What? Now? If you think you're going to touch me, you're going to take a shower first. Otherwise, I'll tighten my wrapper so much that even Madou, who throws the cauris, won't be able to undo it.*[30]

(Laughter.)

OUMOU: *Well said.*

MARIAM: *My marriage counsellor told me if I didn't feel like it, I should put a little sleeping potion in his dinner.*

ASSAN: *And did you do it?*

MARIAM: *You can have too much of a good thing, you know!*

AISSATA: *Yeah, there's a limit to everything.*

OUMOU: *As God is my witness, I don't like to make love.*

MARIAM: *Don't try to tell me, Mariam Koné, that you don't do it. How do you manage?*

OUMOU: *I think about God.*

MARIAM: *Never! You should never do that.*

OUMOU: *If I don't do that, what can I do?*[31]

ASSAN: *So, tell us, does your man know what he's doing?*

ELLA: *Did you try speaking to him about it?*

OUMOU: *Me! God forbid! I slip him a little sleeping pill pretty often, and he falls dead asleep. So, I get a little vacation.*

MARIAM: *But I don't get it. You mean he wants to make love every night?*

OUMOU: *That's what I'm telling you.*

MARIAM: *Oh Lord, I couldn't stand it. I'm not a door you can open whenever you want to go in or out. Even doors get tired.*

AISSATA: *You want to know something? In my house, it's a desert. I'm jealous of you; I'd be up for it, even if it were night and day.*

MARIAM: *Don't you say such a thing in front of me—Mariam Koné.*

---

30. A fôtougounidè, tchètchèdjougouyère bé ban Malilawa,ni min nounbara té côminèguèsopinè, o basôrô o dabara bé cômisotramakôfèla, annwmoussowyère ban ta to Allah dema sa kè, tchè nounou koni, entretien zéro. /Ni you ka slipouyèrèkassasama, Allah kikissi o microbou ma./ Kouma dôlafoounbafè ka fô ka kaslipouw ko koi./ I manimiri ko kelendébékla ka ni da i kèrèfè ko kè li dan bayèréyé, eh Allah minè humm./ Né? Foyi mi maga né la i kassa ma, i bi ko dén sinon ninyé tafé ninsirikè a li Madou kolinifili la té sé ka foni.

31. I djoyidjoyé!/ N'gamayanmaga dé tounbafô ko ni ta la domi, fourakissè ka kadoumini na. /I ya kè ah?/ Kôssôbèkè, ko kadi sa / N'ga a nèguèbôlénfènè ma fôdè. / N'Allah dé tchè, kèlimandinyén./ Kana ni fô né Mariam Koné yésaaaa, é dounbakètchogo di?/ Allah minè./ Ka na kèdè./ Éééé na ma kètén, a doun ka kètchoko di?

AISSATA: *I just did!*

MARIAM: *God in Heaven.*

AISSATA: *I think about God, because if I didn't, even a divorce would be better than what I've got.*

ASSAN: *But you were told, weren't you, that marriage was for better and for worse?*

AISSATA: *Do you think the person who invented that proverb is going to satisfy my desire?*

MARIAM: *Your desire? Since when have women been able to desire?*

OUMOU: *You said it![32]*

ELLA: Maybe you should listen to what your bodies are telling you and make your partners understand it.

MARIAM: First, these aren't our partners. These are our husbands. Partners are for single ladies.

ELLA: I mean sexual partners.

MARIAM: Second, you should stop letting everybody know you have such a satisfactory sex life.

ELLA: You mean you were all virgins when you got married?

AISSATA: No, but we weren't shouting it from the rooftops.

ELLA: How come? I really mean it. Why?

ASSAN: Because it's nobody's business, and because you're worth more when you keep your mouth shut.

ELLA: Worth more for who? Who do you mean?

MARIAM: Everybody. Your family. Your husband.

ELLA: Oh, I thought you were thinking about God. So, how do you keep your husband from knowing you're not a virgin?

(EVELYNE starts to make tea.)

OUMOU *(To EVELYNE.)*: *Put the pot here.[33]*

Sometimes your husband knows it, because he's the one you slept with before the wedding. But the dowry is higher when they think you're a virgin, and if you don't want anybody to know, you'd better have a lot of bank notes to bribe the person who's supposed to verify if your hymen is intact—that is, if you still practice that kind of verification.

---

32. Né ba, est-ce que é ta inhyèrè bé séwa ? Ah kouma bé yé dé dè./ É ya kouma da ti kè na yéwa?/ Djon ? Nééé ? A fôastafouroulah, n'bétokofarifagafoura dé kèn'gadjimin tala, ah n'bakètchokodi. / I djon ka kouma ni famoudoni, don wo don chou dé awbakèwa?/ Awôkè./ N'Allah n'téssé, o kouma né kèraso da yéwa, na yidiyakoumawokouma, i bayèlè/waga ah ? A li so da yèrè bé singuin./ I ti djôn'gakelenfô i yéwa, né ta ni yère té séfoyi la, nô tèali na ko kan ga chi ala, ka kiléala, o kadi yèrèyé oh./ Kana ninfô né Mariam Koné saaa./ A fôlidoun dé filè i yé./ Eh Allah minè!/ N'bémiri Allah dé ma, wallaye, sinon fourousaaayère ma foussa ni niyé./ Ay dè, ko fourouyé pour le meilleur et pour le pire dé yé./ Tchurrrrr né ko môgô mi yoladayesigui o, a lé dé bé na né nèguè da wa?/ I nèguèwa, né banèguè dé banwmoussow la yanwa?/ A fôtougounidè!

33. A blayan!

AISSATA: My darlings, I love him. *How could I not?*[34] He's the one who wanted us to get married. I wanted it too, but, but, I don't know anymore. He holds me back. He sticks to me. *He's stickier than the strongest glue.*[35]

MARIAM: I'm the one who asked mine to marry me. He was taking too long. I was twenty-eight, and we'd been together for ten years. So, I finally said: what about it? As that comedian says, you've been studying me for ten years, so what kind of diploma do you want? Since I came into the world, I had everything I wanted. It wasn't a man who was going to say no to me. He's the love of my life, but I wasn't born to be run by somebody else. Yeah. It's really me who runs him. We should tell the truth here. Everything begins with the woman and everything ends with the woman. When you marry me, I become your sister, your mother, your wife, and your daughter. Add up all the respect you owe—and give it to me.

OUMOU: I love my man too, but it's not really love. You know, it's something else. I don't know what, but when he's not there, I don't miss him. Now there are children and everything, and I like all that, but when there was just the two of us, it wasn't so great. Well, we only went out for two months before we got married.

ASSAN: In my case, we fight all the time about the children. He says he wants more and I tell him two are enough. You're somebody who doesn't make a lot of money, and me, neither; and you want a lot of children? He exhausts me like that.

ELLA: What are you going to do? I hope you don't mind my asking because . . .

ASSAN: He wanted me to remove my coil and I refused. Now it's Mr. "I don't want anything to do with you"—a sex strike.

HAIRDRESSER: You mean men also go on sex strikes? What? *(She clucks her tongue.)* I didn't think they could.

ELLA: If you really think about it, either there's another woman hidden somewhere, or they use their hands.

AISSATA: What are you saying? Another woman hidden somewhere?

ELLA: Or they use their hands. A lot, really a lot of men masturbate, you know.

MARIAM: Where? You can't mean here. You're mistaken. Let him cheat with another woman, I get that. But cheating on me with his hands, no, I'll kill him.

---

34. m'bakètchokodi?
35. a li colle forte ka djourou ta la

ELLA: Come on, you can't really see that as cheating.

OUMOU: If my man has a romantic hide-out, I'll get one too. Yes!

HAIRDRESSER: I was married for five years and I hadn't had any children, so his mother told him to take a second wife.

AISSATA: Did you agree?

HAIRDRESSER: At least I was told. I was lucky. I didn't learn about it the day of the wedding.

ELLA: And you wanted children?

HAIRDRESSER: My marriage depended on it. That's for sure.

AISSATA: We all want children. It is the ultimate consecration.

MARIAM: Did you know there are women who steal children. They pretend they're pregnant for nine whole months.

ELLA: How can you pretend to be pregnant for nine months? Doesn't your husband make love to you? Doesn't he touch your tummy to feel the baby? Doesn't he go to consultations with you?

AISSATA: That's only in movies. He might go to the consultation, but he'll wait for you at the reception. You end up paying the doctor yourself. You think that getting married means you've won, but it's just one battle of many, my dear. Being a woman isn't easy. Is it?

ELLA: If that's what marriage is like, it doesn't make me feel like getting married. I mean, your men weren't like that before they got married. Were they?

OUMOU: It depends. Some change after the wedding.

MARIAM: We change too. Men know only too well how much we want to get married, and that once we're in it, they know we're ready to do anything to stay. But a woman is born for that, right?

ALL (*Speaking together.*): So much suffering.

ASSAN: You're not the one who decides, my pretty. You'll see when your in-laws start putting pressure on you.

ELLA: But mine doesn't have a family.

OUMOU: You're going to marry someone who doesn't have a family?

ELLA: Is that a problem?

OUMOU: Oh no, that's luck!!

(*All burst out laughing.*)

MARIAM: Excuse me, but tell us your secret.

ELLA: I killed them.

(*All laugh again. EVELYNE starts to serve the tea.*)

ASSAN: Anyhow, without a good woman, there's no good marriage and no good upbringing of children. You couldn't bring up children correctly if women hadn't first brought them into the world. Just for that alone, my friends, we ought to be celebrated.

ELLA: You're wrong. One of my colleagues told me that we, women, were created to spend our time asking to be forgiven for having sinned when we made Adam take a bite out of the apple.

MARIAM: It's obvious that guy is a failed abortion, and because it didn't work for his mother, he ended up with only half a brain.

OUMOU: I swear you're right. All their mothers must have thought about abortion. Maybe they should have done it.

EVELYNE: If they were able to, because really, if you take the chance, it's your doctor himself who'll snitch on you. He'll say you asked his advice. *(Clucks her tongue.) Gossips!*[36] Men!

ELLA: But, normally, isn't there some doctor-patient confidentiality?

AISSATA: What normally? I'm telling you, so listen closely, if you go for tests and then you don't show up on time for the results, and if one of your neighbors or your brother or sister happen to pass by, your doctor will tell them to give you the message you need to come get your results. We don't always tell our families why we go to the hospital. But, so much for confidentiality . . . Have you been brain-washed? Do you think you're living in a world of white men?

EVELYNE: Let me tell you what my mother has already told me a hundred times. A man is his stomach and, as my mother would say, what's below the stomach. So, every morning, catch his banana, play with it and he'll be happy all day long. He'll wear one of those stupid smiles and call you to say, "Baby, I miss you, I'm coming home . . ." And before he gets there, fix him a great meal, really great, really heavy. And when he goes to eat and eat and eat and eat, when he'll be full, do you think he'll have the energy to think about anything else? He'll go to bed and then you can watch your telenovelas as much as you want.

OUMOU: She's absolutely right. That's where real power lies. Knowing how to tighten the knot of your wrapper. Your mother got it right, Evelyne. A man is his stomach and especially what's below his stomach. Our mothers did it. Our grand-mothers did it. Us too. Our daughters will do it when it's their turn. That's the way it is. The whole story.

ASSAN: Mine isn't like that. Even if he swallows a whole camel, he still wants to do it.

MARIAM: But what did his parents do to make him come out like that? How did they do it?

EVELYNE: You're something, Mariam Koné!

MARIAM: But I'm telling you it's true. We don't know what position they

---

36. pwapwato

were in when they made him. Maybe you think it's funny, but it has a lot to do with how a child develops, you know.

ASSAN: Oh Mariam!

MARIAM: *Let God be my judge!*[37]

AISSATA: We can't compare men's libido to the State Electricity of Mali, can we?

EVELYNE: What are you saying!

OUMOU: Well, if men's libido cut off as often as our electricity did, we'd bless the electric company.

(Laughter.)

MARIAM: Ella, you know that some of my colleagues think like yours.

ELLA: They do?

MARIAM: They're always telling me to wear a headscarf so I'll be respected outside, in the street.

AISSATA: And all those whatchamacallits pretend to be men.

ELLA: It makes me afraid, really afraid, and I don't know why, because as long as I can remember there wasn't any women-hating in my life. So why am I afraid? Where is this fear coming from?

(She turns towards the public and signals to the HAIRDRESSER to stop working on her braids.)

You know how it feels when someone whistles at you in the street? With his mouth full of suggestions about as clean as a public toilet?

When someone whistles at you, as though you were a dog.

When someone whistles to be able to treat you like a dog if you respond, and to treat you like a whore if you don't. If you give out your phone number, you're a slut, and if you don't give it, you're still a slut.

You know how it feels when they treat you as though you should be ashamed because you're thirty years old and you still don't have a child, when they call you sterile, when your mother-in-law and your sisters-in-law gather in your own home to find a *real* wife for your husband.

You know how it feels when you hear someone say, "That one over there is a real woman because she gives birth naturally and suffers. Not the one who has a C-section."

Your stature as a woman is measured by how much pain you experience when you bring a child into the world.

You know how it feels when you know it's your husband who's sterile, but you decide to allow them to insult you, to take all the shame on yourself, because that's how you were raised, to be quiet, to put up with everything.

---

37. N'Allah dé tchè!

You know how it feels when they start calling you the neighborhood
garbage pail when the guy you've been sleeping with tells all his buddies
and congratulates himself with high fives. Neighborhood garbage pail.
Why am I so submissive?

HAIRDRESSER: As far back as I can remember, I never saw my father raise a
hand or his voice to my mother.

So, why am I afraid? Why am I submissive? Does it come from my own
weakness, my own cowardice?

My fear to think for myself? To want?

Everybody is astonished that I'm speaking out now and not yesterday.

But that's like asking a prisoner to be free in prison, isn't it?

MARIAM: We're prisoners from the moment our mothers felt us inside
them; they, themselves, prisoners from the moment their mothers felt
them.

Saturday, March 28, 2000

We're at Bakadia's house. One razor. Two razors. Three razors. Scissors . . .
A knife. Glances across the room. Fear. Cries. Hands held tight. Legs
pulled apart. Imprisoned. Cries. Cries. Blood. Blood.

Monday, March 30, 2002

I ask my mother why. She tells me to ask my father. I ask my father. He tells
me to ask my aunt. I ask my aunt. She tells me it's life and there's nothing
I can do about it.

It's life and there's nothing I can do.

AISSATA: Friday, August 24, 2012

I walk. I hurt. I hurt. I stop. I look at the sky. I bleed. The sky is black. I
bleed. I hurt.

ELLA: Where is this fear coming from? Where? Where is it coming from?
Why am I afraid and weak?

EVELYNE: Be a woman, a real woman. Be a woman.

They say that everything a woman wants, God wants. So, what am I
supposed to do with that? Is it a way to put me to sleep? Make me twice
a slave?

ASSAN: Is Heaven really there? Being beaten when I am? Bleeding when I
bleed? Crying when I cry? Falling when they force me into the shadows
of shame and fear and guilt and censorship.

Is Heaven really there when I walk alone at night, my stomach tied in
knots?

Does Heaven bleed when people throw stones at me, beat me, swear at me,
look at me with daggers?

Does Heaven cry in its room when I cry in mine?

Does Heaven cry when I cry in the shower?

Does Heaven even hear my lament?

Why should I complain? Be a woman!

ELLA: Just what does that mean?

Today I'm going to let my body speak about where it hurts.

If I put aside my breasts, my vagina, my uterus, my clitoris, my smile, my silence, what am I? Nothing. Nothing at all.

OUMOU: Am I only a body?

I'm not worth much right now, am I? But wait ten years until someone discovers that menstrual blood cures testicular cancer. Then it'll be just a matter of time before someone invents a pump to retrieve the rare pearl I possess. Drink me, don't just eat me!

Be a woman!

AISSATA: Wednesday, June 6, 2013

In front of the door. A chase. I throw a handful of sand at him. He manages to catch me all the same. Takes out a knife. Pins me to the ground. Enters me. I implore Heaven. Help me, please.

ELLA: Why am I submissive? As far as I can remember, I, too, never saw my father raise his hand or his voice to my mother.

Where is this fear coming from if I never saw my father raise his voice or his hand to my sisters?

Where is this submission, this fear, coming from if not from my own weakness?

My own fear of speaking, of thinking for myself.

Of wanting. In ten years, I don't want to see myself become the mirror image of what I don't want today—a person with little ambition and too many regrets. "I know what I should have done, but, no, I didn't do it. Why? I don't know."

But today, this is where we're at *(gesturing to all the women).*

ASSAN: Wednesday, June 6, 2014

I enter. Our bedroom. He's waiting for me. Lights low. I'm afraid. He stares at me. He's behind me. Takes off my boubou. I'm afraid. It's going to hurt. How can I tell him? Should I tell him? Will he understand? Can I look at him? I must keep quiet. I must keep quiet. Keep quiet.

ELLA: Because sometimes I think it's the third world war, but really, it's not: it's not you against me. Me against you. You against her.

But . . .

Nobody ever asks the right question. No one ever asks the right question. No one asks the right question, not even us.

(Pointing to Evelyne.)

What do you do when your prison is made up of all those you love the most and who certainly love you the most?

Everything isn't just black and white. It's often grey, very often. Isn't that true, Evelyne?

Can we really talk about the power of the wrapper?

What have I done?

Too much? Maybe not enough?

What haven't I done enough of?

How did I get to this place?

I'm lost.

They said "the power of the wrapper" and I never tried to understand what that really meant.

Does the wrapper have its own power, or am I the one who gives it power?

Was it a trap? Or wasn't I worthy enough of the power they gave me?

Where and when did I lose myself in the malice of the universe?

But what if, after all, they were right, and I'm the weaker sex and he's the stronger one?

Even if my sex can take razor blades, scissors, insults, humiliation, fists, I'm the weak one, right?

(The other women mimic trial situations, while ELLA watches, astonished.)

LAWYER: It's rape, YOUR HONOR.

JUDGE: What do you plead?

ACCUSED: Not guilty, Sir. She was dressed so provocatively; and she didn't say no as if she meant it. What was she doing out in the street so late at night? Anyhow, everybody has already had her, so one more . . .

JUDGE: I understand.

LAWYER: Domestic abuse, YOUR HONOR.

JUDGE: What do you plead?

ACCUSED: Not guilty.

(Mini-drama: Women v. Society. One of the women begins to walk, the others all speak out.)

SOCIETY: Why did he beat you? You're sure you didn't do something to get on his nerves?

WOMEN: "She was dressed like a slut. So, if she was raped, she has no right to come crying about it. Everybody must have had her. Nobody would marry that one. She's a whore."

"If a woman is successful at the office, for example . . ."

"It's because she slept with somebody to get the job in the first place."

"If a woman appears to be flourishing . . ."

(A woman puts on sunglasses.)

"She's being kept, of course."

"If a woman dates a married man . . ."

"Dirty home wrecker, of course—and even if the man is momentarily blamed, she's the one who will carry the stigma for the rest of her life."

"While a woman is manipulative and calculating, a man is . . ."

ALL THE WOMEN: "Strategic."

"If a woman is ambitious, she's an opportunist; but an ambitious man is . . ."

ALL THE WOMEN: "A visionary."

"A woman is hysterical because she has a uterus, but when a man goes through burn out, it's because . . ."

ALL THE WOMEN: "His penis is too heavy to carry."

(They all laugh.)

MARIAM *(to Ella)*: This is our harem, and if you're here it's because you need something and it doesn't matter what it is. You'll find it here. You're safe here. Here's where you can let it all out. Here's where you can be free to swear, insult, spit, say all the dirty words that cross your mind. Here you can call your husband by his first name and not by a nick name, like Baby, Darling, or Big Daddy.

AISSATA: Here you can call him Madou, Adama, Siaka. Here you can say whatever you think about your mother-in-law who won't stop harassing you to start having babies, who thinks you're not good enough for her son, who thinks she's worth more than you are. You can talk about your husband's underwear, his performance in bed, or his *disastrous* performances in bed.

You can talk about your period, your vagina, your uterus, how you fart when you make love.

You can talk about how his penis is too big or too small.

You can talk about how you want to make love ten times a day without anybody treating you like a sex fiend or a whore.

You can talk about how you don't want to pluck your pubic hair because you like to have a little fleece.

OUMOU: You can talk about your gynecologist, who's better with his fingers than your husband.

You can talk about your husband's premature ejaculations.

You can talk about how you give yourself pleasure all on your own.

MARIAM: Tell us about how you'd like to cut off his penis and make brochettes in curry sauce with it, and serve it up to society. Ha ha ha ha. That way society will know that sometimes it has no taste at all, and it will understand once and for all what you have to endure because society expects you to sleep with your husband every day. It's the so-called conjugal duty.

And even better than that—you can give the finger to this bastard of a patriarchy, to this society that grovels before men.

ASSAN: You can speak of wanting to wear mini-skirts and go out at night without your husband. You can tell us you don't like incense and you don't at all want to attach sexy beads around your waist.

Tell us how old you are without the fear or shame of being judged for not being married.

Tell us how you don't want to have a child or how you only want to have two and not populate a whole village.

Tell us about the illegal abortions you've had to have because the law has decided abortions are against the law.

AISSATA: Tell us more about your illegal abortions and how society would treat you if it knew you had an abortion, but how it would also treat you, by stoning you, if you were pregnant without being married.

ASSAN: Tell us how you lost your virginity.

Tell us about the number of sexual partners you've had in your life.

Tell us of your favorite positions for making love.

Tell us of your desire.

Here, no one is going to judge you.

Here, we support each other and give advice.

MARIAM: Tell us what you want, tell us your desires, your devastation, your pain.

And above all, tell us about yourself, your real self.

Did we say it all, girlfriends?

ALL THE WOMEN: YESS!

MARIAM: This is our dance floor and when we gather together once a week, we put the music on as loud as we can. My dear, we get wild. So, yes, it's a tontine; yes, we wear wrappers. But, my dear, underneath the wrappers is what we're really wearing.

(She pulls a bottle of spirits out of her bag.)

ELLA: So, I should understand this isn't really a tontine? Am I wrong; did my aunt lie to me?

MARIAM: It absolutely is, my pretty. This is the best tontine there ever could be. We all chip in to do whatever we want.

AISSATA: It's really simple. Just listen. We come together to speak about our problems, our anxieties.

OUMOU: We get everything out of our systems and we don't judge. We tell the truth without wounding anybody.

Here, we listen to each other.

Here, no one tells us what we must or must not do.

Here, nobody is better than anyone else.

Here, there is no fear.

ASSAN: We aren't Mme. Diarra, Mme Koné, Mme. Sangaré, Mme. Traoré, Mme Sidibé, Mme Diawara. We're Mariam, Evelyne, Assan, Aissata, Oumou.

AISSATA: We're the kind of women who are very intelligent, very strong, very independent and all of that. Don't you see? Thin, heavy, shaved head, wigged, or braided . . .

OUMOU: We, so respectful, sometimes too respectful, way too . . . We, who hear the disgusting whistles that men direct towards us in the street; we, who've been tempted to respond but always remember what our mothers said, "Are you sure you can educate jackasses, daughters?"

We, who have already had to listen to remarks about our too short skirts, our too tight pants, our see-through tops, our *décolletés*, even when we're wearing wax cloth or bazin or even bogolan. We are women who stay strong in spite of it all—because the fight has only just started, and we are more than ready.

ALL THE WOMEN (*Singing.*):

We'll put the men who dare lie to us in big basins and we'll beat them like they beat damask cloth to make it soft.

We'll put the men who dare hurt us in the soles of our high heels in order to show them how beautifully we can walk.

We'll pummel the crap out of the lives of those men who refuse to pay the cost of spice.

Why don't they put all the idiots who wear us out over nothing in the trunk of a car and give us the keys?[38]

(All burst into laughter.)

(END.)

The author reserves all serialization and dramatization rights. Requests for any of these rights or the translation into languages other than English should be addressed to Jeanne Diama at sophiakjeanne@yahoo.com. Judith G. Miller can be reached at Judith.Miller@nyu.edu.

---

38. Hey mousso trompé tchè min ma nan nèguè an bôn do bazin na, an bé gossikè o kan./ Moussobougôtchè min ma nan tôrô an bo don talon na, ka démarchikènayé./ Na sôngôbôbali mi ma nan tôrô an bo bila kèrèfè, ka négligence djougoubolo kan./ Kô don bali mi ma nan gnani, a bo do môbili la, aw ka clé contact ciné ma.

Ugandan playwright Asiimwe Deborah Kawe, author of *Cooking Oil*.

Cooking Oil

Asiimwe Deborah Kawe

Asiimwe Deborah Kawe was born in Kiruhura, in the South West of Uganda. She is an award-winning playwright, producer, and performer. Also, the co-founder and producing artistic director of Tebere Arts Foundation, a Uganda-based arts organization that supports Ugandan theater-makers at different stages in their career. Tebere Arts Foundation is the principal producer of the Kampala International Theatre Festival, where Ms. Kawe serves as the artistic director.

Previously, Kawe worked with the Sundance Institute Theatre Program; dividing her time between New York City and different cities in East Africa, she led for six years the East Africa initiative, a program that covered the countries of Burundi, Ethiopia, Kenya, Rwanda, Tanzania, and Uganda. Ms. Kawe received a Diploma in Music, Dance and Drama, a B.A. in Theatre and Performing Arts from Makerere University in Kampala, Uganda, and an M.F.A. in Writing for Performance from the California Institute of the Arts, USA.

Kawe writes for stage, radio, and screen. Her stage plays include *Red Hills, Forgotten World, Appointment with gOD, Un-entitled, Do they Know it's Khristmas?, The Promised Land,* and many other short plays and performance texts. Her radio play, *Will Smith Look Alike,* won an award with the BBC World Service African Performance playwriting competition. Asiimwe enjoys creating a safe space for other performing artists, especially those who live on the African continent. Her mission is to mentor emerging artists in her country to think about performing arts as a career option and to work toward making indigenous theater artforms in different Ugandan communities considered part of the mainstream.

Kawe has been a writing fellow at the Akademie Schloss Solitude in Stuttgart, Germany, a guest Artist at Pomona College in California, USA, and a

44 SPEAKING OUR SELVES

playwright in residency at Residenztheater in Munich to mention but a few.

At the 30th Anniversary of the Cairo International Festival for Experimental Theatre, September 2023, Ms. Kawe was given an award for her theater work and leadership on the African continent and the world. Ms. Kawe lives in Kampala with her family.

Asiimwe Deborah Kawe is an editor of *Speaking Our Selves: New Plays by African Women*. Asiimwe is on Instagram as @asiimwe_kawe, X as @adkdaks, Facebook as @asiimwedeborahgkashugi, LinkedIn as @AsiimweDeborahKawe, and on TikTok as @asiimwe0128. For more information about Kawe's work, visit the following websites: www.asiimwedeborahkawe.org; www.tebere.org; and www.kampalainternationaltheatrefestival.com.

An interview with Asiimwe Deborah Kawe is available at https://doi.org/10.3998/mpub.12827650.cmp.2.

ASIIMWE DEBORAH KAWE ON *COOKING OIL*:

In 2006, I had just left my home country, Uganda, for further studies. It was the first time in my life I was going to be away from anything familiar for a very long time. A few weeks after reporting to the university, a very embarrassing story came out in Uganda's local newspapers in which some employees at the Uganda's ministry of health, including three ministers, were implicated in the mismanagement of the Global Fund, totaling up to $51 million meant to fight malaria, HIV, and tuberculosis. For the first time, I was in a position to view my country from outside, to question what I had never thought of questioning before. The story challenged me to ask myself questions about the relationship between Sub-Saharan African countries like mine and the global north.

I knew very little about the politics of foreign aid. The arrest, trial, and eventual acquittal of the three Ugandan ministers was like a theatrical performance, and not a good one at that. It was a mockery of those who were supposed to have benefited from the $51 million to access drugs for the above-mentioned life-threatening diseases, and the U.S. taxpayers where the embezzled money had come from. It was a very bad joke: a display of how the powerful will always get away with a slap on their wrist or no slap at all for the crimes committed. The sad reality is that those who need the aid are unseen, are used as pawns for other people's self-aggrandizement, and that their need is a commodity.

I learned that in some cases, what we perceive as aid (support/assistance) makes our countries poorer and not richer. In fact, some forms of aid are designed that way, as loans that my parents' generation was subjected to pay back, that I am paying back, and that my children and generations to come will be subjected to pay back. Does this kind of aid alleviate or perpetuate poverty?

Lastly, the cycle of dependence in this man-eat-man society. Are the countries that are aid dependent actually independent? How can one boast of political independence if they're economically dependent? Are the leaders of countries that are aid dependent trying to get out of the cycle or do they rather their countries stay in that position because it sustains and indirectly supports kleptocracy.

I wrote the play to try and seek answers to the many questions I had/still have, to unpack my experiences and observations, and also to invite anyone interested into this conversation.

46 SPEAKING OUR SELVES

Cooking Oil
Asiimwe Deborah Kawe

CHARACTERS

Maria/Maria's Silhouette: Spirit. 18 years old. Intelligent, beautiful, looks much younger than her age. Hawks gallons of cooking oil and also smuggles them across the borders of her country. Her ambition—to attain university education.

Hon. Dr. Sir Silver Bibala:[1] Politician. Mid-40s. Eloquent, handsome, loyal to his friends, cunning. His ambition is to build a strong political career; never to allow poverty into his household ever again; he dreams of one day becoming the president of his country.

Bataka:[2] A peasant. Mid-40s. Silver's childhood friend, Maria's father. He lost his property during the war and became very poor. However, with Silver's help, the economic condition of his household has slightly improved. He looks much older than his age. His ambition is to educate his sons (Maria's brothers) and find a day's meal for his family. He runs a retail shop in the nearby trading center. He becomes a haunted man.

Neeza:[3] Housewife. Late 30s. Maria's mother and Bataka's wife. Beautiful but tired. She is a traditional woman who tries to keep out of her husband's way. Her ambition is to kick poverty out of their household and see Maria back in school.

Ndeeba:[4] Fresh graduate social worker. Mid-20s. Turns activist. Nurses political ambitions. Upfront, idealistic. Her ambition is to turn her country into a corrupt-free society. Can she succeed?

A Figure In A Helmet: A faceless, sexless figure that appears to most of the characters in the play. Fate.

Woman 1 & 2: Maria's customers.

Voices: Of the crowd, of journalists; echoes of the characters' dreams.

NOTE ON THE STAGING OF THE PLAY:
The script is written in movements and there are five movements. The Voices may be played by members of the ensemble. Everything is seen as it appears on the minds of the characters. For pronunciations of words not in the English language see footnotes and for the music of the lullaby and the rhyme in Prologue and Movement 1, see end of the play.

---

1. Pronounced as: BEE-buh-LA
2. Pronounced as: buh-TAHK-uh
3. Pronounced as: NEH-zuh
4. Pronounced as: nn-DEH-buh

PROLOGUE

(Middle of the night. One side of the stage is a grave. On the grave, there are exercise books, pens, an empty gallon of cooking oil and a writing "MARIA REST." NEEZA is engaged in some rituals; she prays. Her husband BATAKA stands still like a statue. Maybe he has become a statue. On the other side, NDEEBA types. She must be trying to beat a deadline. All this takes eternity. In the middle of the stage is where the roads meet. As NDEEBA types, MARIA'S silhouette appears behind her. The clock reads 12. Her typing gains momentum as MARIA'S silhouette keeps flickering on the wall behind.)

SILHOUETTE: You need to sleep.
(Beat. A lullaby is heard. The English translation of the lullaby is side by side to the one in the Lusoga[5] language and may appear as subtitles behind NDEEBA as she types.)

Hm..hm . . . omwana[6] alikulila[7] ndhala[8]	Hm..hm . . . the child is crying because it is hungry
Hm..hm . . . omwana alikulila ndhala	Hm..hm . . . the child is crying because it is hungry
Nkanda[9] kusilisa[10] omwana	I've tried to silence the child
Omwana alikulila ndhala	But it is crying because it is hungry
Hm..hm . . . omwana alikulila ndhala	Hm..hm . . . the child is crying because it is hungry
Omwana alikulila ndhala. . . .	But it is crying because it is hungry

(A moment of confusion. The lullaby disappears. NEEZA, having finished her rituals, moves her husband like a statue and they disappear where the roads meet. MARIA appears. She is pushing a wheelbarrow with gallons of cooking oil. She stands where her grave has been. SILVER also appears. NDEEBA types. At an appropriate moment, she will join SILVER'S crowd. MARIA and SILVER overlap in the sections below.)

MARIA: One thousand, two thousand, three thousand	SILVER: One million, two million, three million
MARIA: Three thousand shillings cash!	SILVER: Three million shillings cash!
MARIA: That was not bad!	SILVER: That was not bad!
MARIA: "No pain, no gain" That is my motto.	SILVER: "Silver is your SILVER" That is my motto.

---

5. One of the languages spoken in East Uganda. Pronounced as: loo-SAW-guh
6. Pronounced as: ohm-WAH-nuh
7. Pronounced as: ah-LEE-koo-LEE-luh
8. Pronounced as: nn-DAH-luh
9. Pronounced as: nn-KAN-duh
10. Pronounced as: koo-SEE-lee-suh

MARIA: If only I could make seven thousand shillings between today and tomorrow!

SILVER: If only I could make seven million between today and tomorrow!

MARIA: I would have made ten thousand shillings in just one week.

SILVER: I would have made ten million in just one week

MARIA: If I could make ten thousand shillings each week

SILVER: If I could make ten million each week

MARIA: By the end of the month I would have made forty thousand shillings

SILVER: By the end of the month I would have made forty million

MARIA: That means in a year . . .

SILVER: That means in a year . . .

MARIA: Four hundred and eighty thousand shillings

SILVER: Four hundred and eighty million!

MARIA: That should be enough for my school fees for the next two academic terms!

SILVER: That should be enough for my family's next holiday in the Bahamas!

MARIA: But there is my father; "First, your brothers need to complete secondary school"

SILVER: But there are hungry relatives! "Our son fell into things!"

MARIA: My mother too! "They need to read and speak English like you"

SILVER: Distant cousins ; "We gave him our votes!"

MARIA: My aunties; "It is more important for your brothers to study!"

SILVER: Aunties and uncles; "My son needs a job"; "My daughter has no school fees!"

MARIA: Those I once shared a classroom with; "Poor Maria, she still hawks and smuggles cooking oil!"

SILVER: The entire village whose names I can barely remember; "That man Silver; he should help us, he is the son of the soil!"

MARIA: Two years of hard working . . .

SILVER: Two years of smart calculations . . .

MARIA: Two years of risky selling . . .

SILVER: Where money is, votes will be!

MARIA: Selling to the locals as Father thinks I sell only across the borders.

SILVER: Two years of non-stop lobbying . . .

MARIA: Two years of unfulfilled dream . . .

SILVER: Every political campaign

MARIA: Every beginning of the term

SILVER: Free cooking oil for all!

MARIA: Father sits my brothers and I down

SILVER: Free cooking oil from Silver's shop!

MARIA: "One more year Maria, just one more year!"

SILVER: More gallons to Bataka!

MARIA: My savings go to my brothers again!

SILVER: Two years of practicing eloquent speech

MARIA: Two years of non-stop hawking!

(They both sing their "slogans." Their voices keep increasing until they begin to sound gibberish. It should be noted that in this section, Silver's lines are a little louder than Maria's. A fight for space, a belief that he's entitled to be heard above everyone and everything else.)

SILVER: Ladies and gentlemen!

SILVER: Vote Silver Bibala!

SILVER: You will have silver in your pockets!

SILVER: You will have silver in your houses!

SILVER: Silver is your silver!

SILVER: I pledge . . .

MARIA: Cooking oil here!

MARIA: Cooking oil cheap today!

MARIA: Cooking oil to give your food a new look!

MARIA: Cooking oil to make your food taste better!

MARIA: No pain, no gain!

MARIA: I pledge . . .

(Overlapping ends.)

SILVER: Five years of political liberation

VOICES: Silver Oyee[11]!

SILVER: Five years of economic empowerment

VOICES: Long live Silver!

SILVER: Five years of prosperity for all

VOICES: Silver Oyee!

SILVER: As I lobby and acquire

VOICES: Long live Silver!

SILVER: Aid for you my starving village

VOICES: Silver Oyee!

SILVER: So help me God!

VOICES: Long live Silver!

(Handclapping is heard.)

MARIA: Commitment to my hawking,

Dedication to my dream, focusing on every day's work,

Disregarding every distractive voice So help me God!

SILVER: I like that part of the Bible, which says; "He who does not work should not eat." Man eateth where he. . . .

(Clears his throat.)

MARIA: I don't understand that part of the Bible which says: "You reap what you sow."

SILVER: Hard work! That is hard work! I reap from my hard work.

MARIA: I have sowed hard work, but look at me!

SILVER: Look at me!

MARIA: Very bad!

SILVER: The fruit of my hands!

MARIA: I have worn this dress for the last one year!

SILVER: Marks and Spenser is my trademark.

MARIA: For how long will this poverty be?

SILVER: People are poor because they are lazy!

---

11. A way to cheer someone on. Pronounced as: OH-yeh

MARIA: Three thousand shillings in one day? Makes me somebody!

SILVER: Three million shillings in just one day! I am not a nobody!

MARIA: Today is my lucky day!

SILVER: Today is my lucky day!

MARIA: One thousand shillings goes to Maria's pocket!

SILVER: One million shillings for Silver, eh as a contingency fund!

MARIA: Balance two thousand shillings . . .

SILVER: Balance two million shillings . . .

MARIA: One thousand shillings returns home. . . .

SILVER: One million for my wife and children . . .

MARIA: Five hundred shillings for the border protectors, to keep them off my back.

SILVER: Five hundred thousand for the media, to keep them off my back.

MARIA: Five hundred shillings, contribution to my brothers' school fees.

SILVER: Five hundred thousand, for the inquisitive electorate.

MARIA: One day, I will go back to school.

SILVER: One day, I will become "His Excellency, Mr. President!" Everyone will sing my name!

(MARIA gathers her gallons and takes the cooking oil to potential buyers, calling out, until her voice disappears. SILVER'S dream sequence continues, voices chanting in praise of SILVER.)

MARIA: Eeeeh[12] cooking oil!

A VOICE: We support . . .

VOICES: Silver . . .

MARIA: Cooking oil cheap here!

A VOICE: We love . . .

VOICES: Silver . . .

MARIA: Cooking oil to make your food taste better!

A VOICE: We want . . .

VOICES: Silver . . .

MARIA: No pain, no gain!

A VOICE: Everybody . . .

VOICES: Silver . . .

MARIA: Cooking oil cheap today!

A VOICE: Everywhere . . .

VOICES: Silver . . .

MARIA: Are you buying Sir?

A VOICE: Everyman . . .

VOICES: Silver . . .

---

12. An expression of calling to/getting someone's attention. Pronounced as: EH

MARIA: It will give your food a new look!

A VOICE: Every woman . . .

VOICES: Silver. . . .

MARIA: A golden look to be exact!

A VOICE: Oh oh . . .

VOICES: Silver

MARIA: Cooking oil in plenty.

A VOICE: Eh eh . . .

VOICES: Silver

(SILVER disappears with his "crowd" of supporters; waving.)

MOVEMENT 1

(MARIA appears, pushing the wheelbarrow, she runs across the space looking for an exit, she runs off. A FIGURE with an invisible face appears wearing a helmet; lingers where MARIA has been and disappears. Three men come running on stage, two of them are dressed in military uniforms with the words "The Border Protectors" written on them, the third man is SILVER. SILVER sights MARIA, one of the border protectors aims; SILVER sees him but before he can do anything, the man shoots. There is a scream off stage. Beat. The shooter drops his gun and runs away. The second border protector picks up the gun and follows the shooter. SILVER walks around looking for an exit. He bumps into things. Maybe he has become blind. He finally finds the exit. Beat. MARIA'S silhouette appears again.)

SILHOUETTE: One more day to go. Time to wake up!

(NEEZA and BATAKA appear. BATAKA murmurs. NEEZA prays. The lullaby. NDEEBA is somewhere. She types.)

BATAKA: Four bullet wounds. Two in the back. One through the neck. One at the back of the head.

(BATAKA will chant the line above throughout the following dialogue.)

NEEZA: This is where it all ended for Maria. I have been here before. Every week I come here to make sure my daughter is ok. So that no one kills her vengeance spirit. It all started when my husband accepted that cooking oil. The cooking oil that became our blessing, our curse. The cooking oil that became our source of income after the war. Here I am again. Praying to you, the ALL-SEEING one. Let not my daughter's spirit rest. I have done today's share. Tomorrow will come with its lot.

(She does her usual rituals.)

NDEEBA: Two months in the field, I encountered the charismatic man I had heard about. There was something he possessed. Something I had never seen in any other politician. It was almost tangible. People liked . . .

no . . . loved him. They could access him, and him? He reached out to them and touched their hearts. I was hooked.

(NEEZA and her husband, BATAKA, disappear. SILVER and his crowd appear. NDEEBA joins the "crowd." MARIA will emerge in another space, another time and establish a selling point along the village path. On her cooking oil gallons, the words "NOT FOR SALE" are clearly marked. SILVER rises to stand at a "podium" before a cheering "crowd." It's time to give a speech.)

SILVER: Thank you! Wana inchi, Habari zenu?[13]

CROWD: Nzuri!![14]

SILVER: Our people say that the one who travels the road frequently knows all the potholes.

VOICE 1: He is indeed our son!

VOICE 2: But does the road have to have potholes?

SILVER: *(Beat.)* I was born here. I was raised here. I got my education here. I fought for our freedom here. I understand you well. I know the problems that affect you. I know our successes and I know our failures.

CROWD: Silver oyee!

SILVER: I am a man of the people; I live an ordinary life like you. I stand for transparency and democracy. I will restore this country. I will restore order, I will restore freedom of speech, of expression, of movement.

VOICES: Long live Silver! Long live Silver!

SILVER: Thank you! Thank you! Lend me your ears and give me your hearts. I stand before you in humility and gratitude for the support you have continuously shown me. Many of you, many of your sons and daughters worked with me to defeat greedy, unprincipled, violent and sectarian leaders! Not leaders, dictators! That's what they were. Dictators who frustrated the dreams and aspirations of our country at the very dawn of our independence! Dictators that buried the hopes and faith of generations that were ready and eager to make this country truly our own! Today, we stand at the threshold of making this country an example of what happens when the people are given power to manage their own affairs! That is what I intend to do, as your leader. This country does not belong to the chosen few; we are all called, we are all chosen and we have all been predestined to govern this land. That is what it means to consolidate national unity! That is what it means to have the priorities of our land in the right place. That is what good

---

13. A Kiswahili way of greeting, meaning "Citizens, what's the news?" Pronounced as: wah-NAH in-CHEE her-BAH-re zeh-NOO.

14. Kiswahili word to mean "The news is good" and pronounced as: knee-N-ZOO-lee

COOKING OIL **53**

governance and good leadership mean. We sacrifice individual interests for the good of all. I am here to right the wrongs that have been done in this country; the state inspired violence, unequal distribution of resources, a distorted economy, lack of basic services, marginalization of some groups of people, that is why I am here. I need your hand, I need your feet, I need your brain—I need you! We have enormous challenges facing us in our time, but we are a strong, hardworking, focused, innovative, resilient people! Together . . . I said together . . . I said together . . . *(The CROWD'S excitement is palpable.)* Together, we will transform this land, together we will rebuild this country, together we will determine our own destiny! Trust me with your vote, trust me with your future!

VOICES: Long live Silver!

SILVER: I promise to address issues that affect us to the whole world. . . .

VOICES: Long live Silver!

SILVER: While we starve, while we lack the basic needs of life like food, education, shelter . . . While we die of all sorts of diseases, the world watches . . . The world keeps quiet! This should stop! This must stop!! The solution is with us. The solution is in our hands!

CROWD: Silver oyeee!

NDEEBA: This feels like standing in the presence of god! I want to be this man!

(The CROWD disappears. NDEEBA follows them. MARIA occupies the space.)

MARIA: Eeh cooking oil! Cooking oil cheap today! I will bring it to you right there. No pain, no gain! God bless you sir. Are you buying Madam?

WOMAN 1: How much?

MARIA: One hundred shillings a liter.

WOMAN 1: Oya..ya..yaaaa![15]

MARIA: Don't wail as if you have lost someone.

WOMAN 1: Am I buying a car or a boda-boda[16]?

MARIA: If you and I had cars and motor bikes, would we be here?

(They are joined by another woman. To the second woman:)

WOMAN 1: She is a cheat.

WOMAN 2: Has she increased?

WOMAN 1: There are no gardens of money here!

WOMAN 2: Is it as twice as Silver's?

---

15. A way of exclaiming. Pronounced as: OH-yeah-yeah-YEAH

16. A motor bike taxi that is commonly used in some towns in Uganda.

54 SPEAKING OUR SELVES

WOMAN1: It is four times!

WOMAN 2: Aya..aa..aaa!

MARIA: Even you?!

WOMAN 2: Why are you punishing us?

MARIA: What have I done?

WOMAN 1: She wants us to starve.

WOMAN 2: That money is a lot.

WOMAN 1: We would rather buy from Silver's shop.

WOMAN 2: I will not mind the distance.

MARIA: Why are you complaining?

WOMAN 2: Your price.

MARIA: What price?

WOMAN 1: Of the cooking oil.

MARIA: What about it?

WOMAN 1: It is expensive.

MARIA: I am talking to her.

WOMAN 2: It is expensive.

MARIA: How much is it?

WOMAN 2: *(To WOMAN 1.)* How much is it?

WOMAN 1: Ask her.

WOMAN 2: *(To MARIA.)* How much is it?

MARIA: You know the price.

WOMAN 2: The usual?

MARIA: The usual.

WOMAN 2: I apologize. *(To WOMAN 1.)* Liar.

WOMAN 1: Wretched!

WOMAN 2: *(To WOMAN 1.)* Miserable! Give me one liter. *(Pays MARIA.)*

MARIA: Thank you customer. Bless you.

WOMAN 1: Beggar!

MARIA: I will not allow you to abuse my customers!

WOMAN 1: Which "customers"? I am only seeing one miserable/[17]

MARIA: You have to stop.

WOMAN 1: I don't think that container of yours can even measure a liter! No wonder you have no customers.

MARIA: Where are you from in this village?

WOMAN 1: I am from the next village.

MARIA: That explains it.

WOMAN 1: Reduce the price; that is way too much!

---

17. A symbol, used throughout the script, to suggest that a character is interrupted by the next speaker.

MARIA: That is the lowest I can offer. And as you can see, others are buying.

WOMAN 1: I am not others!

MARIA: You are obstructing me.

WOMAN 1: I am going to Silver's shop.

MARIA: I don't see any roadblock here.

WOMAN 1: They will give it to me at half your price.

MARIA: Eh cooking oil . . .

WOMAN 1: I will go. I am not buying a car or a boda-boda!

(She does not move.)

MARIA: Eeh cooking oil! Cooking oil to give your food a new look!

WOMAN 1: A new look? Hmm! You talk as if this is better than cow ghee!

MARIA: Do you have the ghee?

WOMAN 1: Are there any more animals alive?

MARIA: Then, stop dreaming.

WOMAN 1: And stop overcharging!

MARIA: Eeh cooking oil cheap here today . . .

WOMAN 1: Anyway, I'm on my way to Silver's shop.

(She stays.)

MARIA: Your legs are not tied, are they?

WOMAN 1: I will move when I want.

MARIA: Eeh cooking oil! Cooking oil to give you energy . . .

WOMAN 1: I said I am leaving for Silver's shop now!

MARIA: I heard you the first time.

WOMAN 1: If it was not for my husband who insists we must have cooking oil . . .

MARIA: Maybe he should be the one to do the buying!

WOMAN 1: *(Not at all amused.)* Give me two liters.

MARIA: Buy three and I will give you one free.

WOMAN 1: I am taking two, why don't you give me half a liter free?

MARIA: These are hard times for us all. *(They exchange money and the cooking oil.)* God bless you.

WOMAN 1: Do I have a choice?

MARIA: Are you buying sir? No? No problem! Money is hard to get these days. *(Beat.)* That person again! They do not know that staring is rude. I wonder why people don't just say that they are not buying instead of staring at me. It is ok not to have money! Many people in this area are hard up! It is normal here. *(To the person.)* Ok, next time. Have a nice day!

(She counts the money. Dividing it up by putting some back in her bra, some in her purse, and some in her dress pocket.)

MARIA: Eh, cooking oil! Maria gives it to you at an affordable price. Others will cheat you! *(Pushing her wheelbarrow away.)* What do you say? Cooking oil cheap today.

(NDEEBA appears.)

NDEEBA: Rally after rally, campaign after campaign, street after street, corner after corner, house after house—I followed him. I saw him. I listened to him. I admired him. "The son of the soil" as he is fondly referred to in his village. A village that has suffered misfortunes. A village that was ravaged by war. After the war, the floods hit. After the floods, there was a drought. Then famine hit. Silver contacted Mzazi[18] Relief Aid. That is how I come into the picture.

(SILVER appears, still at a rally. Fantasy projection.)

SILVER: Freedom! Freedom to live! I declare freedom today! Voting Silver, is voting your voice! Silver = Free education. Silver = Free medicines. Silver = Free Anti- Retrovirals. Silver = No taxes. Silver = Flowing money/

CROWD: Long live Silver! *(Beat.)*

VOICE 3: Keep talking, we want to hear your voice, only your voice!

VOICE 1: Silver! We are starving!

VOICE 2: Are you going to bring back the rains?

SILVER: *(To himself.)* That's damn! Do I control nature! Be calm Silver. BE CALM.

VOICE 3: My bicycle broke down!

SILVER: *(To himself. Frustrated.)* Do I look like I'm a bicycle mechanic? *(To the CROWD.)* A sugar plantation!

VOICE 3: A sugar plantation?!

VOICE 2: Will the sugar plantation fix his bicycle? Maybe you should give him a boda- boda!

SILVER: I beg your pardon?

CROWD: Boda-bodas for your supporters!!

SILVER: *(To himself.)* This is getting out of hand! *(To the CROWD.)* But . . . I can't afford boda-bodas for the entire village.

VOICE 2: What was that? Did you hear what he said? Everyone listen to the man we supported!

(Everyone speaks at the same time. CROWD is getting out of control.)

SILVER: Listen to me! Please listen . . . alright . . . Send two representatives to my office tomorrow. *(The CROWD goes wild.)*

CROWD: Long live Silver!

---

18. A Kiswahili word to mean "parent," pronounced as: mm-ZAZ-ee

SILVER: Every able-bodied man in this village will get a boda-boda and a communal sugar plantation! *(To himself.)* Do not allow them to ask any more questions. *(To the CROWD.)* You the electorate will get to choose the name of the plantation! Note to self . . . . pause for clapping and cheering. *(He pauses, nothing happens.)* Thank you! Thank you! More sugar plantations! The second sugar plantation will be named after . . . Note to self . . . point to someone you will have identified in the audience and pause for cheering . . . will be named after YOU!!! I am a man of the people. Voting me is voting your voice! *(One handclap is heard. Beat.)*

CROWD: What else are you giving us?

(SILVER had not anticipated more "requests." He has to end the rally now.)

SILVER: Thank you! Thank you very much! God bless us all!

(Voices in the crowd are persistent. "We want a new road," "a school close by for our children," "a new roof for the Church," "the Mosque needs new windows," "a ball for our youths' football team," . . . the voices disappear and the setting transforms into a bar. SILVER, NDEEBA, and BATAKA all sit at the same table. They are happy.)

SILVER: Cheers!

BATAKA: To the guest among us.

SILVER: A welcome to our circle.

NDEEBA: I feel at home already.

(They all drink.)

SILVER: And to our usual ritual

BATAKA: Every night we pledge. To stand for each other

SILVER: To defend each other

BATAKA: To protect each other

SILVER: In good times and bad times

BATAKA: To be honest with each other and not to stab each other in the back

SILVER: We welcome you to this ritual

NDEEBA: I don't understand

SILVER: For you to be our friend

NDEEBA: For me to be your friend?

BATAKA: That is all we need.

NDEEBA: I am already your friend!

SILVER: For you to take an oath!

NDEEBA: I have to take an oath?

SILVER: Never to betray us.

NDEEBA: Never to betray you?

BATAKA: And to support us in our work.

NDEEBA: I will support you in your work!

ALL TWO: We will support you in your work!

(NDEEBA is taken up by this and starts uttering whatever comes to her mind.)

NDEEBA: I will stand by your side!

ALL TWO: We will stand by your side.

NDEEBA: I will never betray you!

ALL TWO: We will never betray you.

SILVER: Whatever we ask

NDEEBA: Whatever you ask.

SILVER: You will do.

NDEEBA: I will do?

BATAKA: For our friendship's sake.

NDEEBA: That, I don't understand.

SILVER: You will support our work?

NDEEBA: I will support your work.

SILVER: That is all we ask.

NDEEBA: That I will do.

BATAKA: You are now us.

NDEEBA: I am now YOU?

(SILVER starts the children's rhyme "Three blind mice." The two men join hands and dance in a circle around NDEEBA. They may encourage the audience to sing along in English.)

SILVER: Embeba Ishatu[19]	Three blind mice
Zikairuka[20]	Three blind mice
Zaza ow'omukazi[21]	See how they run
Omukazi[22]	See how they run
Yaziha omubazi[23]	They all run after a farmer's wife
Omubazi	Who cut off their tail with a carving knife
Gwazicwa emikira,[24] emikira	Did you ever seen such a sight in your life
Yareta oburofa, oburofa[25]	As three blind mice
Bwamara'bantu![26]	Three blind mice

---

19. Pronounced as: ehm-BEH-bah EE-shah-TOO
20. Pronounced as: zih-KAI-EE-roo-kuh
21. Pronounced as: ZZAH-zuh oh-WUHM-kah-zee
22. Pronounced as: oh-M-kah-zee
23. Pronounced as: yeah-Zee-ha oh-M-bah-Zee
24. Pronounced as: goo-WAH-zee-chu-WAH em-in-CHEE-ruh
25. Pronounced as: Yeah-RAY-tuh oh-BOO-raw-fuh
26. Pronounced as: boo-WAH-ma-ruh a BUH-N-too

(BATAKA begins to speak the lyrics to the song underneath SILVER and NDEEBA'S dialogue.)

BATAKA: Embeba

SILVER: Tomorrow we will need fifty . . .

NDEEBA: Fifty what? . . .

BATAKA: Ishatu

SILVER: Fifty gallons . . .

NDEEBA: Of ? . . . /

BATAKA: Zikairuka

NDEEBA: What are you talking about?

SILVER: Of cooking oil . . .

BATAKA: Zikairuka

NDEEBA: Of cooking oil? . . .

BATAKA: Zaza ow'omukazi omukazi

SILVER: Make them a hundred . . .

BATAKA: Yaziha omubazi omubazi

NDEEBA: A hundred gallons?

BATAKA: Gwazicwa emikira emikira

SILVER: Fifty for you and I . . .

BATAKA: Yareeta oburofa oburofa

NDEEBA: Fifty for you and I? . . .

BATAKA: Bwamara'bantu

SILVER: The rest for Bataka . . .

BATAKA: Yazicwaho emikira emikira

NDEEBA: The rest for Bataka? I don't understand! . . .

BATAKA: Embeba Ishatu

SILVER: In the name of the brotherhood.

NDEEBA: I can't do that!

(The circle breaks, Bataka stops speaking the lyrics to the song.)

SILVER: You have to. Everyone benefits.

NDEEBA: I cannot.

(Overlapping.)

SILVER: Even the wanainchi. The masses.	NDEEBA: No.
SILVER: That's the norm.	NDEEBA: May be it shouldn't be.
SILVER: It is kind of expected.	NDEEBA: Forget it!
SILVER: You pledged.	NDEEBA: I didn't realize . . .
BATAKA: You took an oath.	NDEEBA: That it involved . . .
SILVER: An oath is an oath.	NDEEBA: Taking what is not mine . . .
SILVER: Everyone does it. It is yours . . .	NDEEBA: And share it with you . . .
BATAKA: Yours by right . . .	

60 SPEAKING OUR SELVES

(SILVER and BATAKA join hands, NDEEBA is unsure whether she should join in. The two resume singing the Embeba nursery rhyme. She is back to the present. She types.)

NDEEBA: Two things I must mention in this chapter of the report: One, I was not involved in the cooking oil deal. Two, how useful has our aid been? Has this village got better? Is the poverty gone now? How about the death of a teenage girl?

(At MARIA'S grave. NEEZA prays.)

NEEZA: The floods destroyed my crops after the war. After the floods, there was a drought. A long and painful drought followed. That was the beginning of the famine. That is how my husband contacted Silver. And that is how Silver gave my husband that cooking oil. You, THE ALL KNOWING! You, THE ALL SEEING! There is nothing I have mentioned that you do not know already. But I have one question, just one? Was it too much for you to let her realize her dream? It was just one dream, just one. Why did she have to be this? A pile of earth! A mold! *(Talks to her daughter's grave.)* Does anything in here see my tears, hear my voice? Then rise! Crack the earth and push through. Come my daughter. Come. Follow them, in their houses, in their big offices, in the big buildings, during those important meetings, in their big cars, follow them. Come. Haunt them! *(She disappears. MARIA appears somewhere still hawking cooking oil.)*

MARIA: One, two, three, four, five, six, . . . Twelve men! All carrying sacks of charcoal! I wonder how many trees have been cut down today! Hey! You, I am talking to you! At that rate, do you think the rains will ever come?! Eh? If you continue selling charcoal don't expect rains here! But remember, after selling your charcoal come back here and buy cooking oil! What do you do? People must cook. People must eat. And they need charcoal to cook food. No charcoal no eating. *(Beat.)* DEFORESTA-TION. I first heard that word from my geography teacher. *(Imitates.)* "Today, we are talking about effects of DEFORESTATION!" *(MARIA stops the reminiscence.)* Oh school! My school? Girls' boarding school, prestigious secondary school only for the clever and the rich. Maria is not rich, but she is bright. "Grooming for the Future!" That was our motto. But look at me now. My school: "Sell cooking oil only across the borders!" Father speaking Silver's orders! My uniform: A dress with a pocket, a bra, a size bigger for the money, and an extra purse! My song: Cooking oil here! Cooking oil cheap today! My motto: No pain, no gain. In my dreams, I see myself on my graduation day. I first go to the salon. They fix my hair. *(She looks at herself in the "mirror"—the audience.)* Not bad! Of course, I am not in these tatters. I am in an expensive silk dress.

The dress is not long. It is just slightly above my knees. Expensive jewelry gracing my neck and wrists. Gold Stiletto shoes on my feet. Before going to the main campus for the ceremony, Father, Mother, and my brothers, Martin and Manuari go with me to Afro Studio: Cheers everybody! Time for snap shots! Say cheezzzz or cheerzzzz! Snap shot one: Maria alone. Cheezzz! Full length. Nice body. Pretty face. Lawyer of the year! Next: Maria alone. Portrait. Serious look. A lawyer's look. Next: Maria, Papa and Mama. Cheerzzz. Proud parents. The lawyer's educators. Next: Maria, Martin and Manuari.[27] Proud brothers. Following in their sister's footsteps. Next: The whole family. Cheezzz! Proud family. Important family. That has produced the best. My graduation gown is too long! I can't walk well in it, I am removing it. "You must keep it on your dress is short!" Oh Mother. "Did you run short of fabric?" Even you, Father?! *(She now becomes a news anchor holding a microphone.)* Dear viewers, I now bring you a brief interview with one of our graduates today. She emerged the best student from the Faculty of Law, Maria Kakazi[28] Bataka. Maria, how do you feel about your achievement?

(She holds the Microphone to an imaginary MARIA. But before she answers, SILVER appears.)

SILVER: Ahaaaa! A mouse cannot be sure of surviving the cat's trap if the cat is still hunting!

MARIA: I am not a mouse.

SILVER: Sure you are!

MARIA: Stop calling me a mouse! My name is Maria Kakazi. . . .

SILVER: "Born on December 25th and that is why they gave me the name Maria"! Isn't that the way you introduced yourself to me? Remember? It was on Christmas Eve, remember? My family and I had arrived from the city that same evening. I had decided that I would spend the festive season with my electorate. You knew we were there. You must have thought: the Member of Parliament is around, he has money and everybody talks about his generosity. Then you came. Where is that beautiful voice coming from? I asked myself. Then, I opened the window and there you were! My kids joined me . . . gosh, they fell in love with your singing right away! Remember? My goodness, one of them even wanted to go with you! "I am fundraising for school!" you said. Under the moonlight, neat braids pulled backwards, pink round chiffon dress, a little tight around your bust . . . and the wind, the wind

---

27. Pronounced as: mahn-WAH-ree
28. Pronounced as: kuh-KAH-zee

kept blowing your dress in all directions, revealing your cream petticoat underneath. It was quite a distraction and you seemed embarrassed by it all. Remember? You then held the dress between your thighs and kept singing. Under that moonlight, your body looked so . . . so . . . vulnerable, like you needed someone to protect you. In that moment, for the first time in my life, I was glad I didn't have a daughter. I asked you how much money you needed for your school term. Remember? *(Beat.)* And your face, God, your face was determined and beautiful and mysterious . . . I remember thinking to myself . . . poor kid! God, you looked so . . . so . . . I don't know, I wondered how old you were . . . that night I thought about you. *(Beat. Embarrassed.)* Are you going to remain standing there like an electric pole or what? *(Beat.)* Let's come to the point. What brings you to this side of the village? I am sure your father has told you that I am the only one supposed to sell to the locals. I have given you some weeks of grace and that is it! If you don't stop; I will have to inform your father. *(Beat. Stares at MARIA indecisively.)* I am sure, you have become an overgrown eucalyptus tree and you will need a bulldozer to remove you. *(SILVER goes over to her and attempts to carry her. This is a dance. A dance of power and control.)*

MARIA: Leave me alone! Do I look like I'm in a wrestling ring?

SILVER: The dumb speaks!

MARIA: Why don't you leave me alone?

SILVER: Because I don't want you to be in trouble.

MARIA: Because you don't want you to be in trouble.

SILVER: I have provided your father with legal documents for you to sell across the border.

MARIA: Why should I walk ten kilometers, pushing fifty liters, carrying ten more liters on my head when there is market here?

SILVER: Because this is my market!

MARIA: You make a lot of money in YOUR politics.

SILVER: There is no money in politics! It is all about sacrificing, serving the people!

MARIA: Whatever! I used to sell to these people in peace. When you saw that father was making some money, you decided to take the market away from us.

SILVER: Now, watch your mouth! I don't really need cooking oil money.

MARIA: You are very right. Your hands can land on any money they want. Why can't you allow me to sell my cooking oil here?

SILVER: You have legal papers to sell across the borders.

MARIA: Legal papers or not, I will continue to sell to these people.

COOKING OIL **63**

SILVER: You will land yourself in trouble, little Mary!

MARIA: You know what . . .

SILVER: Now that's my girl!

MARIA: I am not your girl, and I was going to say that I don't like you!

SILVER: It does not matter. I like you.

MARIA: I don't!

SILVER: One day, you will.

MARIA: In your dreams . . . if you dream.

SILVER: I like you . . .

(She breaks the dance.)

MARIA: Then allow me to sell some cooking oil here . . . please.

SILVER: Maria that is not the way the world works. I am looking ahead into the future. The incumbent president has told me that I am top on his list, among the people he is considering to succeed him.

MARIA: So?

SILVER: So?! I need to build a strong financial stand ahead of time.

MARIA: So?!

SILVER: So, every source that can bring me money must be tapped.

MARIA: I thought you said you don't need cooking oil money?

SILVER: That is not exactly what I said.

MARIA: I wonder why people trust you!

SILVER: Because we are all human, Maria.

MARIA: Some people say this is not how you used to be. They say that you have changed.

SILVER: This is not heaven where the angels dwell.

MARIA: I think the people are right.

SILVER: And them? Are they still the same? Those same people keep asking for more and more.

MARIA: Mr. Silver, think about my father, the man who has been working hard to get you votes here. How does he benefit? Why don't you allow his daughter, the daughter of your best friend, me, to sell cooking oil here?

SILVER: Your father may be the vice president or a senior presidential advisor.

MARIA: *(Sarcastically.)* You are such a man of your word!

SILVER: Now you think that you are being clever? *(MARIA starts pushing her gallons towards the exit. Beat.)* Don't you need a ride today?

MARIA: No.

SILVER: Why not?

MARIA: The chains you circle your rides with . . .

SILVER: I am just a barking dog. I never attack, I never bite, I just bark! *(He barks. He laughs.)* That was supposed to be funny. *(Beat.)* Come on; let me help you push that stuff to my car. *(SILVER takes the wheelbarrow. MARIA lets him.)* You hardly sold anything. That is why you should have allowed to live with us in the city. You seemed excited about the idea, and then changed your mind just like that. Was it your mother?

MARIA: Do you think I don't hear stories of poor girls who are convinced by powerful people like you to go live with them in the city. They promise to pay for their education, and do you know what happens to these girls? They end up becoming your servants, your children's nannies and sometimes/

SILVER: I am your Member of Parliament, it is my responsibility to make sure that my constituency is well taken care of, especially, the girl child. I would have treated you like a daughter.

MARIA: Since I have a father already, maybe that wasn't necessary.

SILVER: Ok! So you don't want to be treated like a daughter, maybe, then you should marry me, and then I would take care of everything including your education.

MARIA: *(Takes the wheelbarrow from him.)* Thank you. I will walk.

SILVER: *(Takes the wheelbarrow from her.)* That was supposed to be another joke!

MARIA: Are you going to give me back the wheelbarrow?

SILVER: I know you need the ride. You will need the strength for tomorrow, because I won't allow you to sell from here. If I were you, I would be reasonable, get into Silver's pick-up truck for a nice ride back to Maria's mother.

MARIA: Sometimes I wonder what Father and Mother would say if I told them the things you tell me.

SILVER: You would do that? Even after what I have done for you? Why would you even think of doing such a thing? You don't have to like me if you don't want to. But I also don't want you to abuse my kindness. When I tell you not to sell cooking oil here, I expect some respect. Do you ever hear yourself the way you talk to me? You have no slight respect for me! *(MARIA chuckles.)* You think I don't deserve any? *(Silence.)* Eh? You keep quiet again. I know how to get you move and how to make you talk.

MARIA: If you try carrying me again, or touching my stuff, I will scream. *(She starts pushing her wheelbarrow.)*

SILVER: I was seeing you.

MARIA: What?

SILVER: On "T.V."

MARIA: On T.V.?

SILVER: At your "graduation ceremony."

MARIA: What are you talking about?

SILVER: In a new dress!

MARIA: Ah!

(Overlapping.)

SILVER: And high heeled shoes . . .	MARIA: You have . . .
SILVER: In the photo studio . . .	MARIA: You have no right . . .
SILVER: Your graduation gown was long . . .	MARIA: To spy . . .
SILVER: Your dress was short . . .	MARIA: To spy on my . . .
SILVER: High above the knees . . .	MARIA: On my thoughts. . . .
SILVER: Your thoughts were loud.	MARIA: Don't touch me.
SILVER: I know your dreams . . .	MARIA: They are my dreams!
SILVER: To share . . .	MARIA: To keep.
SILVER: You need money . . .	MARIA: To go to school . . .
SILVER: And to look good . . .	MARIA: Finish High School . . .
SILVER: Like any other girl . . .	MARIA: Go to university . . .
SILVER: Get out of those rags . . .	MARIA: Get a career . . .
SILVER: Maria! *(SILVER pushes some money to her.)* For you.	

(Overlapping stops.)

MARIA: What for?

SILVER: Get a new dress

MARIA: I don't need . . . I can't take money from you anymore!

SILVER: Go to the salon

MARIA: All I need is . . .

SILVER: Get shoes . . .

MARIA: I don't think . . .

SILVER: Take it.

MARIA: I'd rather . . .

SILVER: Here, it's for you.

MARIA: I . . . *(MARIA first hesitates but after a thought, she takes the money. SILVER pushes the wheelbarrow. MARIA contemplates. She follows SILVER.)* It will be a loan!

SILVER: *(Beat.)* A loan. You said it.

MOVEMENT 2

(The setting transforms into BATAKA'S compound. It is a different day. MARIA is holding a small mirror and she shapes her eyebrows with a

razorblade. Her mother, NEEZA, is peeling cassava but keeps glancing at her daughter. They do their activities in silence.)

NEEZA: Get me water to wash this cassava, or else customers will come and find nothing to buy.

MARIA: *(Beat. Smiling to herself. Absent mindedly . . .)* Uh?

NEEZA: Is there something that I should know of?

MARIA: Did you ask for something?

NEEZA: You are smiling to yourself.

MARIA: Did you ask for water?

NEEZA: What makes you happy?

MARIA: Do I always have to be miserable?

NEEZA: Lately, you're paying a lot of attention to your looks.

MARIA: Did you have a bad day, Mother or what?

NEEZA: How did the sales go today?

MARIA: They went well.

NEEZA: Are you still selling to the locals?

MARIA: Was it drinking water you asked for?

NEEZA: I think they have been giving you a lot of money; is that why you are happy?

MARIA: Mother. . . .

NEEZA: Are you rich now?

MARIA: What?

NEEZA: Are you rich?

MARIA: What does that mean?

NEEZA: Do you have a lot of moneys?

(Beat. Something is on MARIA'S mind.)

MARIA: Where is it, Mother?

NEEZA: Where is what?

MARIA: Mother, please! I will die.

NEEZA: This is not a riddle session.

MARIA: Mother, I am serious! I will die.

NEEZA: Whom are you threatening?

MARIA: I mean it!

(She moves to the exit.)

NEEZA: Maria!

MARIA: Mother, you have no idea what I go through. I am about to realize my dream of going back to school. There is nothing I have not done for you or Father or your sons!

NEEZA: They are your brothers.

MARIA: This will kill me!

NEEZA: Your tongue is too fast for me. Sit down here.

(She does not. NEEZA gets an envelope from her inner garment.)

MARIA: Give it to me.

NEEZA: Not so fast!

MARIA: Give it here, Mother!

NEEZA: Maria, this is a lot of money. Where did you get it?

MARIA: Don't I work? Everyday? What do you call pushing that thing? WORK!

NEEZA: Are you quarreling with me?

MARIA: *(Loud silence.)*

NEEZA: Let us talk, ok?

MARIA: No!

(NEEZA puts back the envelope in her garment. Beat. MARIA is about to go, she changes her mind, and sits down.)

NEEZA: Maria, what is going on? You no longer tell me how much money you make.

MARIA: I don't want to tell you anymore.

NEEZA: Why not?

MARIA: Because you never defend me before Father. If you had defended me right from the beginning; at least, one of the boys would have waited to join secondary school and I would have finished high school.

NEEZA: Maria, am I not the one who has been keeping your savings? Secretly? You know how much I want you to go back to school. There is something about this money that you are not telling me. What is it?

MARIA: I only got it yesterday/

NEEZA: You are lying. I saw this money two weeks ago.

MARIA: I got it from Silver.

NEEZA: Silver?!

MARIA: It is a loan.

NEEZA: A loan?

MARIA: I will pay the money back.

NEEZA: How?

MARIA: *(She breaks down.)*

NEEZA: Why did Silver give you money?

MARIA: To buy a dress and shoes. But I was not going to use it to buy those things.

NEEZA: Since when did Silver start taking care of you?

MARIA: Mother stop! Is he not our member of parliament? Is it not his responsibility to make sure his constituency is well taken care of, especially the girl child!

NEEZA: Hm! You sound like him already! Instead of selling cooking oil you go to the city to beg money for shoes and dresses!

MARIA: Who said anything about the city?

NEEZA: You tell me.

MARIA: The city is four hours away. Would I have been coming back home every day?

NEEZA: Who knows?

MARIA: Mother! *(Beat.)* I was keeping it to top up my savings for school.

NEEZA: I want you to take this money back to Silver! I don't want people to exploit your situation, Maria!

MARIA: Like Silver is the only one exploiting my situation!

NEEZA: *(Enraged.)* What? Who else is exploiting you?

MARIA: You and Father!

(Beat. NDEEBA appears.)

NDEEBA: Hello.

NEEZA: Hello.

(Silence.)

NEEZA: Are you lost?

NDEEBA: No. I believe I am in the right place. You must be Mrs. Bataka?

NEEZA: Who are you?

NDEEBA: Ndeeba.

NEEZA: What can we do for you?

NDEEBA: I have come to speak to you about something.

NEEZA: What?

NDEEBA: Cooking oil.

NEEZA: Are you one of Maria's customers?

NDEEBA: No.

MARIA: Uh, you! Ndeeba, finally we get to meet! I know who you are! The new woman working for Mzazi Relief Aid. The only woman who rides a motorbike in this village! The one telling people not to buy my cooking oil . . .

(She begins loading gallons of cooking oil on her wheelbarrow.)

NDEEBA: Not your cooking oil only, all the cooking oil being sold in this village!

NEEZA: What?

MARIA: You are always roasting your cassava. You never get to know such things.

NDEEBA: Maria, can we talk about this cooking oil thing?

MARIA: I am not talking to you about anything.

NDEEBA: Maria, it is for your own good.

COOKING OIL 69

MARIA: My job is to sell. I only talk to those who are buying. Would you like to buy some?

NDEEBA: Maria, please . . .

MARIA: Where did you stop in school?

NDEEBA: Where is this going?

MARIA: Your level of education.

NDEEBA: I have a degree in Social Work and Administration.

MARIA: Where did you get the money to go to university? *(Beat.)* Come on degree woman! Where did you get the money?

NDEEBA: My parents gave it to me.

MARIA: Well, mine don't have it.

(She begins pushing the wheelbarrow.)

NDEEBA: You do not have to make corrupt choices to achieve your dreams.

MARIA: What? *(Beat.)* I have read something like that somewhere . . . *(Beat.)* What would you do if you were me?

NEEZA: That woman is mad, leave her.

MARIA: No, Mama. She is not mad. She is normal. Someone made her the judge among us. I am sure she has never taken anything that doesn't belong to her, her entire life!

NDEEBA: It is not like that.

MARIA: What would you do, if you were me?

NDEEBA: Maria, you can read English. Tell your mother that on those gallons, there are words "NOT FOR SALE."

NEEZA: So? Our Hon. Dr. Sir Silver gave us permission!

MARIA: I have a mind to tell you to go to hell!

NEEZA: MARIA! Excuse my daughter's behavior. *(To MARIA.)* Inside the house. Now! (MARIA stays. NEEZA gives her a murderous glare. MARIA is adamant. To NDEEBA.) Now, why don't you leave? All of us here have work to do. Or, go talk to my husband in the trading center.

NDEEBA: That is where I was before coming here.

NEEZA: And he asked you to come and talk to us?

NDEEBA: How can all of you fall for Silver's lies?

MARIA: If you are interested, I have something to say. People know the truth, they know that it is not his cooking oil, they know it is not for sale.

NDEEBA: Why do you sell it to them?

MARIA: Why does Silver sell it and why do they buy it?

NDEEBA: I don't know.

MARIA: There is nothing for nothing here. If they refused to buy it today, tomorrow, Silver would tell your bosses overseas "there is no more famine here" and do you know what your Bosses oversees would do?

70 SPEAKING OUR SELVES

NDEEBA: No.

MARIA: They would believe him and take the aid away. People buy this cooking oil because; they know that Silver will make sure that we get posho[29] and beans until the rains come. Degree woman, there is nothing for nothing here!

NDEEBA: You seem a very intelligent girl; why are you doing this?

MARIA: I thought I told you the reason already. (Beat.) Can I ask you question?

NEEZA: Madam, my daughter asks lots of questions, I suggest you go away.

NDEEBA: It is alright, she can ask.

MARIA: Thank you. That is the problem here. People are afraid to be asked questions and to ask questions. Silence reigns in this place.

NDEEBA: You may ask your question.

MARIA: The selling of cooking oil has been going on for a while. The Mzungu[30] who was here in your position, didn't mind us really. He was friends with my father, Silver and many other villagers. Why do you care? Why don't you let us just be?

NDEEBA: Because I think your father and Silver are taking things that do not rightfully belong to them.

MARIA: And you think your bosses overseas don't know that?

NDEEBA: I don't know. Maybe they do.

MARIA: How can you not know? You work for them.

NDEEBA: Maybe they don't know.

MARIA: But maybe they do and it is not a big deal. Why do you want to make it a big deal? I am working for my school fees here. Why is that a bad thing?

NDEEBA: Because you are doing it at other people's/

NEEZA: I don't care whether you are against our cooking oil business. All I know is that there have been improvements in this home! I mean compared to the rest of the villagers! Look at this, cassava! And a whole gallon of cooking oil. If it was not for Hon. Dr. Sir Silver to give my husband a deal.

NDEEBA: A bribe.

NEEZA: No, a deal!

NDEEBA: It is a bribe!

MARIA: Aah! Another word I have read somewhere!

NEEZA: Stop using big words to confuse us! Who do you think you are? Because we are not studied like you, because we do not ride a motorbike like you, you think we don't dream?

---

29. Corn meal. Very common in East Africa. Pronounced as: POE-SHO

30. An East African word for a white person and pronounced as: Moo-ZOO-n-goo

MARIA: Ndeeba, even people like us dream. Do you know what I dream of?

NDEEBA: What is your dream?

MARIA: I sell cooking oil to get out of here.

NDEEBA: Why do you want to go away from here?

NEEZA: Maria, you have to leave now. You are getting late for your evening selling.

MARIA: There you go again Mother! Shutting me up! You and Father always shut me up when I talk about my dreams! Do you think I don't dream? *(To NDEEBA.)* If I don't fight for myself, no one will fight for me. *(Beat.)*

NDEEBA: I will fight for you!

MARIA: You?!

NDEEBA: *(Beat.)* Yeah, I will find a way of fighting for you.

MARIA: Do you know how I feel pushing this thing every day?

NDEEBA: No.

(She pushes her wheelbarrow out.)

MARIA: Eeeeh, cooking oil! Cooking oil cheap here! Cooking oil to make your food taste better. No pain, no gain!

(Beat. NEEZA calls out to her daughter.)

NEEZA: Don't forget to return that money to the owner! *(Beat. Realizing that NDEEBA is looking at her. To NDEEBA.)* What?

NDEEBA: Why do you enslave her?

NEEZA: Woman, you have come wearing many jackets. Do you now want to teach us how we should parent our own children?

NDEEBA: No.

NEEZA: I don't think you love Maria more than her mother.

(Beat. BATAKA appears.)

BATAKA: Are you still spreading your gospel?

NDEEBA: Mr. Bataka, I was about to leave.

BATAKA: What are you waiting for then?

NDEEBA: Whatever happens, at least, I warned you.

NEEZA: About what?

BATAKA: She is threatening to inform her bosses that we are selling the cooking oil!

NEEZA: Don't do that as if you have no soul. You saw that girl. You saw her passion for school. Do you think we enjoy taking things that don't belong to us?

BATAKA: Do you think we like living in a place like this?

NEEZA: Don't you think, I would also want to know that I earn some money in other ways?

BATAKA: Do you think we enjoy seeing Maria pushing that wheelbarrow every day?

NEEZA: Don't you think, we would want her to go back to school?

BATAKA: Did she not always come first in class?

NEEZA: Listen Ndeeba, I never went to school, my father died when I was young . . .

NDEEBA: I am sorry. . . .

BATAKA: *(Showing signs of boredom.)* Ugh! Don't tell that story again!

NEEZA: Why not?

BATAKA: It is not relevant here.

NEEZA: It is my story. I will tell it all the same.

BATAKA: Don't you think some of us get bored of that same old story?

NEEZA: My mother could not afford fees for all of us . . .

BATAKA: Oh, please stop.

NEEZA: But I told myself, that I will educate my girls. When I got married to this man . . .

BATAKA: Don't put me in your story.

NEEZA: I will put you in my story. When I got married to this man, I found that he studied but never went to university.

BATAKA: Don't begin telling my story! Stick to yours.

NEEZA: We both vowed that we would work hard to send our children to school.

BATAKA: I think you should go.

NEEZA: That is why we sell this cooking oil. For our children to study.

NDEEBA: And Maria?

BATAKA: We have tried to give her an education. She is a good child. All she needs is patience. She will go back to school.

NEEZA: Don't tell her to stop selling cooking oil without giving her another alternative.

MOVEMENT 3

(Late evening. MARIA is by the village path with empty gallons counting money. She still has the envelope that she was fighting over with her mother in the previous movement. The sound of a motorbike; she stops.)

MARIA: I really hate it when people just stare at me without a word! Hey! You! Whoever you are, I am remaining with a liter of cooking oil. It will cost you fifty shillings only. That is half the price. No pain, no gain! Are you buying? You know how much it will cost you at Silver's? Three times the price I am giving you! This is your golden chance! *(The sound of the motorbike is heard receding.)* This person again! Who are they? Whatever they want, why do they hide behind that mask of a helmet, they

COOKING OIL **73**

appear as if they are faceless. Every day, they stand there and stare at me. They come at a time like this, to just stare at me! Every time I try reading the number plate of their motorbike, they ride away, leaving a cloud of dust behind them. *(Beat.)* Mine will be a car! A big car, and I will drive it the way Silver drives his car, not the way he drives the truck, no, the way he drives his Hummer *(imitating Silver)* with just one hand on the steering wheel and the other resting on the window. Waving to people once in a while. *(She is now Silver.)* "This is a good one. Very conducive for our impassable roads. Comes in handy when I am visiting my constituency. It can reach anywhere. I can even drive it through a cave or a lake."

(She looks at the envelope with the money she got from Silver. Confusion. Uneasiness. Indecisiveness. The sound of the bike is heard approaching. MARIA hides the envelope. Beat. NDEEBA moves towards MARIA.)

NDEEBA: You have been here for a while.

MARIA: Did you see that person?

NDEEBA: What person?

MARIA: The one who stares at me.

NDEEBA: Who stares at you?

MARIA: The one who rides off when I try to move closer.

NDEEBA: What are you talking about?

MARIA: The person who gives me chills.

NDEEBA: Is that supposed to be a joke?

MARIA: The one who makes me think of death.

NDEEBA: You are not making sense.

MARIA: You must have met that person.

NDEEBA: Where?

MARIA: On a motorbike.

NDEEBA: When?

MARIA: On your way here.

NDEEBA: Didn't see anyone.

MARIA: On a motorbike?

NDEEBA: No.

MARIA: Wearing a helmet?

NDEEBA: NO.

MARIA: I fear that person.

NDEEBA: Who is he?

MARIA: Maybe a she.

NDEEBA: A woman?

MARIA: Maybe . . .

NDEEBA: You saw that person?

MARIA: There!

NDEEBA: Your eyes are tired Maria. There is nobody.

MARIA: Gone.

NDEEBA: How are you today?

MARIA: The sales were great, thank you.

NDEEBA: I didn't ask about the sales.

MARIA: I am remaining with something little. Would you like to have it?

NDEEBA: Well, you know I can't . . . *(MARIA starts pushing her wheelbarrow.)* Maria!

(MARIA stops.) Give it to me. *(She does. NDEEBA then gives her a lot of money.)*

MARIA: Wo!! I don't have change for that.

NDEEBA: You can keep the change.

MARIA: This is a lot!

NDEEBA: I know.

MARIA: So?

NDEEBA: I have not forgotten.

MARIA: What?

NDEEBA: My promise.

MARIA: Which one?

NDEEBA: Helping you to go back to school.

MARIA: Oh . . .

NDEEBA: My contribution . . .

MARIA: I can't.

NDEEBA: Why not?

MARIA: I can't pay back!

NDEEBA: Pay back?

MARIA: What's your price?

NDEEBA: Price?

MARIA: Yeah.

NDEEBA: Nothing.

MARIA: You just want to help me?

NDEEBA: Yeah.

MARIA: Why?

NDEEBA: Well . . .

MARIA: Are you like Silver?

NDEEBA: What do you mean?

MARIA: He says he wants to help me but there has to be a price.

NDEEBA: Have you paid him?

MARIA: I am not a dump.

NDEEBA: Your mother told me.

MARIA: Told you what?

NDEEBA: Silver's money. The loan.

MARIA: Oh Mother!

NDEEBA: Did you return it?

MARIA: Y..e..s.

NDEEBA: That is good. You did well.

MARIA: Thank you, for the money I mean. *(Beat.)*

NDEEBA: Maria, this cooking oil has to stop.

MARIA: Not again!

NDEEBA: Things are getting complicated.

MARIA: I have to get home now!

NDEEBA: You have to hear! *(MARIA pushes her wheelbarrow.)* Maria . . .

MARIA: Ndeeba!	NDEEBA: Look here!
MARIA: Look at me!	NDEEBA: It's for your good!
MARIA: What haven't I done?	NDEEBA: The selling must stop!
MARIA: The wheelbarrow every single day!	NDEEBA: There will be another way . . .
MARIA: Except for Christmas and Easter days . . .	NDEEBA: Patience is what you need . . .
MARIA: Maria becomes a night angel . . .	NDEEBA: But the cooking oil must stop

(MARIA breaks into a Christmas carol, "Ding Dong Merrily on High.")

MARIA: Ding Dong merrily on high,

In heav'n the bells are ringing

Ding Dong! Verily the sky

Is riv'n with angel singing . . .

NDEEBA: What is all this?

MARIA: It is Christmas Eve!

NDEEBA: I don't understand . . .

MARIA: Do you see me Ndeeba?

NDEEBA: I don't see you Maria.

MARIA: I start at 7:30 on Christmas Eve.

NDEEBA: Where are you?

MARIA: In the village.

NDEEBA: Where?

MARIA: From house to house.

NDEEBA: What are you doing?

MARIA: Taking good news around . . .

NDEEBA: What good news?

76 SPEAKING OUR SELVES

MARIA: Of our saviour's birth . . .
NDEEBA: I am lost.
MARIA: A song for a coin.
NDEEBA: Why?
MARIA: Fundraising to go back to school.
(NDEEBA gets into MARIA'S world and throws her some money. MARIA continues to sing lyrics from "Ding Dong Merrily on High," and its refrain.):

MARIA: Gloria, Hosanna in excelsis!   NDEEBA: That girl can surely sing.

(NDEEBA throws her more money. MARIA moves to another "house.")
MARIA: Good tidings I bring!
NDEEBA: No coin for you!
MARIA: The line is: Take your songs of poverty away!
NDEEBA: Take your songs of poverty away!
(MARIA moves to another "house" and sings the first lines.)
NDEEBA: Our own children are not in school!
MARIA: It is now Easter Eve!
NDEEBA: Three hymns before we give you a coin.
MARIA: I sing my voice hoarse.
(NDEEBA throws her more money. MARIA bows and moves to another "house," and while doing so, she paraphrases 1 Corinthians 15:4.)
MARIA: He died and was buried but on the third day He arose!
NDEEBA: Go away beggar!
(She sings the refrain from the Christian hymn, "Up from the Grave He Arose"):

MARIA: He arose!   NDEEBA: Your father has more money
                                          than us!
MARIA: He arose!   NDEEBA: You sell us our own cooking
                                          oil . . .
MARIA: Hallelujah Christ arose! NDEEBA: And you want more money
                                          from us? *(Beat.)*

MARIA: That was cruel!
NDEEBA: What was?
MARIA: What you said about me selling people their own cooking oil.
NDEEBA: That is what people say, Maria!
MARIA: One day my name will be all over newspapers . . .
NDEEBA: When Maria?
MARIA: On my graduation day. Do you see me Ndeeba?
NDEEBA: I see you Maria.
MARIA: The university chancellor will call out my name . . .
NDEEBA: Ladies and gentlemen, I now call upon . . . Maria Kakazi Bataka!

(Hand clapping is heard. MARIA whispers something to NDEEBA.)

NDEEBA: That's right! The best law student this academic year . . .

MARIA: I have to shake the chancellor's hand . . .

NDEEBA: I see you Maria . . .

MARIA: He wants me to give a speech . . .

NDEEBA: I see you Maria.

MARIA: I will first introduce my father to you.

(NDEEBA stops playing along.)

NDEEBA: I think you should go home now!

MARIA: Father, I can't go home now, I have not even given my speech!

NDEEBA: I am your father now? I thought I was the college chancellor.

MARIA: Father, all these people turning up for my graduation ceremony!

NDEEBA: Maria.

MARIA: Miss Maria!

NDEEBA: Miss Maria?!

MARIA: Look at you Father! People, this is my father! Aren't you happy for me, Father?

NDEEBA: It is getting late Maria. Stop your games.

MARIA: I never played games. There were always problems! Then came the selling of cooking oil! The first thing my father would say was . . .

(Looks at NDEEBA, who is blank.)

MARIA: "The gallons are empty." *(NDEEBA complies.)*

NDEEBA: The gallons are empty!

MARIA: It would be followed by . . . "How much did you make today?"

NDEEBA: How much did you make today?

MARIA: He would have me surrender the money. Do you remember father? You would tell me to kneel.

(NDEEBA has now fully absorbed herself into the role of MARIA'S father.)

NDEEBA: Maria, you don't speak to your parents on your legs! *(She kneels.)* Give me the money for today's sales!

MARIA: But Father . . .

NDEEBA: Maria, always remember you have to wait until your brothers are far in school!

MARIA: I have to wait until my brothers are how far in school?

NDEEBA: They are my first priority!

(MARIA gives her "father" money and gets up.)

MARIA: One evening, Father told me that I was to stop selling cooking oil to the locals.

(BATAKA appears to MARIA.)

BATAKA: From now on, it is going to be only across the borders.

MARIA: I can't, Father!

BATAKA: You must!

MARIA: And the border protectors?

BATAKA: Here are the papers.

MARIA: And the other side of the border?

BATAKA: Some coins to keep them off your back.

MARIA: And the distance, Father?

BATAKA: Silver offered to get someone from his farm to always give you a ride.

MARIA: You don't know Silver, Father!

BATAKA: Silver is my friend.

(At this point SILVER appears but MARIA does not see him.)

MARIA: Silver is a fox.

BATAKA: Is that the way you talk about grown-ups? Do you know how kind that man has been to us? Do you want to go back to school?

(BATAKA disappears.)

NDEEBA: Stop it, Maria.

MARIA: I have not finished delivering my speech.

NDEEBA: It is getting late, you should go home.

MARIA: (Continues with her speech.) Silver's free things were never free.

NDEEBA: Maria!

MARIA: The weeks of grace . . .

NDEEBA: Stop . . .

MARIA: The rides . . .

NDEEBA: That's enough . . .

MARIA: The money . . .

NDEEBA: I've heard . . .

MARIA: He always asked for a price.

NDEEBA: Enough!

MARIA: Father, let me tell my story!

NDEEBA: Look, I am Ndeeba. I am not your father . . .

MARIA: Then, there was someone in a helmet . . .

NDEEBA: That person again!

MARIA: The one who always stared at me . . .

NDEEBA: You've already told me about that person.

MARIA: The one whose face I never saw. . . .

NDEEBA: You said that before!

MARIA: My skin would coil . . .

NDEEBA: It is all in your mind.

MARIA: They looked like you!

NDEEBA: Looked like me?!

COOKING OIL 79

MARIA: Walked like you!

NDEEBA: Walked like me?!

MARIA: Their figure cut the figure of death . . .

NDEEBA: My figure does not cut the figure of death!

MARIA: I think it was the angel of death.

NDEEBA: I am NOT! *(Breath.)*

MARIA: At the border, I would run into the protectors. "Arms Up!"

NDEEBA: I give up!

MARIA: I would put up my arms! What have I done wrong? I have the papers, authorizing me to sell across the borders. "And to the locals?" they would ask. I . . . I . . . "Silver says we arrest you when we catch you selling to the locals!" I will not do it again. "Run! Maria, run!" They would scream. I would run as far as my legs would carry me . . . Thinking any time a bullet would eat my flesh . . . "Stop" They would shout. Then someone would call out . . . "Give us something small, we won't bother you again." *(MARIA throws some money at NDEEBA and continues running.)* I have to give up my savings again or they shoot me. After running while pushing the wheelbarrow for almost three kilometers, I have no more strength to run. I stop! They catch up with me. "Aim, one, two . . ." Please don't shoot! *(Breathes out.)* I get out my last savings, I had hidden it in my bra! That is all I have. One of them, stinking with booze, checks my bra, looks at my breasts, and forcefully touches them. I push his hand away and he laughs. I run again. Tears rolling down my cheeks. *(Beat.)* Then I would drag my legs back home with enough for only my brothers' school fees. Some days were hard, really hard. But look at me today . . . My graduation!!

NDEEBA: You have to go now!

MARIA: Why? No more gallons! Today is my graduation! Silver should see me today! With my prize money, I will pay back his loan . . . full with interest! He will know that I was no joke!

NDEEBA: MARIA!

MARIA: Why do you shout my name? *(MARIA sees SILVER.)* Oh, my god! *(She flees leaving the gallons behind. SILVER attempts to run after her. NDEEBA blocks him.)*

SILVER: *(After MARIA.)* You take my money, you take my market away, you show me no respect, who do you think you are?

NDEEBA: You have no shame! I will pay you back your money!

SILVER: *(To NDEEBA.)* I see! You are the one confusing the girl! I am not interested in your payment.

(They stare at each other. They hate each other!)

MOVEMENT 4

(The setting in this movement evolves to suit the action. A room—maybe SILVER'S office.)

SILVER'S VOICE: *(In BATAKA'S head.)* Grab when your hands are still capable of grabbing something and your mouth can still chew . . . eat before any man . . . or woman munches and swallows you.

BATAKA: I was always against taking things that are not mine. Believed in hard work. But what do you do where everyone is under pressure to acquire much wealth? What do you do in a society where good actions are irrelevant? What do you do where honesty leads to nothing? What do you do where social relationships have become business relationships? What do you do where there is nothing for nothing? What do you do? It all started when he gave me the gallons. Now I see things and hear voices saying "stop."

(NDEEBA appears. Maybe she is BATAKA'S other conscience/his other part/ his other voice.)

NDEEBA: Stop!

BATAKA: I can't stop!

NDEEBA: You have to.

BATAKA: How will I support my family?

NDEEBA: You have made enough!

BATAKA: How about my sons' education?

NDEEBA: Invest what you have made.

BATAKA: It is not enough!

NDEEBA: How much is enough?

BATAKA: Just few more gallons and I will stop!

NDEEBA: Beware Bataka!

BATAKA: Beware of what?

NDEEBA: The investigation . . .

BATAKA: Those ones come and go.

NDEEBA: The law. . . .

BATAKA: I can't stop.

NDEEBA: Justice . . .

BATAKA: It depends.

NDEEBA: The trial . . .

BATAKA: The trial?

NDEEBA: In court . . .

BATAKA: What are the charges?

NDEEBA: Community exploitation.

BATAKA: Only?

NDEEBA: And bribery. . . .

BATAKA: That's common.

NDEEBA: And CORRUPTION.

BATAKA: What?!

NDEEBA: You are found guilty.

BATAKA: Enough!

NDEEBA: Handcuffs. . . .

BATAKA: And Silver?

NDEEBA: Scot-free!

BATAKA: How?

NDEEBA: You are his sacrifice.

BATAKA: What next?

NDEEBA: You must pay back for all the cooking oil you took . . .

BATAKA: But I can't afford it!

NDEEBA: Prison!

BATAKA: Prison?!

NDEEBA: Maximum . . .

BATAKA: Sentence?

NDEEBA: Deadly!

BATAKA: What? How many years?

NDEEBA: Life!

BATAKA: STOP!

(As NDEEBA disappears, NEEZA appears. She is only in BATAKA'S mind.)

BATAKA: And who are you?

NEEZA: I am your wife Neeza.

BATAKA: Why is your image obscured Neeza?

NEEZA: The light is dull in here.

BATAKA: I have been given a life sentence.

NEEZA: I have heard.

BATAKA: It feels like a bad dream. They have just announced it. Are my children aware?

NEEZA: Only Maria knows.

BATAKA: Tell Maria to come and address these people.

NEEZA: She had to go and sell the remaining cooking oil.

BATAKA: All along, you knew that Maria was selling to the locals! Why didn't you tell me?

NEEZA: You wanted me to force you to listen?

BATAKA: Why has the whole world turned against me?!

NEEZA: I am here. I know that you did this for us.

BATAKA: I know this is all Silver's doing.

NEEZA: I always told you to be careful of that man.

BATAKA: And the issue of Maria!

NEEZA: Leave Maria out of this.

BATAKA: She has to defend me.

NEEZA: Do not subject her to this as well!

BATAKA: I never allowed her to sell to the locals!

NEEZA: I told you it was Silver behind it. He gave Maria weeks of grace . . .

BATAKA: Gave Maria weeks of grace?

NEEZA: To sell to the locals. Maria told me this.

BATAKA: Maria told you this?

NEEZA: And I told you this!

BATAKA: I don't remember!

NEEZA: You should have done the selling yourself.

BATAKA: And who would have run the shop?

NEEZA: You would have done both.

(Overlapping:)

BATAKA: All I was trying to do was get you out of . . .	NEEZA: Do you remember me saying. . . .
BATAKA: Your tattered dresses . . .	NEEZA: I do not like you involving Maria in this cooking oil business.
BATAKA: Mismatched sandals . . .	NEEZA: You said: "I cannot talk now. I have an important meeting with Hon. Dr. Sir Silver."
BATAKA: Your face was no longer bright and beautiful . . .	NEEZA: I said: "It will take only a few minutes."
BATAKA: Poverty had curved deep holes around your eyes!	NEEZA: You said: "Today is the day when I am meeting the big man!"
BATAKA: Your breasts were no longer firm and strong . . .	NEEZA: You were always rushing, Bataka, saying;
BATAKA: They were a threadbare pair of socks on your bony chest.	NEEZA: "I have to go to the city to conclude another deal with my friend Silver."
BATAKA: The skin at the back of your hands . . .	NEEZA: Silver had become your life . . .
BATAKA: Had become an old mat or a cloth that has been chewed by a goat.	NEEZA: You ate Silver, walked Silver and even dreamed Silver
BATAKA: Your hands were no longer smooth and soft . . .	NEEZA: Another day, I had found Maria with a lot of money . . .
BATAKA: They had become hard and rough . . .	NEEZA: Did you even listen to me?
BATAKA: Like the bark of an overgrown tree.	NEEZA: Do you remember what you said?

BATAKA: Your feet that were once smooth . . .

NEEZA: "Just roast your cassava!" That is what you said.

BATAKA: Had turned into little cracks like a crashed calabash.

NEEZA: After that, I left you to do whatever you wanted.

(Overlapping stops.)

BATAKA: And my children. . . .

NEEZA: They are also my children . . .

BATAKA: I did all this to put a smile on your face.

NEEZA: Since you seem to blame everyone but yourself, it is better to. . . .

BATAKA: Please don't go Neeza. Don't leave me alone. *(He starts running after the imaginary NEEZA.)* Tell Maria to come and tell these people that I was not even aware that she was selling to the locals!

(SILVER appears. Beat.)

SILVER: Bataka! Are you going to remain standing there like a statue? Bataka, can you hear me?

BATAKA: Do you now think that I am deaf? Is Neeza going to come back?

SILVER: What's the matter?

(BATAKA starts as if waking up from a nightmare.)

BATAKA: Voices inside my head . . .

SILVER: What were the terms?

BATAKA: Only across the borders.

SILVER: Then you sold to the locals, making exuberant profits!

BATAKA: There were no exuberant profits and you know it!

SILVER: Do you have anything to say in your defense?

BATAKA: I was not aware that Maria was selling to the locals.

SILVER: Liar. Your cooking oil should be taken away!

BATAKA: Ok.

SILVER: Ok what?

BATAKA: Take it away!

SILVER: Bataka, what was that?

BATAKA: I am tired. My daughter is tired. We can't do this anymore.

SILVER: Why the sudden change?

BATAKA: You can have back the cooking oil! It will give you more money for your next political campaign!

SILVER: I am not a selfish man. We all want to eat where we work. But when you stand in Silver's way . . . My issue is that, my market was here, your market across the borders.

BATAKA: You and I know that cooking oil is not for sale here or across the borders.

SILVER: Have you forgotten where you came from?

BATAKA: No.

SILVER: Gaping shoes on your feet!

BATAKA: I remember.

SILVER: Then, I gave you a shop.

BATAKA: I remember.

SILVER: A well-stocked shop.

BATAKA: I remember.

SILVER: After yours was burnt down!

BATAKA: By your opponent's supporters!

SILVER: I did you a favor.

BATAKA: I was campaigning for you!

SILVER: What does that mean?

BATAKA: I deserved it!

SILVER: I didn't have to do it!

BATAKA: I had worked hard for you!

SILVER: It was for friendship's sake!

BATAKA: It was a compensation!

SILVER: Look at you! You wear neckties because of cooking oil!

BATAKA: So tight around my neck . . . because of cooking oil!

SILVER: Look at your sons, both in Secondary School; because of cooking oil.

BATAKA: But my daughter is at home!

SILVER: You were a nobody . . .

BATAKA: I was somebody . . .

SILVER: Your name was Bataka . . .

BATAKA: That was me . . .

SILVER: Now you are MISTER Bataka!

BATAKA: I don't know who I am!

SILVER: Everyone here would do anything to trade places with you.

BATAKA: My place burns.

SILVER: *(Softly. This is what drives him.)* I will tell you what burns. Poverty burns! Do you recall my torn pair of shorts as a young boy?

BATAKA: You do not have to go there!

SILVER: Do you remember how the whole school used to laugh at me?

BATAKA: Don't.

SILVER: Selling roasted nuts . . .

BATAKA: That was then.

SILVER: How I would be chased out of classes because I had not finished paying school dues?

BATAKA: The past is past.

SILVER: Do you remember how you used to share your lunch with me?

BATAKA: So?

SILVER: I promised to reward you one day.

BATAKA: It has nothing to do with the cooking oil.

SILVER: It has everything to do with poverty and my promise.

BATAKA: You are not poor anymore.

SILVER: And you are not . . . well, you don't have your property anymore!

BATAKA: Why don't I have it anymore?

SILVER: You lost it in the war.

BATAKA: Who waged that war?

SILVER: But, I never forgot you.

BATAKA: Who justified that war?

SILVER: I gave you free cooking oil to sell!

BATAKA: Who said that those leaders were greedy, corrupt, and sectarian?

SILVER: That was a huge sacrifice!

BATAKA: My property became the sacrifice.

SILVER: I made provisions.

BATAKA: Yes, you pushed us across the borders.

SILVER: Got you papers to cross freely.

BATAKA: Bataka's market ten kilometers walk.

SILVER: All the documents were legal.

BATAKA: That was not fair on me, Silver!

SILVER: Signed and stamped by the right people!

BATAKA: And on the other side of the border? I asked.

SILVER: Bataka, will always cross freely to and fro.

BATAKA: "I don't control the other side" you said.

SILVER: You accepted the offer all the same.

BATAKA: How many choices does a beggar have?

SILVER: You are not a beggar, damn it! You are a friend.

BATAKA: Our relationship has changed, Silver!

SILVER: Not in my eyes, Bataka!

BATAKA: I am a servant and you are the master!

SILVER: You are a brother, Bataka!

BATAKA: You have changed, Silver!

SILVER: You have changed.

BATAKA: We have changed.

SILVER: Damn you, Bataka! You are doomed! If you want, stay in your poverty.

BATAKA: I don't know who I am . . .

SILVER: I will stay here . . .

BATAKA: I want to stop . . .

SILVER: What has got into you? What are you murmuring about?

(Beat. BATAKA slips into hallucinations again.)

SILVER: The man shall face the courts of law. Take the stand!

(SILVER forces BATAKA to take a certain position and face "the judge," who is SILVER. The accusing "voices" may be played by characters with minor roles.)

VOICES: Raise your right hand and place your left on my Bible *(which is his palm)* and repeat these words after me! Do you swear to tell the truth and nothing but the truth so help you God? *(BATAKA does not say anything.)* The accused is sworn in my Lord!

SILVER: *(As the judge.)* You may proceed!

VOICES: It is stated in your testimony that you have been smuggling cooking oil across your country's borders! How do you plead, Bataka? *(Beat.)* My Lord, the accused admits that he has been stealing people's cooking oil that was given to him for free distribution.

SILVER: *(As the judge.)* How does the accused plead?

VOICES: *(As the prosecutor.)* The accused pleads guilty, my Lord. It is also stated in your testimony that not only did you smuggle the cooking oil across the border, with your permission, your daughter, sold it to people in your community. How do you plead, Bataka? *(Beat.)* My Lord, the accused also admits that he allowed his daughter to sell cooking oil to people in his community. My final question, Mr. Bataka, in your own words you say that you and Hon. Dr. Sir Silver Bibala have been friends for more than twenty years. Why are you trying to implicate such a man of integrity in your shoddy deals of cooking oil? Is it not true that it was your own decision to sell this cooking oil? *(Beat.)* My Lord, the accused is very remorseful and. . . .

SILVER: *(As the judge.)* This court will go for a ten minutes recess . . . May the accused see me in my chambers?

(BATAKA appears transfixed. He is looking at something—MARIA appears in his mind dressed in military clothes.)

BATAKA: Maria! What are you doing wearing military clothes?

MARIA: You sent for me?

SILVER: Don't pull those silly strokes of being insane on me again!

BATAKA: First go and remove those military clothes.

MARIA: Mother says that you want me to stand the trial on your behalf.

SILVER: If you don't stop this nonsense, I will have you beaten.

BATAKA: Go and dress up properly.

SILVER: Bataka!

BATAKA: Maria has come!

SILVER: Stop that!

BATAKA: Maria, tell them. Tell them that I never gave you permission to sell to the locals!

SILVER: I will have you confined . . .

BATAKA: Let Maria first tell you the whole truth.

SILVER: . . . to a mental institution!

BATAKA: Come on Maria tell him!

SILVER: Where is that Maria that you are talking about?

BATAKA: Right here!

SILVER: Where?

BATAKA: What has happened to you Silver? You cannot even see?!

SILVER: You are stretching my patience.

(All this time, "MARIA" has been moving slowly next to where SILVER is standing. She has a "knife" in her hand. BATAKA is "seeing" all this.)

BATAKA: Maria! What are you doing?! *(He throws himself in front of SILVER and starts struggling to take the knife away from "MARIA.")* Run, Silver! Run! Maria has a knife! She wants to stab you! *(SILVER stands confused. He is visibly frightened.)* Run for your life, Silver! Maria, I can't allow you! Let bygones be bygones! Silver is a friend! He'll always be! We will be doomed if you do this! Run Silver! Run for your life!

(SILVER disappears. "MARIA" overpowers her father and gets to SILVER'S chair which she stabs several times as BATAKA helplessly looks on.)

MARIA: You are free.

BATAKA: Finished.

MARIA: Free at last!

BATAKA: He was my friend.

MARIA: I am your daughter.

BATAKA: He tried to save me!

MARIA: I have saved you!

BATAKA: From poverty.

MARIA: From prison.

BATAKA: You have killed him.

MARIA: To free you!

BATAKA: He was a peaceful man.

MARIA: I am not violent.

BATAKA: Soon, the police will come!

MARIA: I hear the siren.

BATAKA: It will be my turn!

MARIA: You have done nothing wrong!

BATAKA: Silver is dead.

MARIA: Maria is guilty.

BATAKA: I will stand trial for you!

MARIA: I want to stand trial for me.

BATAKA: Let me!

MARIA: Father, the siren!

BATAKA: No one will touch you!

MARIA: When I was young, you would say that!

BATAKA: My little Maria!

MARIA: I am a big girl now!

BATAKA: You are still my little angel!

MARIA: I will take care of myself!

BATAKA: No one will harm you!

MARIA: I am big and strong!

BATAKA: I will hold your hand . . .

MARIA: It is too late, Father!

BATAKA: Help you cross the road . . .

MARIA: I have crossed the border all alone!

BATAKA: On your way to school!

MARIA: There is no more school.

BATAKA: After school, we will play hide and seek.

MARIA: *(MARIA is taken up by the childhood memory.)* Or the tag/plague game!

BATAKA: Maria! You are the one with the plague!

MARIA: No, Father. You are the one with it!

BATAKA: That means you are going to chase me.

MARIA: No! You are the one supposed to chase me!

(BATAKA starts chasing his daughter around. She enjoys it. It is a father-daughter moment.)

BATAKA: What do I do to you when I catch you?

MARIA: You pull my nose!

BATAKA: You have no nose!

MARIA: I do!

BATAKA: Where is it?

MARIA: Right here.

BATAKA: Where?

MARIA: Here on my face!

BATAKA: Do you have a face?

MARIA: Of course, Father, everyone has a face!

BATAKA: Where is your face?

COOKING OIL **89**

MARIA: Right here!

BATAKA: I do not see it.

MARIA: Right here.

BATAKA: Can I touch it?

MARIA: Yes, Father you can touch my face!

("MARIA" moves closer to BATAKA, who pulls her nose.)

BATAKA: You now have the plague!

(She attempts to run but it is too late.)

MARIA: I was just showing you my nose!

BATAKA: In the process you got the plague.

MARIA: It is my turn now.

(The same lullaby sung in the Prologue is heard. She begins chasing him. The sound of a siren.)

MARIA: The police!

BATAKA: Whatever happens . . .

MARIA: Nothing will happen.

BATAKA: Remember that I love you . . .

MARIA: I will sort it out!

BATAKA: And, I am sorry!

MARIA: It will be alright, Father.

BATAKA: It was foolish on my part!

(The sound of the siren gets closer.)

MARIA: I was left with three liters only . . .

(She begins to move.)

BATAKA: Do not go alone.

MARIA: I have to.

BATAKA: Wait! *(The lullaby dies out. "MARIA" disappears.)* Maria! *(SILVER appears. BATAKA gains composure.)* I must go now!

SILVER: The ambulance is here!

BATAKA: Why?

SILVER: To take you to a mental institution.

BATAKA: I am mad now?

SILVER: If you are not, why do you see things we do not see? And why are you not admitting that you gave Maria permission to sell cooking oil to the locals, and why do you want to give up the cooking oil deal? Uh? Because Ndeeba has promised to give you money?

BATAKA: That's not true!

SILVER: To take your daughter back to school?

BATAKA: Those are lies!

SILVER: Does Ndeeba want you to give evidence against me?

BATAKA: That's not true! It was all about. . . .

SILVER: Equal gallons!

BATAKA: Equal shares . . .

SILVER: Equal territories and respecting each other's boundaries.

BATAKA: That was my vow!

SILVER: Your oath!

BATAKA: That if we will ever cross . . .

SILVER: Each other's boundaries? I would become a dog!

BATAKA: I would become a cat!

(SILVER starts barking like a dog that has seen his enemy. BATAKA also charges at SILVER. They both get on all fours and get into a dog/cat fight. The dog gets on top of the cat and is busy devouring into the cat. The "cat" escapes and stands in a corner visibly scared of the "dog"! It becomes a dance, until the cat is overpowered. BATAKA runs away. SILVER chases him around. BATAKA escapes as the setting shifts to NDEEBA.)

BATAKA: I need to get Maria from the border.

NDEEBA: Why?

BATAKA: I am running away from this village.

NDEEBA: Why?

BATAKA: They are following me!

NDEEBA: Who?

BATAKA: Let's find Maria.

(The setting shifts to the village path where MARIA is transacting her business. MARIA is counting lots of money. She has never been this happy.)

MARIA: From Silver, two hundred thousand shillings cash! Cooking oil, fifty thousand shillings cash! From Ndeeba, one hundred thousand shillings cash! (The sound of a motor bike.) Eh, cooking oil, only three liters left . . . You buy two, you get one free! No pain, no gain!

(WOMAN 1 appears.)

MARIA: Only three left.

WOMAN 1: Give me two.

MARIA: And I will give you the remaining one free!

WOMAN 1: Thank you. (Beat.) What are you staring at?

MARIA: That person in a helmet is there again!

WOMAN 1: I do not see anyone.

MARIA: There!

(Something else attracts the woman from the opposite direction.)

WOMAN 1: Look!

MARIA: What?

WOMAN 1: There are men running towards us. They are armed!

COOKING OIL   91

MARIA: Where?

WOMAN 1: Let's run away Maria! This way!

MARIA: Not that way! There is that person in a helmet!

WOMAN 1: Run Maria, run!

(*MARIA bends down to pick up the gallons, as the money falls from her purse. She starts picking it up.*)

WOMAN 1: Forget the money and the gallons! Run!

(*MARIA does not. The woman leaves her. Four rapid gunshots.*)

(*Black Out.*)

MOVEMENT 5

(*This movement opens with the lullaby that we heard in the Prologue. It fades as the rest of other people's voices come in. NEEZA silently prays. Her husband stands still. NDEEBA continues with her report. Voices of journalists at SILVER'S office door as SILVER tries to bar them from entering. These could be accusing "voices" of the crowd.*)

NEEZA: Here I am again, praying to you Ruhanga wangye.[31] This prayer is not of thanksgiving for the cooking oil. It is to tell you that it was a blessing and a curse. I seek redress. I seek justice. I seek fairness. When her spirit is avenged, I will not bother you again.

NDEEBA: And full stop! There! All finished! I have been on this for a week! For seven days I have sat here, to make sure I finish this report! So that no one denies the truth. It all started when I was posted in this village. When the commission of inquiry sees this. . . .

VOICE 1: Hon. Silver, what do you have to say about the girl's shooting?

SILVER: It was unfortunate.

VOICE 2: Where was she getting the cooking oil from?

SILVER: How do you expect me to answer a dead girl's question?

VOICE 3: Is it true that you had given her permission to smuggle the cooking oil?

SILVER: Who bewitched you, journalists?

VOICE 4: Is it true that you ordered her killing?

SILVER: (*Pleadingly.*) It was never meant to be this way.

VOICE 4: Who then is responsible for her death?

SILVER: I am not a killer!

VOICE 5: Is it true that Mzazi Relief Aid Country Director is also under investigation in relation to the cooking oil?

---

31. My God in Runyankore language spoken in South West of Uganda. A prayer. Pronounced as: roo-HER-n-guh wuh-N-jay

92   SPEAKING OUR SELVES

SILVER: I tried to stop him . . .

VOICE 4: Stop who?

SILVER: *(Thinking aloud.)* He was drunk. Gun in hand. It was too late.

VOICE 5: Are you admitting that you had a hand in the girl's death?

SILVER: *(Realizing what he has just said.)* Leave my corridor now!

(The questions are asked simultaneously; voices 3, 1 & 2 at first and then voices 3, 4 & 5.)

VOICE 3: Do you think your political career is over?	VOICE 1: Hon. Silver, will Mzazi Relief Aid close down here?	VOICE 2: Where is the girl's body?
VOICE 3: There is cooking oil in your shop	VOICE 4: Where were you getting it from?	VOICE 5: What's the future of your political career

(He closes the door, shutting off the journalists' voices. He disappears. The door is pushed open, as NDEEBA appears.)

NDEEBA: Silver, time to answer for your crimes, the president of Mzazi Relief Aid and the police are here . . . *(Silver is gone. NDEEBA is shaken.) (Beat.) (MARIA'S silhouette appears behind NDEEBA, she looks up, and the silhouette disappears. NDEEBA looks at Silver's empty comfortable chair, she longs for it, hesitates, sits in it, stands, looks at it again, and makes the DECISION to sit in it. The silhouette appears again.)*

SILHOUETTE: Time to go Ndeeba! The report is over!

(A moment of confusion. NDEEBA turns, but she is unable to catch whatever it is that is talking at her. Instead, she looks at the clock, which reads 12 o'clock in the afternoon. Beat. The lullaby from the Prologue is heard. The lullaby fades. Beat.)

SILVER'S VOICE: Who is that person in a helmet?

NDEEBA: *(NDEEBA starts and stands at attention.)* Silver! Is that you? Where are you?

SILVER'S VOICE: Someone in a helmet!

NDEEBA: Someone in a helmet?!

SILVER'S VOICE: That person looks like you!

NDEEBA: Stop that!

SILVER'S VOICE: It is beckoning me. Beware, Ndeeba! That chair burns.

(NDEEBA takes the audience in, frightened as she points to the audience):

NDEEBA: There! Someone in a helmet!

END

COOKING OIL 93

(A) Music and lyrics of "Omwana Alikulilandala," transcribed by Audrey Kukunda.

(B) Music and lyrics of the nursery rhyme, "Embeba" ["Three Blind Mice"], transcribed by Audrey Kukunda.

The author reserves all translation, serialization, and dramatization rights. Requests for any of these rights should be addressed to Asiimwe Deborah Kawe at dasiimwe@gmail.com or asiimwekawe@gmail.com.

Tanzanian playwright Penina Muhando, author of *Nguzo Mama*.

Nguzo Mama

Penina Muhando

Penina Muhando Mlama is Professor Emeritus at the University of Dar es Salaam, Tanzania where, for many years, she served as Professor of Creative Arts.

Her academic areas of concentration are African theater, Theater for Development, and theater in education. She has been actively involved in the movement that sought to affirm the existence and value of African theater that suffered considerably at the hands of the colonial forces that relegated African cultural and artistic expression to the so-called primitivity.

Muhando's research, including her graduate studies, as well as her artistic creativity and theater performance, have focused on interrogating and affirming the essence of African theater and the effort to put it on the same pedestal as any other theater tradition in the world.

She chose to write plays using African theater performance approaches that largely depart from some of the acclaimed Eurocentric Aristotelian yardsticks. The underlying essence of her plays is her attempt to highlight African theater performances. Storytelling and dance performance techniques are some of her favorite artistic media with which she employs various African approaches to character development, performance, audience participation, stage management, audience control, and narration. *Nguzo Mama* is one of her plays where Muhando plays around with African performance techniques through storytelling and dance. The same is true also for her other plays including *Lina Ubani* and *Pambo*.

Muhando has published eight plays in Kiswahili including *Hatia* (Nairobi: East African Publishing House, 1972); *Tambueni Haki Zetu* (Dar es Salaam: Tanzania Publishing House, 1973); *Heshima Yangu* (Nairobi: East African Publishing House, 1974); *Pambo* (Nairobi: Foundation Books, 1975); *Nguzo Mama* (Dar es Salaam: Dar es Salaam University Press, 1983), which is published in English (translated by Joshua Williams) for the first time in this volume, *Speaking Our Selves: New Plays by African Women* (Ann Arbor: University of Michigan Press, 2025); and *Lina Ubani* (Dar es Salaam: Dar es Salaam University Press, 1984). In 1976, *Talaka si mke wangu* appeared in J. M. Mbonde, ed., *Michezo ya Kuigiza* (Dar es Salaam: Tanzania Publishing House). Muhando co-authored *Harakati za Ukombozi* with Amandina Lihamba and Ndyanao Balisidya (Dar es Salaam: Tanzania Publishing House, 1983).

Muhando made a deliberate choice to write her plays in Kiswahili, Tanzania's national language, as part of another movement she strongly supported—that of promoting Africa's indigenous languages, which she believes have the same power for artistic expression as any other language in the world.

Muhando is one of the pioneers of the Theater for Development movement in sub-Saharan Africa. She worked with grassroots communities in Tanzania, Zimbabwe, and Cameroon, using theater to identify, analyze, and seek solutions to development challenges. Her book, *Culture and Development: The Popular Theatre Approach in Africa* (Uppsala, Sweden: Scandinavian Institute of African Studies, 1991), captures her experiences in this area.

Muhando applied her experiences in Theater for Development to design, in collaboration with Amandina Lihamba, the TUSEME model, where theater performance is employed to empower girls to acquire self-confidence and self-esteem to identify, analyze, challenge, and combat gender-based inequalities, including patriarchal cultural practices and attitudes, gender-based oppression, and violence. TUSEME (meaning "Let Us Speak Out" in Kiswahili) was first applied in Tanzanian secondary and primary schools. As the Executive Director of the Pan-African Forum for African Women Educationalists (FAWE) between 1998 and 2007, Muhando introduced TUSEME to some twenty countries across Africa. In 2016, Muhando was awarded the UNICEF "Changemaker Award" for Empowerment of Girls through the TUSEME model.

In her career at the University of Dar es Salaam, she served as Head of the Creative Arts Department, Dean of the Faculty of Arts and Social Sciences, and Deputy Vice Chancellor for Academic Affairs. She also held the Mwalimu Nyerere Professorial Chair in Pan-African Studies.

Muhando has also published books and numerous articles on the performing arts, Theater for Development, education, and gender. Her publications include a series of co-authored, gender-focused handbooks published in 2005 by FAWE in Nairobi: *Gender Responsive Pedagogy: A Teacher's Handbook; Empowering Youth through TUSEME; Let Us Speak Out: A Teacher's*

Handbook; and *The Gender Responsive School: A Handbook for Education Practitioners.*

Muhando has served as chairperson on several boards in Tanzania, including the Tanzania National Arts Council, the Tanzania Commission for Universities, and the St. John's University of Tanzania. She has served as a member of many boards in Tanzania, while her international board memberships include the International Youth Foundation, The Open Society Foundation, The Alliance for African Partnership Foundation of Michigan State University, and the Geneva-based South Centre.

An interview with Penina Muhando is available at https://doi.org/10.3998/mpub.12827650.cmp.13.

PENINA MUHANDO ON *NGUZO MAMA*:

The understanding of the play, *Nguzo Mama*, may benefit from a review of the historical context from which it emerged. The 1970s, when this play was written, was a time of serious post-independence struggles for the liberation of humankind in Tanzania and Africa at large. One important branch of such struggles was the liberation of women from the forces of patriarchy, which, in collaboration with other economic and political forces of exploitation, bound women to unacceptable oppression and subjugation.

Since Tanzania's political independence in 1961, women rose to fight for their rights through various social, economic, and political movements. At the political level, many women across Tanzania were united through the Umoja wa Wanawake wa Tanzania (Tanzanian Women Union) (UWT), the women wing of the then-ruling party, the Tanzania African National Union (TANU). Other civil society organizations also strived to uplift the lives of women economically, socially, and culturally.

The struggle for women's liberation then was, however, fraught with challenges. Low levels of understanding of the deeply rooted patriarchal and other forces of gender inequality led to some ineffective approaches to combating the causes of women oppression. *Nguzo Mama* is a glimpse into that struggle and its challenges.

Even though *Nguzo Mama* speaks to the struggles for gender equality of the 1970s, it is still relevant to the current gender equality struggles in Tanzania and elsewhere. There is no denying the fact that significant achievements have been recorded in the attainment of gender equality in Tanzania, as manifested in increased access to education for girls and women at all levels; women's access to resources, including land; and increased recognition and legislation of women's rights. Access to political leadership has also seen rising numbers of female parliamentarians and cabinet ministers, with the country getting her first female President in 2021. These achievements notwithstanding, the struggle for gender equality is yet to see its conclusion. Many patriarchal structures portrayed in *Nguzo Mama* are yet to be dismantled and the negative cultural attitudes against women's rights are still present in a significant number of citizens today. *Nguzo Mama* is therefore as valid today as it was when it was written.

Nguzo Mama has been used as an approved textbook for Literature and Kiswahili subjects in Tanzanian secondary schools and universities. It has also been staged in various secondary schools across the country.

Nguzo Mama
Penina Muhando
Translated from the Kiswahili by Joshua Williams as *The Pillar of Motherhood*

CHARACTERS

Storyteller
The Women of the Chorus:
    Madam 1
    Madam 2
    Madam 3
    Madam 4
    Madam 5
    Madam 6
    Madam 7
    Madam 8
Messenger
Girl
Totolo: A local drunk.
Shaba: Madam 1's husband.
Sudi: Madam 2's husband.
Chairman: Chairman of the Advisory Committee.
Chizi: A madman.
Child: Madam 2's child.
Voice: Sudi's friend.
Maganga: Madam 5's husband.
Kiando: Madam 7's late husband's brother.
Makange: Madam 7's late husband's brother.

NOTES ON SETTING, PLAYING STYLE, AND LANGUAGE
BY JOSHUA WILLIAMS

Penina Muhando gives no indication of where exactly the action of *Nguzo Mama* takes place. This is in keeping with the fluid, lyrical, and largely non-naturalistic playing style the play demands. However, it is clear from the text, and from the note on the text that she prepared for this anthology, that Muhando had Tanzania in mind as she wrote—and, more to the point, Tanzania in the late 1970s and early 1980s. (*Nguzo Mama* was first published in Kiswahili in 1982.) The music and dance called for in the script locate one immediately in the Tanzanian cultural landscape, as do the styles of dress that Muhando delineates for Madam 1–Madam 8. The distinction she makes at several points between the coast and the interior of the country is another kind of shorthand for longstanding questions of race, ethnicity, religion, and national belonging. Taken together, these details indicate that although this is surely an allegory, it is nevertheless one that takes very seriously the diversity of women's real experiences in postcolonial Tanzania, and the many political tensions to which that diversity gives rise. The English language is an imperfect medium for Muhando's lyricism, her wit, her political insight, and the unique synthesis of storytelling, song, dance, and dialogue that she pioneered in plays like *Nguzo Mama*. I have tried to retain at least some sense of the shifts in rhythm and tone in the text of the Kiswahili original by translating both sung and spoken verse passages into English free verse; naturalistic dialogue in the original appears here as prose. I leave it to readers— and, hopefully, one day, performers—to re-imagine what has been lost in translation, and to bring this remarkable play fully to life.

SCENE 1

(A large, thick pillar lying on its side on the stage. To one side of the pillar hangs a small slate with the words "Pillar of Motherhood" written on it. A STORYTELLER sits downstage, warming herself in front of a fire, facing the audience. She stays this way for the entire play. We hear full-throated singing from offstage.)

CHORUS *(Singing.)*: Pillar of Motherhood, Pillar of Motherhood
Shall we adorn you with flowers?
How should we adorn you?
(As the song continues, MADAM 1 enters dancing lelemama, following the beat of the music. She is dressed fastidiously in the coastal style. She dances facing the pillar. She goes to the center to lead the call-and-response, still facing the pillar.)
MADAM 1: Should we adorn you with gold?
Should we adorn you with silver?
Kohl, henna, and perfume?
How should we adorn you?
(The CHORUS responds.)
MADAM 1: Should we adorn you with light?
Kanga cloth from overseas?
With earrings?

How should we adorn you?
(The CHORUS responds and continues to sing. MADAM 1 joins in and continues to dance the lelemama as she circles the pillar. She ululates.)
MADAM 1: Ai ai ai ai ai ai ai!
(She tries to lift the pillar but cannot. She dances offstage.
The song continues and MADAM 2 enters dancing kiduo, singing along with the music. She is dressed like a peasant, a farmer from the coast. She dances facing the pillar, leading the call-and-response.)
MADAM 2: Which hoe do you want?
The one with the long handle or the short one?
A clay pot with a small mouth?
Or a basket in the Gogo style?
How should we adorn you?
(The CHORUS responds.)
MADAM 2: With scores and scores of children?
Our aunts and uncles' children?
Or with ugali porridge?
With beans and milk?
How should we adorn you?
(The CHORUS responds. She ululates.)
MADAM 2: Lu lu lu lu lu lu lu lu lu!
(The song continues. MADAM 2 tries to lift the pillar but can't. She exits.
The song continues and MADAM 3 enters singing, dancing the rumba. She is wearing kitenge cloth in the Congolese style. She dances the rumba facing the pillar, leading the call-and-response.)
MADAM 3: Should we adorn you with Benzes?
Should we adorn you with Volvos?
Which number plate?
The ST or the SU?
How should we adorn you?
(The CHORUS responds.)
MADAM 3: Or maybe with cake?
What are you drinking?
Beer, whiskey, wine?
And a roast chicken too?
How should we adorn you?
(The CHORUS responds.)
MADAM 3: Hooray for the Pillar of Motherhood, oyeeeeeeeeeeee!
(She tries to lift the pillar but can't. She exits. The song continues a little longer and then stops. Silence falls.)

STORYTELLER: A story! A story!
AUDIENCE: Come here, story!
STORYTELLER: A story! A story!
AUDIENCE: Come here, story!
STORYTELLER: A long time ago
In the olden days
The time of our grandfathers'
Grandfathers
Good people lived
In the village of Patata

That village prospered, oh, it prospered
Its people were good and kind
They were born and they grew
Patata came to be praised in every corner of the world
It sparkled—on the surface
With the laughter of its people
Many coveted that Patata-ness and wanted to find it

But the women of Patata
They knew their faults, their weaknesses
Trouble and confusion loomed in Patata
Progress did happen, yes, but it was hemmed in by danger
Because those who bore children were sorely oppressed
And seen as less than human
No matter the fact that they were the ones
To bring development
And raise society up

How did this happen?
No one knew
But there, in Patata, in their home
There was more and more confusion
And Patata's progress was in danger

One day, early in the morning
The villagers of Patata were shaken from sleep
By the clamor of drums, a clarion call
(The drums cry out. Enter a MESSENGER.)

MESSENGER: When the drums ring out, there is a reason
People of Patata, listen
When the drum calls
Let those with no children
Carry stones on their backs
We have found the Pillar of Motherhood
To rescue us from our distress
Wake up, people of Patata!
The ancestors have chosen
To give you the Pillar of Motherhood
To take away your troubles
So, hurry now, wake up!
Lift the Pillar of Motherhood, raise it up
Today—today—right now
Let's say goodbye to despair
Let's get back to progress and development
When the drum calls, it has a message
(The MESSENGER exits. The drums ring out again.)
STORYTELLER: Upon hearing this, the people of Patata were filled with
    happiness
Those who bore children
Their beds could not hold them
They ran to see for themselves
With their babies on their backs
This, their Pillar of Motherhood

The men also got up
And followed behind
To see about this Pillar of Motherhood

As soon as they arrived, they saw for themselves
What had been written
In beautiful handwriting, enormous letters:
PILLAR OF MOTHERHOOD

A cry went up:
"All right, everyone, let's make the pillar stand"
The women rushed quickly to the pillar
To try to lift it

But the men of Patata
Bent their path toward home
They turned back around, got back into bed
Went back to sleep
Waiting for the sun to come up
And breakfast to be made

In their hearts, they thought—
And yes, some said it openly—
"It says 'Pillar of Motherhood' there
This Pillar of Motherhood is mothers' business
Let's leave them to sort it out"

Others asked
Because they were confused:
"How can we abandon this task?
Isn't the development of Patata
Work for men and women both?"

But they still followed along with the others
Remained silent
And waited for development
To happen
One of them, just one, made up his mind:
"When the mother of my children comes back
I will say I sympathize"

Nevertheless, at the Pillar of Motherhood
Abandoned
The women, children on their hips, struggled
They didn't ask questions
They were used to it, poor things, every job being dumped on them
It was even written in books
That women worked sixteen hours every day

They rushed to the Pillar of Motherhood
To take its weight in their hands, raise it up from beneath
They tried and they tried
But they couldn't shift it at all

Oh, what should we do, people of Patata?
There must be a secret
To making the Pillar of Motherhood stand
We must search and search until we find the secret way

They put their backs into it
Devoted themselves to investigating
To revealing the secret
Of how to lift the Pillar of Motherhood
CHORUS (*Singing.*): Pillar of Motherhood, Pillar of Motherhood
Shall we adorn you with flowers?
How should we adorn you?
(*As the song continues, MADAM 4 enters clapping her hands. She moves to the beat of her clapping. She wears a kitenge and a head wrap. She leads the call-and-response.*)
MADAM 4: Pillar of Motherhood hoyeeeeeeeeeeeeeeeee!
Should we adorn you with applause?
Or sweet, sweet words?
Should we make donations?
How should we adorn you?
(*The CHORUS responds.*)
MADAM 4: Even better, let's have meetings
And maybe also marches
We can make declarations, pronouncements
And broadcast them far and wide
How should we adorn you?
(*The CHORUS responds.*)
(*As the song continues, MADAM 5 enters, matching her gait to the madogori beat. She is carrying a small pot filled with hot coals. She puts it down in front of the Pillar of Motherhood. She lights incense and makes a lot of noise as she speaks.*)
MADAM 5: Who are you? Hey, tell me, who are you?
What do you want? Gold? A necklace?
A white kerchief or a black one?
Let go! Give up! Let go!
(*The CHORUS responds.*)
MADAM 5: Who are you? Are you from Arabia?
From land or sea?
Get out! Leave! Get out!
Get out of here and don't come back!

(The CHORUS responds.)
(MADAM 5 tries to lift the pillar but can't. She exits. As the song continues, MADAM 6 enters. She doesn't sing. She walks like a prostitute. And she is dressed like a prostitute. She goes to the Pillar of Motherhood and circles it, acting flirtatious, as if she were soliciting.)
MADAM 6: So, what do you say?
That devil of yours is stubborn, no?
(She's loitering, drifting from place to place.)
(The CHORUS responds.)
MADAM 6: I know this city, my friend.
I've been around.

MPs, poor guys, priests and sheikhs
Young and old
You see me, you hit the brakes
No one passes me by
You'll stand up for me
(The CHORUS responds.)
(She tries to lift the Pillar of Motherhood but can't. She leaves. As the song continues, MADAM 7 enters. She doesn't sing. She's dumbfounded, unsure what to do. Her clothes are normal, ordinary, unremarkable. She walks around in confusion. She looks at the Pillar of Motherhood and doesn't know what to do. She's reluctant even to touch it. She leaves.
As the song continues, the GIRL enters. She doesn't sing. She wears a school uniform. She moves nervously, constantly changing direction. She crosses now to the left, now to the right, now down toward the audience—but she doesn't go to the Pillar of Motherhood. Now voices of different kinds call to her from all the different parts of the stage. Each voice calls to the GIRL to come that way but as soon as she starts in that direction another voice calls out to her and she turns and follows that one instead.)
MADAM 1 *(Voice.)*: Hey you, come here!
MADAM 2 *(Voice.)*: Come! Come here.
MADAM 3 *(Voice.)*: Here! Aren't you listening?
MADAM 4 *(Voice.)*: Come quickly!
MADAM 5 *(Voice.)*: Come here! Here!
MADAM 6 *(Voice.)*: Come here! Run!
MADAM 7 *(Voice.)*: Child, you aren't listening. Come here!
(The GIRL doesn't know what to do. She doesn't know which way to go. She tries to leave the stage using all the various exits. Finally, she leaves the way she originally came.

The CHORUS continues. MADAM 8 enters. She doesn't sing. She wears modern clothes. She carries an armful of books, six or so. She moves in a businesslike manner, like a civil servant. She goes over to the Mother Pillar. She sings a little. She opens her books and reads a bit here and there. She looks at the pillar. She goes out the way she came in—not the way MADAM 1–MADAM 7 exited.)

CHORUS *(Singing.)*: Pillar of Motherhood, Pillar of Motherhood
Shall we adorn you with flowers?
How should we adorn you?

SCENE 2

STORYTELLER: The truth is, they were perplexed
The people of Patata
"This Pillar of Motherhood has come to us at no cost
And we can't lift it
But let's not give up
No—let's find a way"
They met together
To air their thoughts
(MADAM 1, MADAM 2, MADAM 3, MADAM 5, MADAM 6, and the GIRL enter. They sit in the audience. MADAM 4 enters and comes right down in front. She claps her hands and they join her. She stands ready to give a speech.)
MADAM 4: Pillar of Motherhood hoyeeeeeeeeeeee!
AUDIENCE: Hoyeeeeeeeeeee!
STORYTELLER: Statements were made—declarations, manifestos
And greeted with applause and ululation
They poured out by the thousands
And fierce arguments raged back and forth

The mkwaju beat and the ngokwa dance
Their spirits were washed clean
The people of Patata

But the Pillar of Motherhood was still not standing
(MADAM 8 enters with thick, strong ropes in her hands.)
MADAM 8: All right, listen. You all know that the Pillar of Motherhood cannot stand unless we hoist it up with ropes. So, come here, all of you, and take these. We'll tie them on the Pillar of Motherhood and then we all can pull.

(MADAM 1, MADAM 2, MADAM 3, MADAM 5, MADAM 6, and the GIRL come up from the audience. Each of them takes a rope and ties it on some part of the Pillar of Motherhood.)

MADAM 8: Everyone, tie your ropes tight so they don't slip when we pull on them. Ready? All right. Now each of you take your rope and go to one side or the other.

(They all arrange themselves.)

MADAM 8: Oh, Madam Two, I can see your rope is very short. Wait a moment—I'll go get another one that's longer.

(She exits.)

MADAM 1: It's true, right, without a doubt—if we pull together, the Pillar of Motherhood will stand.

MADAM 2: I don't know why we didn't think of this earlier.

(MADAM 4 enters.)

MADAM 4 *(Shocked.)*: Eh! What are you doing? Who told you to do this? Who was it?

MADAM 5: Madam Eight showed us the technique.

MADAM 4: Ah, so Madam Eight has started with her nonsense. Where was she before? When the Pillar of Motherhood appeared, we didn't see her here. She wasn't at the procession. Only now, as we start to plan it all out, she starts running her mouth, making demands. Where was she all this time? Forget it. Drop those ropes. Let go of them, right now. Let's go. They're waiting for us.

(They all start to leave.)

MADAM 4: That Madam Eight and her nonsense!

(She sees that MADAM 8 is coming and exits quickly.)

MADAM 8: Hey, sisters, why are you leaving?

(She stands there, shocked, with her ropes in her hands.)

MADAM 8: This Pillar of Motherhood won't ever stand.

(She exits the way she came.)

STORYTELLER: Wherever they went
Misunderstanding blossomed
This one: "let's do it this way"
That one: "let's do it that way"
Patata was festooned with heat, adorned with fire
Each of them did it her own way
Putting her faith in what she did
To lift up the Pillar of Motherhood

Madam Two decided
If she brewed beer and sold it at the club
She'd get some money—money would show the way
And the Pillar of Motherhood would stand
(*MADAM 2 enters with barrels of kangara homebrew and drinking bowls.*
She sets up shop. Two men, TOTOLO and SHABA, enter.)

TOTOLO (*Laughing.*): Look at this, even Madam Two is brewing booze these days. Tsk tsk tsk.

SHABA: We're going to enjoy our booze this year. The whole village—full of booze.

MADAM 2: Hey, that's progress. This year we'll stand on our own two feet. Come on in, you're welcome.

TOTOLO: Now that this Pillar of Mamahood has come, we drunks will have a good time. Bring me a pint.

MADAM 2: You want one too, Shaba?

SHABA: Come on, man, first pour some out for us to taste. How do we know if it's any good?

TOTOLO: Hey, man, that's true. Let us taste some so we can see if you really know how to brew our beer.

MADAM 2: Oh, all right, is that how it is—you're going to insult me? Fine, taste this. See for yourselves.

TOTOLO (*Drinking.*): Mmm! Hey, this is definitely booze. I swear to God, it's booze. Here.

(*He gives it to SHABA.*)

SHABA (*Drinking.*): Hey, man, it's true. Bring the beer!

(*TOTOLO and SHABA sing and dance.*)

TOTOLO & SHABA: Fill our mugs!
Bring us a pint!
Fill our mugs!
Not just halfway!
Fill our mugs!

MADAM 2 (*Ululating.*): Lu lu lu lu lu lu lu!

(*She makes them a place. They sit down and drink.*
SUDI enters. He's already drunk.)

SUDI (*To MADAM 2.*): Hey, give me the money you got so far.

MADAM 2: Eh! Why should I give it to you?

SUDI: The money. Quickly. Or I'll put you in your place.

MADAM 2: I don't want a fight. This is the same beer you drank at home for free when you were short on cash. Now I can't even make some money without you grabbing it. And you know at home our pots are only full of problems.

SUDI: Shut your mouth. I'll beat you—in front of your boyfriends.
(*He grabs her.*)
SHABA: Hey, Mister Sudi, stop with that babytalk, all right? Not around
here.
(*SUDI turns toward SHABA.*)
SUDI: What did you say? I'm talking to my wife and you're saying it's
babytalk? Is this your wife?
TOTOLO (*To SHABA.*): It's Sudi, man, ignore him—he's already drunk.
SUDI: Who's drunk? Did you get me drunk?
(*He turns back to MADAM 2.*)
SUDI: Hey, your boyfriends made you uppity, now you refuse to hand over
that money. Give it to me, now.
(*He hits MADAM 2. She runs away crying. SUDI follows her. TOTOLO and
SHABA follow them out as well.*)
STORYTELLER: Brewing beer brought her grief
Madam Two's trials and tribulations never cease
She earned money from her homebrew
But the money wasn't enough
To make up for all the trouble she went through

Meanwhile
Others followed in the footsteps of Madam Two
And beer flowed everywhere
Patata was besieged—beer was king
Drop your work and drink instead

Whatever money people made
Was spent on alcohol
And that Pillar of Motherhood
Stayed there in the dirt

Then came Madam One
Her idea was to start a workshop
Weaving things for the home
If she sold handicrafts, and got money
How could the Pillar of Motherhood not stand?
(*MADAM 1 enters with some other women. They lay out mats and sit down.
Each one makes something. Some of them weave tablecloths; some of them
other decorations for the home; some of them mats.*)

MADAM 1: Our work is going well. The embroidered cloth we sent to the trade shows has already all been sold.

ANOTHER WOMAN: Even the ones we gave the Teachers College are all sold out.

MADAM 1: See? Didn't I tell you we'd make money?

(MADAM 4 enters.)

MADAM 4: Ladies. How is everyone? How's the work going?

(Everyone responds that they are fine.)

MADAM 4: Madam One, I see your efforts are picking up steam. This is the kind of thing we want, not the confusion people like Madam Eight are sowing. But it's not just this. We've been fighting hard for handicrafts. Now handicrafts are all over Patata. Handicrafts should be emphasized in our schools. Every school will teach this subject so that our children know how to sew, how to dress well, how to beautify their homes.

MADAM 1 *(Ululating.)*: Lu lu lu lu

(Everyone responds with more ululating. MADAM 5 enters carrying a great heap of embroidered cloth. She throws it all down.)

MADAM 5: Oof, I am just fed up.

MADAM 1: How did it go on your trip? Why have you come back with all this cloth?

MADAM 5: There aren't any buyers.

ALL: No way! It can't be!

MADAM 1: No, it can't be. It cannot. Just admit you didn't go. I tell you— laziness is what is holding us back.

MADAM 5 *(Angry.)*: Oh, so now you're saying I'm lazy, is that it? I went around the whole town, lugging all of this, and now you're telling me I'm lazy. I told you—people don't want to buy. Or did you want me to give it to them free of charge?

MADAM 4: But why would they refuse to buy, just like that, when everyone was buying in the beginning?

MADAM 1: They were falling all over themselves, squabbling with one another.

MADAM 5 *(Angrier.)*: Everywhere I went, they told me they had already bought enough. Now how am I supposed to force them?

MADAM 1: Eh, please. To do business you have to ease people into it, coax them into buying.

MADAM 4: That's it, yes. A little smooth talking here and there. You think they will just give you their money and done—no fuss, no questions asked?

MADAM 5: Fine. You take all of this—and you go sell it yourselves.
(She storms off.)
MADAM 4: Is this how it's going to be with this project?
MADAM 1: Forget about that Madam Five. She doesn't have a head for it.
People, it's getting late; we're out of time. Let's divide up this cloth so that
we can sell it in our own neighborhoods.
(They divide up the cloth.)
MADAM 4: That's a good strategy. Let's make sure that when we meet next
week each of us has sold her portion.
(They all exit.)
STORYTELLER: All the women went around
They knocked on every door
In every house they entered, they found cloth already
The table was already covered
"Why not buy a spare set?"
"Hey, no thank you
Why should I buy one from you, my sister
When I know how to weave myself?"

The women continued weaving
Cloth piled up
And money didn't

The handicrafts craze faltered
And then it died
Leaving that gang of weavers behind
And the poor Pillar of Motherhood
Stayed right where it was

It also happened then that Madam Eight
Got together with her colleagues
Teachers like her
They talked among themselves
Gave each other good advice:
"Let's start with the problems
In our own profession
Let's remove the hurdles
That keep us from doing our work the way we should
When these obstructions are gone
The youth will be well-educated

And if all of Patata is educated
The Pillar of Motherhood will stand"

So, they had a meeting
In the workplace
To uncover the secret of what held them back
And seek out actions they could take

But alas!
Even before they had settled down in their seats
Trouble fell upon them
They were summoned to the council chambers
To answer charges
(The CHAIRMAN of the Advisory Committee enters and sits. MADAM 4 enters and sits immediately to his right. MADAM 8 enters and sits a little apart.)

CHAIRMAN: Madam Eight. You've been called before us because some news has come to the attention of the Advisory Committee. We'd like you to give us an explanation of a few miscellaneous things.

(Pause.)

CHAIRMAN: Briefly, the issue is that we've heard that you formed a little group to block the efforts of your sisters here in Patata to lift up the Pillar of Motherhood. What is more, your group is composed exclusively of teachers and discriminates against non-teachers. What is even more than that, your group has been having meetings to plan smear campaigns against your sisters and their efforts.

STORYTELLER: Alas!
Madam Eight was shocked—oh, she was shocked!
How had it come to this?
Poor thing, she didn't know why she had been summoned
The letter she had gotten was short
It said:
"Come to the Chairman's office at nine"
It must have been that Madam Four

Even though the charges were serious
She wanted to laugh
She let a smile slip through
Her mind raced:
"How should I answer them?

Should I tell these imbeciles they're spinning lies?
Should I tell Madam Four to stop spying on me?"

She held back
Withdrew inside her heart
And had a heart-to-heart with herself:
"Let's be cautious, my friend
Stay away from trouble
These adversaries of yours
Have costumed themselves as leaders
And the hats that leaders wear—
As far as I know—
Conceal gray hair, scars, baldness
Thoughts of all kinds, good and bad
Also, around here at least
A leader shows the way
Leading us into plenty
Or into the lion's mouth
Paths are narrow here
Whoever is in front is the one who can see
And Grandmother told me
A leader is never defeated"
Madam Eight thought all of that
And decided to stay silent

MADAM 4: You see, Chairman? This is contempt! I told you she was
   disdainful. Now you see!
CHAIRMAN: Madam Eight. If you remain silent, how are we supposed to
   understand you? I'm asking you, in my capacity as Chairman of the
   Advisory Committee, to explain yourself. Why did you do these things?
STORYTELLER: Madam Eight stared at them
And spoke to herself inside her heart:
"Today I will see for myself
What will happen"

MADAM 4: So now you don't talk. Out there—that's where you think you're
   strong. But if you're asked to speak, you don't speak. Weren't you the
   chairwoman of your meeting? You want to take over chairpersonships
   by force. Why don't you come forward and run for the position, earn
   your votes—if they really want it to be you? Chairman, I told you: some
   of those teachers don't in fact like this Madam Eight. She just forced her
   way into the limelight. If they love her so much, then why are these

same teachers coming to me to reveal their plans? Speak so that we can
hear you.

STORYTELLER: Madam Eight's anger was rising in her throat
But she mastered it
She bit her tongue so words would not come out

She stared at them and thought:
"They are partners in this
They worked it out; they conferred
Their plans are ready to sink me
So I won't give them the chance
Until I see their endgame"
Silent she remained
And held their eyes

They stared
They stared
They stared each other down
The Chairman grasped for something to say
Madam Four could barely keep her seat

CHAIRMAN: Madam Eight, are we to conclude that you have no respect for
these proceedings and that is why you will not speak? Do you know
what the consequences of this kind of behavior are? I would like us to
consult with each other so that the matter can end here, but it looks like
you want the matter to go far. I implore you not to disrespect this
hearing and answer the questions you were asked.

STORYTELLER: Anger ebbed and laughter rose
She forced it down
Not wanting to be accused of something else
What was wrong with them?
Two people—one, two—
Had turned themselves into a committee
"What constitution says a chairperson
Can a hold a hearing on their own
Or get help from people
Who aren't even on their committee?
Do a judge and plaintiff make a court?
I have never heard of such a thing!
This hearing is a sham
I won't trouble myself with speaking"

Silent she remained

CHAIRMAN: Madam Eight, as a leader myself, as Chairman of the Advisory Committee, I advise you—for your own safety—disband that little group you formed. If there are issues you want to talk about just bring them to your leader, Madam Four, so that she can put them on the agenda for the regular meetings. This practice of forming so many little groups is not allowed.

STORYTELLER: Madam Eight thought to herself:
"So being a leader or a chairperson
Gives someone the power
To do things the opposite way
From how they're normally done
How can a person make threat after threat
And claim it's just advice?
How can a person hand down judgement
Having only heard the accuser's side
Without the accused there to hear?
How can a person judge the accused
Without knowing what she thinks?
And, oddest of all
How can a chairperson
Without a real committee
Sit in judgement on these charges?

Alas!
This is the reason so many people
Dream of being chairs themselves
Because the job is easy
You just do things arbitrarily
Poor Patata! No wonder
Confusion is everywhere"

CHAIRMAN: The second problem—let me tell you—is that there isn't a single person who has permission to hold a meeting without the approval of this office. Also, it's a requirement that someone bring this office the minutes for everything that's done here in Patata. That's a rule and everybody knows it. Hence, when you go back, you must abide by my decisions.

STORYTELLER: Oh, alas!
Madam Eight had never heard this rule

In ten years of doing this work
Holding hundreds of meetings at her workplace

Madam Eight herself had been a Secretary
And even a Chairwoman
But still had never heard, not once
That every single workplace meeting
Had to be approved
By the office of the Advisory Committee

Alas for this strange day!
If big men schemed to bring you down
They'd use every method at their disposal
Even powers they hadn't been given

She thought and thought
And suddenly realized she had to change course:
"You'll be slaughtered
In the silence you've wrapped yourself in
Better to explain to them
That you know the law
They don't have enough—
From what they've said—
To hold you
If you don't tighten your belt
You will die"

MADAM 8: My apologies, Chairman. I'm hesitant to accept your verdict.

MADAM 4: You hear her insolence. I told you myself.

MADAM 8: I'm speaking with the Chairman. And Chairman, I ask you, as Chairman, to protect my right to speak. Even though I am not a leader I know that I have the right to speak. I can't accept your verdict until you explain to me what exactly the charges against me are. The explanations I've been given here so far haven't mentioned the charges themselves so that I can understand them.

MADAM 4: Chairman, she just wants to throw us off course. She wants to bring in all those fancy degrees they're always showing off. And that is precisely the problem. Those teachers, especially Madam Eight here, always put on airs with their degrees. They don't know that the very citizens they look down upon are the ones who made it possible for

SPEAKING OUR SELVES

them to study until they got those degrees. And once they get their degrees, what do they do with them? Nothing. Nothing at all. Completely hopeless!

MADAM 8: Chairman, explain to me why I was called here only to be insulted. Did we come here to call each other names?

MADAM 4: Eh, someone needs to tell you the truth.

MADAM 8: Chairman, I ask that I be informed of the charges against me. What is my offense—having degrees, or something else?

CHAIRMAN: Listen, Madam Eight, I have told you that you must explain to us why you formed your group, why it's for teachers exclusively, and why you're standing in the way of the task of lifting up our Pillar of Motherhood.

MADAM 8: All right, if those are the charges, I'll give an explanation. However, I ask that I be allowed to give it in writing.

MADAM 4: Would it kill you to speak—right here, right now? Aren't you the Chairwoman of your little group? A Chairwoman must always be ready to defend herself without writing it all down. Don't play the scholar here.

CHAIRMAN: I think you can explain yourself here and now.

STORYTELLER: The hidden agenda of this hearing
Was becoming clear
Madam Eight was shocked
Where did this requirement come from?

"People are full of surprises
Because my old friend Madam Four
Has a leadership position
Which she got without following procedures
She has concocted these allegations
And the Chairman called a meeting
Without the Secretary or members of the committee"

Poor Madam Eight
Silent she had remained
What was said was said
And insults piled on
But she never interrupted the Chairman

Poor Madam Eight
Her rights had been denied

The Chairman was furious
She had to speak
To tell the truth
To hell with what would happen

MADAM 8: Chairman, I don't agree. If I am charged, I have the right to respond however I like. I will respond in writing. Everyone involved will get a copy. I will bring it tomorrow, I promise. Once you've read my explanation you can sit in judgement. But before that I will not accept your ruling—or any advice you give.

STORYTELLER: Now it was the Chairman's turn, and Madam Eight's
To be flummoxed
They didn't know what to do
If you cook pumba you have to eat it
They left—to wait and wonder
What the taste of their dish would be

What happened thereafter is not wise to tell
Lest children hear and lose faith
I'll just say one thing:
That Pillar of Motherhood of theirs
Still lay on the ground

CHORUS (Singing): Pillar of Motherhood, Pillar of Motherhood
Shall we adorn you with flowers?
How should we adorn you?

SCENE 3

STORYTELLER: There's still more to the story
All sorts of occurrences, spread all over
In every corner of Patata
If I start to tell you all of them
We'll have to stay here until tomorrow
And the story still won't end

But there was one person, an artist, hard-working
The people of Patata called him Chizi
The mad one
Not that he was really mad
They called him a madman
Because he didn't care

120 SPEAKING OUR SELVES

If you were a big shot or a commoner
Publicly or privately
He would tell the truth
Playing his marimba
Adorning his words with the music he played
He spoke the truth

Those who were wise listened
But—unfortunately—
The leaders, corrupt as they were
Never found the time
To stop and hear
What this so-called madman had to say
If only they had listened to him
The Pillar of Motherhood would be standing
(CHIZI enters. He sings and plays the marimba. He dances from time to time
during his song. And sometimes he speaks without singing.)
CHIZI: I'm Chizi, I'm the madman
Listen to my marimba
Which I made
With my own hands

Listen to my voice
Like a bird in the bush
But first—
There's one thing I don't like
Don't look me in the face
My mama gave birth to me
And I had an ugly face
But mama is beautiful
Without a doubt
I don't know my papa
'Cuz mama won't tell me
Who he happens to be

Hey, my people, how did I know my face was ugly?
One day someone came to our village
He was a white guy who happened to be Black
I made my marimba ring out
And did a dance for him

That's how we welcome guests in my place
And show our happiness
This out-of-towner saw my face
And straightaway said
(*Exaggerated English or American accent.*):
    My God[1]
My God—whatever that means
I'm a madman, I don't know
When I asked, they told me
It means your face is ugly
My God!

So, leaving my face alone, okay
Let's look at Patata
I am sad
And I don't understand
What is happening here
I've lived a long time
And I've seen many things
The plague of diarrhea
Famines named for gunnysacks
Also cholera
The war with those German guys
And the one with tricky Amin
But what is happening now in Patata
I don't know if I should call it a war or a plague

Let's call it hunger, maybe
Like the one that gnaws at me
I see it all the time
Hunger never leaves my side
They say I'm lazy
But it's not my fault
I learned to loiter
Since I sucked at mama's breast

---

1. In the Kiswahili text of *Nguzo Mama*, Chizi says "My God" many times—in English. I've italicized each instance here. Since Chizi is imitating the "white guy who happened to be Black," I suggest that the actor playing him in an English-language production use an exaggerated accent whenever speaking this phrase. This should create something akin to the effect of hearing a Kiswahili-speaking Chizi pepper his speeches and songs with absurd *my God*-s. No other character speaks any English at all in the original play. – JW

Okay, let's say it's hunger
That has come into Patata
Hunger for unity
For cooperation
We're jealous of each other
And neglect, it grows like weeds

I see you looking at me
Thinking Chizi, he's a madman—
Unless you have a proposal
For another name to call me?
(Pause. To the audience.):
Any ideas?

You see these people?
They don't like democracy
If I say everybody calls me mad
Am I mad?
Or is it you?
You who sit and stare at me
Leaving a few people, just a few
To do whatever they want

I tell you, there is fear
All over Patata
Those who know the truth
Have wrapped themselves in silence
Or like Chizi here
They laugh

So keep your seats
Keep laughing
As confusion grows
Your Pillar of Motherhood
Will stay there on the ground
(He hears something. He looks into the distance and sees people coming. He quickly changes his song. As he exits.):
I have a girl, she's flat as a board
Flat as a board hey hey
(MADAM 1, MADAM 2, MADAM 3, MADAM 4, MADAM 5, MADAM 6,

MADAM 7, and MADAM 8 enter. They cross to the Pillar of Motherhood.
Each of them is carrying a rope and readies herself to haul the pillar up.
In this scene, one event flows fluidly and continuously into another. The work
of hauling on the ropes continues without a break even when a character
leaves. It continues without stopping. If desired, the work of hauling on the
ropes can be done to the beat of a drum and the singing of work songs when
there is no other action on stage—and silently when there is.)
STORYTELLER: As confusion grew
They sat down and strategized:
"My friends, unity is strength
Disunity is weakness
Let's go forth, all together
To raise the Pillar of Motherhood
With all our strength
Our blood and sweat"

And so they rushed to the Pillar of Motherhood
And got straight to work
MADAM 4: All right, Madam One, Madam Two, Madam Three: Pull! Really
     pull!
(They pull. The Pillar of Motherhood starts to lift a little off the ground.
Madam 1 stops pulling to speak to Madam 5.)
MADAM 1: I say, where did you buy that kanga?
MADAM 5: Eh, didn't you hear that they're in stock? I bought this one
     yesterday at the Arab's shop.
MADAM 1: Are there any left?
MADAM 5: They're still selling them now. You didn't see the queue when we
     passed by?
(MADAM 1 drops her rope.)
MADAM 1: Hey, I'm going, I'm not going to miss this new design.
MADAM 8: Sisters, where is Madam One going now?
(MADAM 1 is about to leave.)
MADAM 1: Eh, sisters, I'll be back. But I'm not going to miss out on that
     kanga.
(SHABA enters. To SHABA.):
MADAM 1: It's like you knew
Coming here at just the right time
Give me money, man, to buy a kanga
I'm not missing this new design
Give me the money today, all right

To get the kanga

It's been three months since I've seen new ones

SHABA: I told you I haven't got any money. You want me to steal?

MADAM 1: How you get it is your business

But me, I've got a kanga to buy today

(They chase each other off.)

STORYTELLER: They pulled

They pulled

They pulled some more

They sang songs

To give themselves strength

(They sing a work song—whichever one—as they pull on the ropes. A child is heard crying off-stage.)

CHILD *(Voice.)*: Mama! Mama! Mama! Mama, the baby is crying.

(MADAM 2 quickly drops her rope and runs toward the sound of the voice.)

MADAM 2: Sisters, that's my kid.

(She runs into SUDI, who is drunk.)

SUDI: Eh, where have you been all this time? I came here a while ago. The baby's crying and crying—I don't know where you are—

MADAM 2: What, man, you couldn't figure out how to comfort her?

SUDI: Who's gonna comfort her? The baby's hungry.

MADAM 2: Her food is there. Why didn't you feed her?

SUDI: Hey, what's your job again, huh? But first bring me some food. I'm hungry.

(MADAM 2 brings him some food.)

SUDI: You finished washing my clothes? Bring them here. I wanna wear that outfit. I'm going out.

MADAM 2: They aren't dry yet.

SUDI: Not dry yet? What? They've been drying since this morning.

MADAM 2: I washed them in the afternoon. This morning I woke up early to work in the field. When I came back, I had to cook for the kids—there wasn't any water—I went to fetch some.

SUDI: Oh, shut up! What am I supposed to wear now? I'm telling you, dry them by the fire. I wanna go back to where I was. There was very good booze I left behind. You want the other guys to finish it off? Dry those clothes before I beat you.

(MADAM 2 exits.)

SUDI: And bring me some water to drink too!

(A voice from off-stage.):

VOICE: Mister Sudi, are you there?

SUDI: I'm here, man, come in.

VOICE: No, man, I'm going. If you don't come soon, that beer's gonna be all gone, man. Everybody's heading over there.

SUDI: Wait for me, I'm coming.

(He abandons his food.)

SUDI: Hey, Mama Njiti, where are my clothes?

(MADAM 2 enters with water.)

SUDI: Drink your water yourself.

(He leaves. MADAM 2 gathers up the dishes and exits.)

STORYTELLER: Madam Two knew life's bitterness
She longed for a miracle:
That she'd have many hands
And very long arms
So she could fulfill all the duties
That had been placed on her
One hand to raise her baby
Five for her other children
And more, maybe three
For all her husband's endless needs

She wanted so badly
For her husband's hands to be hers too
Because he only ever used them
To drink, never to work
She wanted more hands to do the farm work
She needed two to hold the hoe properly
To harvest the crops
So her family could eat
She wanted her arms to be long
To cook, to fetch water
To pound the grain and chop the firewood
While she was working in the fields

And now she wanted still more hands
To lift up the Pillar of Motherhood!
She didn't know how many she needed
Try and imagine:
If she had enough hands
What sort of being would she be?

MADAM 4: All right, sisters, heave!

(They pull.)

MADAM 4: Sisters, why are you doing it so lazily?

MADAM 8: You know there's less power on that side now that Madam One and Madam Two have gone.

MADAM 4: I'm telling you, we won't get far like that. People's hearts aren't in it, that's what the problem is. Heave!

(A work song.

Madam 6 sees something in the distance. To MADAM 5):

MADAM 6: Hold on, can you take my rope for a minute?

(She crosses quickly to another part of the stage and stands there. She brushes off her clothes and makes herself look nice. Then she starts wandering around acting flirtatious, moving slowly like a streetwalker. After a moment, MAGANGA enters. MADAM 6 goes up to him. They laugh together. MAGANGA signals that she should follow him. MADAM 5 sees what they are doing. She quickly drops her rope and goes after them.)

MADAM 5: Hey, Madam Six, you primitive. You're taking my husband— right in front of my eyes?

(MAGANGA hurries off. MADAM 6 turns around and looks at MADAM 5 contemptuously.)

MADAM 6: Don't squawk at me.

MADAM 5: I see what you're up to, preening like that.

MADAM 6: You said you had a husband?

MADAM 5: Watch your manners.

MADAM 6: Hey, first tell him to watch his manners. He came on to me. Where were you?

MADAM 5: You're such a whore. Every single man . . .

(She hits MADAM 6. MADAM 6 grabs her and holds her tight so she can't move.)

MADAM 6: Your whore husband came up to me.

MADAM 5: Let go! Let go of me! You bitch!

MADAM 6: Your bitch husband chases all the single ladies.

MADAM 5: You're so stupid, you savage. Let go!

MADAM 6: Your stupid husband—dumbstruck, mesmerized by women.

MADAM 5: Let go of me!

(She squirms, trying to free herself, but can't get loose.)

MADAM 5: Let go of me. You're the most primitive, savage—

MADAM 6: You're the primitive, fighting with your whore husband.

MADAM 5: Let me go! Let me go!

(MADAM 6 holds her even tighter.)

MADAM 6: Listen to me. I'm telling you the truth. You're like my little sister.

I don't want your man. Even if you gave him to me free of charge I
wouldn't want him. He's not a man. Think about it.
(She lets go of MADAM 5 and starts to leave.)
MADAM 6: A man-whore like that isn't worth troubling your heart.
*(MADAM 5 sits down on the ground and bursts into tears. And then she stops
and starts to wail.):*
MADAM 5: Misery! Misery! Misery!
My children are miserable
They have no clothes
They have no food
My children play hungry
My children sleep hungry
My husband burns through all our money
On women
What do I do?
What do I do with all this misery?
What do I do to make it stop?
(She starts to cry again. She exits, still weeping.)
STORYTELLER: She goes and she goes and she goes
The sound of her crying all the way home
She finds her children held by hunger
"Mama, don't cry—I'm hungry," her little one tells her
Her tears dry up that instant:
"If I sit and cry my children will die
Of hunger
What do I do?"

And that Madam Six also went home
She never came back
Never touched the Pillar of Motherhood again
"I'm not used to hard work
I depend on the softness of my hands
If I rough them up pulling the rope
How will I feed myself then?
Let those idiots waste their time
I look for time
And I find none
If only I had the time to catch more men
Because one or two is of no use
Prices are shooting up

And where am I supposed to get the time
For the Pillar of Motherhood?"
And having said that, she took to the streets

MADAM 4: All right, heave!

(They pull on the ropes and sing work songs.)

MADAM 3: All right, sisters, I'm leaving. You see that Volvo? It's come for me.

MADAM 4: Don't joke around, let's get to work.

MADAM 3: I'm not joking, sister. We're going to a party with my husband at seven o'clock. Hey, I have to help him keep his job, yes? Or else what shall I eat?

MADAM 8: Let's just keep going a little longer.

MADAM 3: You only say that because you've got a job with a salary. Even if you get divorced you can be independent—but what about me? If you want, I'll make a donation rather than do the work myself. Sorry. Goodbye.

(She starts to leave.)

MADAM 3: Also, I can't come tomorrow either. My husband and I are throwing a party at our house for his colleagues, so that's why I won't be here.

(She exits.)

MADAM 8: All right, sisters. Those of us who don't have men to trifle with us—and those of us who have husbands but they aren't big shots—let's keep going.

MADAM 4: Heave!

(They start singing and pulling on their ropes—but without success.)

MADAM 4: Oh no! I just remembered. I'm late for a meeting of the Committee on Promotions—and I'm the chairwoman. You know how hard we are working to make sure women get high positions since we are always forgotten. We have to hold this meeting.

MADAM 8: You're leaving too? Again?

MADAM 4: Now what am I supposed to do, with all the duties I have? You are the ones who elected me—here, there. I have to do it all. But I'll be right back.

(She exits.)

MADAM 8: All right, heave!

(They pull.)

(KIANDO and MAKANGE cross the stage carrying a bed. On top of the bed they've piled miscellaneous kitchen things: pots, plates, spoons, and so on. MADAM 7 sees them and drops her rope. She runs up to them and tries to block their path.)

MADAM 7: Ha! So, my in-laws have come back. You're taking everything. Even the bed. Even the plates. Where will I sleep? Where will I cook?

KIANDO: Hey, it's good we found you. We looked for you everywhere. Bring us the money you hid from us.

MAKANGE: You've hidden our brother's property, woman. You don't even fear the dead!

MADAM 7 *(Crying.)*: How many times do I have to tell you? Your brother died. You took all the money. You snatched my children away from me. You took everything. But still you're saying I hid money away somewhere.

(She weeps.)

KIANDO: You're not fooling us with those tears. Show us where you hid the money. Or you will be in serious trouble.

MAKANGE: We're leaving now, but when we come back you had better have our brother's money ready.

(They leave. MADAM 7 exits crying.)

STORYTELLER: She wept, Madam Seven, oh, she wept
She had no one to turn to for help
Her husband died, his brothers came
They took all the money, not even leaving her five cents
The vessels and all the clothes
They distributed amongst themselves
Madam Seven felt her spirit crack
Watching those brothers
How they squabbled over money they hadn't even earned
"This is my chair" "That hoe's mine"
"These are my pants" Chaos prevailed

She wanted to die, to follow her husband
When she saw all five of her children
The youngest only three years old
Driven off like goats
They went with the brothers, for shame
The aunt who took them in
Didn't even know their names
And now, on top of all that
Her in-laws came back to sweep up
And carried off the broom
Putting the blame on her
For hiding money away

How will she tell them
That what they took was
All her effort, all her sweat, alone
The children, beloved, she raised all on her own
While their father soaked himself in beer
The money the brothers wanted
All flushed down the toilet

Madam Seven cried—oh, she cried
And the Pillar of Motherhood, back there
Still lay on the ground
(*MADAM 8 hauls on the rope by herself. She sings work songs. She doesn't know which way to pull.*)
MADAM 8: I'm wasting my strength for nothing.

SCENE 4

STORYTELLER: They were all demoralized, confused
Especially Madam Eight
They went home, their spirits aggrieved
Early in the morning
When they were still in their beds:
The rumble of drums
(*Drums.*)
MESSENGER: When the drums ring out, there is a reason!
Listen, people of Patata
When the drum calls
Let those with no children
Carry stones on their backs
The elders who gave it to us have decided
That the people of Patata
Don't want the Pillar of Motherhood
If you really wanted it
Then why is it still lying there on the ground?
So, they've decided to take the Pillar of Motherhood back
And take it somewhere else
Where it will be put to good use
Or stick it in a museum, if they have to
(*Drums.*)
When the drum calls, it has a message!

The elders have decided
To give you three more days
If the Pillar of Motherhood is not standing by then
It will be taken away
You know what will happen then
All of Patata will miss the Pillar of Motherhood
Because without a Pillar of Motherhood
Whose house can stand?
(Drums.)
When the drums rumble, there is news!
(Drums. He exits.)
STORYTELLER: Terror seized them
Those who bore children
Their beds could not hold them
They leapt up, not knowing what to do
There was commotion
This one here, that one there
This one this way, that one that way
Their husbands, on the other hand
Burst out laughing
Some of them said "They look like fools"
"Since when have women been people?"
Were they all born yesterday?"

Some women, quick to anger
Made a ruckus
"We can do it" they said
"Let us show these savages
Who are accustomed to oppressing us"

The husbands of these women thought
"The coming of the Pillar of Motherhood
Has awakened the women
They have started thinking of many things
Something they never did before
If that Pillar of Motherhood stands
We will be the losers
Better it stays on the ground
Or goes back to where it came from
It will cause us calamity
If it ever stands"

Confusion spread
Patata fretted, thick with words
But the women girded themselves and got to work
"What will become of Patata
If we lose the Pillar of Motherhood?"
CHORUS *(Singing.)*: Pillar of Motherhood, Pillar of Motherhood
Shall we adorn you with flowers?
How should we adorn you?
STORYTELLER: Chizi had heard the drums
He got up quickly, stretched out his hand
And took up his marimba
(CHIZI enters.)
STORYTELLER: He hurried to the Pillar of Motherhood
And squeezed himself into a corner
To see what there was to see
He tensed his fingers on the marimba's tines
Ready to pluck
He cleared his throat and coughed twice
So his voice wouldn't catch
I'll turn the story over to him
To rest my throat for a while
CHORUS *(Singing.)*: Pillar of Motherhood, Pillar of Motherhood
Shall we adorn you with flowers?
How should we adorn you?
*(As the song continues, MADAM 1 enters singing, dancing lelemama,
following the beat of the music.)*
MADAM 1: Should we adorn you with gold?
Should we adorn you with silver?
Kohl, henna, and perfume?
How should we adorn you?
(She exits. The CHORUS responds.)
CHIZI *(Singing.)*: My friends, I'm shocked
By Madam One's words
This gold and silver
And all this perfume
Where will she find them
When she spends her time
Sitting at home
Gossiping
With her feet up?

I've never seen her work
Or even break a sweat
Tell me, where can you get gold and silver
Without doing any work?
So that I can also go
And scoop it for myself
(*The CHORUS continues. MADAM 2 enters to the beat of the kiduo dance,
singing.*)
MADAM 2: Which hoe do you want?
The one with the long handle or the short one?
A clay pot with a small mouth?
Or a basket in the Gogo style?
How should we adorn you?
(*She exits. The CHORUS responds.*)
CHIZI (*Singing.*): This one, Madam Two
There's sadness in her soul
She'll die poor, destitute, like me
But I'm shocked
What does this woman eat?
Truly, I've never seen anyone stronger than her
But that husband of hers
I don't know what she feeds him
Madam Two does all the work
Mister Sudi eats the fruits of it
All of Madam Two's sweat
Ends up in the pub
Where Mister Sudi boozes day and night
One day I'll ask him
Which love potion he gave to Madam Two
So that whenever I am lucky enough
To get a wife
She should be like her
A wife who accepts every hardship
Bears my children and babies me
Grows my food and cooks for me
Washes my clothes and finds me beer
I'd get all of that!
And I'm *my God!*
(*SUDI wanders by. He's drunk and singing "Top Up My Drink."*)
SUDI (*Shouting.*): Hey, Mama Njiti!

(He exits.)

MADAM 3 *(Singing.)*: Should we adorn you with Benzes?

Should we adorn you with Volvos?

Which number plate?

The ST or the SU?

How should we adorn you?

(She exits. The CHORUS responds.)

(CHIZI laughs long and hard.)

CHIZI *(Speaking.)*: I just had to laugh, my friends. That one, Madam Three, is my aunt. For the love of God. They told me she was my aunt. My papa was born first and she was next. One day . . . wait, I'll show you.

(He crosses the stage and intercepts MADAM 3.)

CHIZI: Good day.

(MADAM 3 looks at him contemptuously.)

MADAM 3: Chizi, are you crazy, why did you follow me home? Come on, get out of here. We have an engagement with some visitors.

CHIZI: Where am I supposed to go? Aunty, your brother disowned me and now you're chasing me away.

MADAM 3 *(Angry.)*: What did you say? Get out of here, quickly. Right now. Hey, this guy wants to embarrass us in front of our guests.

CHIZI: Aunty, I'm hungry.

MADAM 3: Get out.

CHIZI: Aunty, I don't have any clothes.

MADAM 3: Don't call me aunty. Take your calamities and go. If you come back, I'll call the dog to bite you.

(She picks up a rock with which to hit him. CHIZI runs back the way he came.)

CHIZI: *My God!* You saw that! You know, Aunty is the Chairwoman of the Proper Upbringing Committee. She herself is not employed. But she takes her husband's title as her own. In fact, she's the one who really holds the title, if you know what I mean.

(The CHORUS continues. MADAM 4 enters clapping her hands. She moves to the beat of her clapping.)

MADAM 4: Should we adorn you with applause?

Or sweet, sweet words?

Meetings, donations, demonstrations?

How should we adorn you?

(She exits. The CHORUS responds.)

CHIZI *(Singing.)*: I'll say it softly

So I don't go to jail

It's not that I'm afraid of jail
They have free food there
But my grandma told me
All human beings are equal
But some are more equal than others
And she's one of those
(He raises his voice.):
If you ask me, Chizi
What name should we call her?
(He points to his mouth.)
Madam Words, Madam Words!
(He's shouting now.):
Madam Words! Greetings!
Listen to me, to Chizi
I have something to say

Once, I proved my point
By following her around
She did not want to stop
And waste her time
She poured out words—
I kid you not—
For a whole entire hour
(MADAM 4 addresses the audience. She speaks non-stop.)
MADAM 4: We've thought of all of that. We've passed many resolutions and
we're so thankful they've all been adopted. Children's upbringing,
especially given that this year is the Year of the Child, we're opening
children's centers for the little ones all over Patata. We're putting special
emphasis on projects, all kinds of projects: bars, clothing stores,
handicrafts associations, cooking, restaurants, and a lot more besides.
Power to the women. That's a problem we're focusing on. Women will be
given positions, we've already prepared a list. We're finding MPs,
managers, ambassadors, et cetera. Some have already been given these
positions, as you know. Also let me remind you of our demonstrations.
Don't forget that. We have to show our gratitude that women are getting
recognized, getting positions. On that note, don't miss Saturday, one
o'clock, let's all come, my friends. The marriage law will be changed. One
man, one wife. Oh yes, and this habit of getting beaten—we don't want
that. Also issues with schoolgirls getting pregnant everywhere, impreg-
nated by people in high positions, destroying the lives of our children.

This is not acceptable, my friends. Also young girls throwing their babies in the garbage—there is a seminar next week to discuss this, it's a major source of shame. We are working on all these issues. Yes, and this subject, the subject of how to raise our children . . .

(CHIZI sings as MADAM 4 exits.)

CHIZI: Good day, Madam Words
That's enough words for me
Today I have stopped
I won't ever tease you
I have stopped, I have stopped
I don't want to be asked
About what you have said
Lest I start saying many things
I'm Chizi the madman
Everyone knows

(The CHORUS responds. MADAM 5 enters to the madogori beat. She doesn't sing. She just laughs, almost shouting.)

MADAM 5: Ha! Ha! Ha! Ha!

(She exits. The CHORUS continues.)

(CHIZI addresses the audience.):

CHIZI: Oof, why are you all looking at me? You talk. I'm tired. Or do you think she is also my aunty? No. I don't even know her. I don't understand a thing. You decide for yourselves.

(He sees MADAM 6 coming.)

CHIZI: No, this I can't. I don't want trouble coming my way.

(He runs and hides.)

(MADAM 6 does not sing.)

MADAM 6: What? Still so stubborn?

(She loiters a bit, walking here and there.)

MADAM 6: We'll see
I've already told you:
You see me, you hit the brakes
No one passes me by

(She exits. The CHORUS continues.)

(CHIZI comes back out, watching her go, and singing.):

CHIZI: I have a girl, she's flat as a board
Flat as a board hey hey

I'm so afraid of that woman
The one she fought with

Is my sister
My poor sister
Died—because of that man
I don't want to talk about it
I didn't come here to cry
Even though you think I am mad
My tears are expensive
I'll never shed them
On account of that man
(*MADAM 7 enters. She doesn't sing. She's confused. She doesn't know what to do. She looks this way and that. She leaves.*)
CHIZI (*Singing.*): Poor Madam Seven
They have scrambled her brains
They have broken her mind
I feel sorry for her
One day I went to see her
Maybe I really am mad
"Good day"
"Good day"
"Madam Seven, explain to me
What is this Pillar of Motherhood?
Seems to me that here in Patata
Everything's all mixed up
And everywhere I turn
I hear 'Pillar of Motherhood'
What is it?"
She answered me well
With kindness and compassion
"My son, I have no idea
Maybe ask Madam Four"
But just the other day
She was named Secretary
Of some committee or other
Dunno which one
I forget
(*The CHORUS continues. The GIRL enters. Voices call out to her and she follows each one when it calls.*)
MADAM 1 (*Voice.*): Hey you, come here!
MADAM 2 (*Voice.*): Over here! Come!
MADAM 3 (*Voice.*): Here! Aren't you listening?

MADAM 4 *(Voice.)*: Come here! Right here!
(The GIRL exits the way she came in.)
CHIZI *(Singing.)*: Maybe it's for the best I don't have a child
Hey, parents, tell me:
How do you raise yours?
If there's someone here who knows
Stand up and share

I heard my grandmother singing once
"I don't know a thing
Just how to give birth, that's all"
Now don't go around singing that song, okay
It's from the girls' initiation ceremony
I got hit with a stick
When I sang it one day
You all see me, Chizi, as mad
But everyone I'm looking at
All of you, with your children
The one thing you know more than me
Is childbirth

"Children are the nation of tomorrow"
I've heard people say that
When that nation of tomorrow arrives
If I'm already dead
Please go and resurrect me
So I can see for myself
I'll make a new marimba
So I can sing about it properly
(The CHORUS continues. MADAM 8 enters with her books. She pages through them.)
That Madam Eight
I'm afraid to go near her
Afraid to be told *my God*

They hate her so much
Especially Madam Four
But when I listen to her carefully
Even though I'm *my God*
Her words are true

But her compatriots
Don't want to hear them
Why? I have no idea
(*He peers off.*)
Aunty is coming
Goodbye!
(*He runs off. MADAM 1, MADAM 2, MADAM 3, MADAM 4, MADAM 5, MADAM 6, MADAM 7, and the GIRL enter, moving fast. They quickly encircle the Pillar of Motherhood.*)

MADAM 4: Get rid of those ropes, they'll just get in the way. Today it has to stand. It must.

MADAM 8: Sisters, let's talk it through.

MADAM 4: Aah! We don't want to talk. Talking—words—that is what has slowed us down. All right.

(*They try to lift the Pillar of Motherhood, but it doesn't move.*)

MADAM 4: Lift!

MADAM 8: But without ropes the Pillar of Motherhood can't stand. Sisters, we have to be smart.

MADAM 1: Save it for your scholar friends.

MADAM 4: Lift!

(*They try to lift it, but it doesn't move.*)

MADAM 4: Lift! Lift!

(*They struggle to lift it.*)

(*TOTOLO and SHABA cross on one of their jaunts.*)

TOTOLO: What's it all about, huh—all that noise the women are making?

SHABA: Shhhh, don't talk so loud. If they hear you, you are in trouble.

TOTOLO: Eh, it's nothing. Just words. They're making a racket, not doing anything of any use.

SHABA: As for me, I don't like this insolence they're teaching one another. They're so stubborn after, when they come home.

TOTOLO: Hey, man, that's it. Me, my wife barely spoke. Then she went to these meetings—poof—she sharpened her tongue.

SHABA: I gave mine a smack and forbade her to go again.

TOTOLO: Is that so? Then why is she right over there? Isn't that her in the red kanga? Hey, you're messing with me.

SHABA: These days she's going again. But there is one rule. When she comes home she's my wife and that's it.

TOTOLO: My friend. Let's get out of here so that we are not associated with this lady stuff.

SHABA: Ah, that would be a scandal. Let's go fast.

(They exit.)
MADAM 4: Lift! Lift!
(They try to lift it, but it doesn't move.)
MADAM 8: Sisters, we have to use our brains as well. Let's use the ropes. Let's go get tools and use them.
MADAM 4: Lift!
(They struggle to lift it.)
MADAM 8: Let's work with the men as well. The Pillar of Motherhood has value for everyone.
MADAM 4: Lift!
(They struggle to lift it.)
MADAM 8: Let's call all the children—they're the nation of tomorrow.
MADAM 4: Lift! Lift!
(They struggle to lift it.)
MADAM 8: All right, let's have a look first to see why it's not moving . . .
MADAM 4: Lift! Madam Eight, shut up!
MADAM 1: All your talk just makes us lazy.
MADAM 4: If we're not united we can't do anything.
MADAM 8: Lift! Lift! All right, everybody, let's sing. It will stand up! It will!
(Everyone struggling to lift the pillar sings):
ALL: Pillar of Motherhood, Pillar of Motherhood
Shall we adorn you with flowers?
How should we adorn you?
MADAM 4: Lift!
STORYTELLER: Since Chizi ran away
Let me finish the story

They struggled and struggled
To lift the Pillar of Motherhood, there
The first day passed

They struggled and struggled
Day and night
To lift the Pillar of Motherhood, there
The second day passed
Today is the third day.
(To the audience.):
Should I go on, or not?
Should I go on, or not?
(Pause.)

That's the end of my story.

CHORUS: Pillar of Motherhood, Pillar of Motherhood
Shall we adorn you with flowers?
How should we adorn you?

The author reserves all serialization and dramatization rights. Requests for any of these rights or the translation into languages other than English should be addressed to Penina Oniviel Mlama, University of Dar es Salaam, Creative Arts Department, PO Box 35044, Dar es Salaam Tanzania, or penina_2000@ yahoo.com. Joshua Williams can be reached at jdmwilliams@gmail.com.

Burundian playwright Claudia Munyengabe, author of *Le Roi Est Mort, Vive la Reine*.

Le Roi Est Mort, Vive la Reine

Claudia Munyengabe

Author and actress, Claudia Munyengabe, studied political science and international relations at the Lumière University in Bujumbura, Burundi. She later became interested in art. A supporter of Burundian cultural development, she actively participates in such activities as performing experimentations, festivals, workshops, soap opera productions, and community sensibilization to promote Burundian art through theater.

Munyengabe's career is marked by a free commitment to dramatic writing. Her most recent play, *Le Roi Est Mort, Vive la Reine* (2021; translated from the French and Kirundi by Rivardo Niyónīzígiye as *The King Is Dead, Long Live the Queen*, 2024), was presented in the fifth edition of Buja Sans Tabou (2022), a theater festival that takes place every two years in Burundi with the aim of promoting artistic freedom of expression.

Claudia Munyengabe is also an author of *Point zéro* (2019), which was performed as part of Staging Times, a project based on a concept which explores different dimensions of how visual and performing arts can interact. By linking photography and theater, the project creates a network between artists from six African countries (Mali, Burkina Faso, Kenya, Burundi, Malawi, South Africa). The design of the project follows a ping-pong format: pictures of the photographers provide a source of inspiration for the theater artists. Vice versa, their plays and performances, based on the photographs, will again generate new images. *Point zéro* was inspired by photos taken by photographer Sarah Waiswa and performed in Bujumbura as part of the fourth and fifth edition of the Buja Sans Tabou Festival, and later in Rabat, Morocco in the first edition of their African theater festival (2023). *L'Acide* (2020) was created for the commemoration of the "International Day of the Rights of the Child" and was produced at the French Institute of Burundi. *Trirīriri-ri* (2022), which was created to commemorate "World Day Against

Trafficking in Persons," toured Burundi. *Sagwa* (co-written with Burundian author Laura Sheïlla Inangoma [2018]) is the result of a peacebuilding training course organized by "Never Again Rwanda." The play looks back at the composition of the national anthem and the issues surrounding Burundi's independence on July 1, 1961. *Sagwa* was performed in Bujumbura in January 2019.

Munyengabe also writes short stories, among them "Ne m'enterre pas," in *Au-dessous du volcan* (Sepia Editions, 2019) and "*à l'autre bout du monde*" in *Cewije Collections* (Cewije Editions Design, 2015). The author's dream is to meet young people and to bring to their awareness the emergency for reflection and artistic creation in Africa.

An interview with Claudia Munyengabe is available at https://doi.org/10.3998/mpub.12827650.cmp.5.

HISTORICAL NOTE BY RIVARDO NIYÓNĪZÍGIYE:

Since the reign of Ntare I Rushatsi Cambarantama, the first monarch of the Kingdom of Burundi (contested dates of his reign, 1680–1709), Burundians celebrated Umuganuro, the sowing festival. During those yearly ceremonies, the Mwami (the king) blessed the sowing, so that the harvest would be good and abundant. It was also an opportunity to celebrate the new year together from the closest to the furthest servants of the Palace. Most of the rites during the festival were directed by women although some were degrading for them. For example, the function of Mujawibwami, a female court worker, whose role was to chase away the guests of the court, presenting herself naked and pissing in the midst of the crowd coming from all over the kingdom was a real disgrace. Queen Ririkumutima, nicknamed Bizima Bitazimiza Mwezi, favorite wife of King Mwezi Gisabo and one of his great advisors, chose to abolish that role of Mujawibwami.

Ririkumutima insisted that one of his sons succeed the king, but his sons were not eligible and Mwezi Gisabo could not allow it. Longing for power at all means, after the death of Mwezi Gisabo in 1908, she became the queen mother of Mutaga Mbikije, a position that was reserved for the biological mother of Mutaga Mbikije, who had been assassinated presumably under the orders of Ririkumutima so that she becomes the queen mother.

At the same period, Burundi was being occupied by the Germans. Friedrich Robert von Beringe, a German commander, tried his best to divide the country to make it totally a German colony. His *divide et impera* rule ended with the indirect rule by Grawert, his successor, leading to the Kiganda treaty of June 6, 1903, the official starting point of German colonization in Burundi. Even to these white officials, Ririkumutima engaged in negotia-

An etching of Queen Ririkumutima (ca. 1850–1917), one of the 13 women married to Burundi's King Mwezi Gisabo (1852–1908). She was considered his favorite wife and counsel. Queen Ririkumutima is the historical inspiration for Munyengabe's fictional character, Bizima.
Source: https://reinesheroinesdafrique.wordpress.com/2016/06/13/limpitoyable-re ine-ririkumutima-la-mwamikazi-reine-qui-usurpa-le-titre-de-mugabekazi-reine -mere/

tions, presented herself in meetings, and made demands; these were uncommon behaviors considering the place of women in the Burundian society at that time. She is known as one of the queens who participated actively in the political affairs of the kingdom, but singularly known for her strong character, determination, and exceptional negotiating skills.

CLAUDIA MUNYENGABE ON *LE ROI EST MORT, VIVE LA REINE*:

Le Roi Est Mort, Vive la Reine was written for the fifth edition of Buja Sans Tabou (Bujumbura, Burundi, 2022), a theater festival promoting the freedom of expression. This edition's theme was "Memories . . . ," the memories that are kept about Burundi. I felt a great need to focus the research on Queen Ririkumutima (1850–1917).

This play unveils the elements of history that really existed in Burundi. The play goes further by imagining from within the character of Bizima her thirst for power and how far she could have gone to reach the throne. As the story takes place in Queen Bizima's mind, surrealism captures her conviction that she possesses and acts upon, during a historical period when, indeed, a woman is very important, but unrecognized, in the construction of a society's movement toward equality. For me, I'm able to manifest this relationship between inner and outer selves through dreams or flashes of imagination. The ambitions of Ririkumutima with her vision of the female condition, represented by Bizima in the play, are presented as a dream or

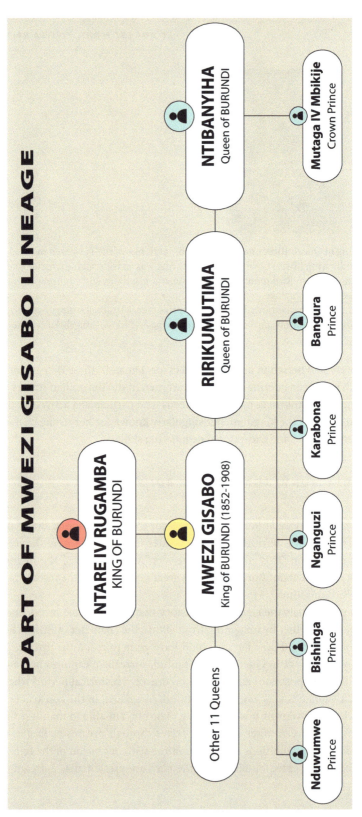

A chart identifying the immediate lineage of King Mwezi Gisabo and his marriage to Queen Ririkumutima, with whom he has 5 sons.

imagination that perhaps women of today could materialize. The play wants to transcend the times where the language used in the text is sometimes classically historical (for instance, the scenes between Bigoro and Bizima) and sometimes contemporary (such as the scenes of recruitment in a manicure-pedicure salon and in the nightclub). Only a dream, or surrealism, can easily offer this possibility.

It is critical that the Kirundi language is preserved as part of the translation. Some poetic words or concepts in Kirundi, such as seasons' names and the names of clans, do not have their direct equivalent in English, French, or other Indo-European languages. Translating them solely into English decreases the deepness and takes the reader away from the real meaning. For the sake of originality and keeping the real meaning of the poetic rhythm and voice, I've chosen to keep them in Kirundi. The English translation appears to the right of the Kirundi text in order to preserve the reader's flow and comprehension of the text in the English language.

148 SPEAKING OUR SELVES

Le Roi Est Mort, Vive la Reine
Claudia Munyengabe
Translated from the French and the Kirundi by Rivardo Niyónīzígiye as *The King Is Dead, Long Live the Queen*

CHARACTERS

Bigoro: A man, 67 years old, the King of Burundi from 1852–1908.

Bizima: A woman, 50 years old, the Queen and wife of Bigoro.

Mujawibwami (Muja): A young woman, 20 years old, a servant of the kingdom.

Birenge: A 45-year-old German colonial commander. His real name is von Beringe, a resident of Urundi (Burundi) from August 1902 to February 1904.

The clients: Eight people (five girls and three boys in their 20s).

Three couples: Three young couples in their 20s.

Bizima's rebel troops: 80–100 young people, of whom the majority are women, between 15 and 20 years old.

Intore: The King's army. Around 50 skilled and dynamic men, between 15 and 40 years old.

SETTINGS

The play takes place in multiple locations throughout Burundi. The play's historical actions occur non-chronologically between 1880–1907. Other actions occur in the present and future.

SCENE 1

(Total darkness. It's night-time. 1907. BIGORO and BIZIMA are in the King's bedroom. We hear only voices in heat, whispering sensually, murmuring, then shouting passionately.)

BIZIMA: Tell me, my invalid warrior with frisky eyes. You, who are unique among humans. Tell me that I am the most vigorous and terrible Queen of your herds.[1]

BIGORO: Yeeees!

---

1. As in, a herd of cows. In Burundian culture, a woman is compared, flatteringly, to a cow.

BIZIMA: Tell me that when I pass, you are aroused and stare at me.

Tell me, stubborn and foolish fellow, that I am the most loved and cherished of all your cows.

Tell me that you will drown in my breasts and never want to be saved. That you will die if I die.

BIGORO: Oh yes, yes.

BIZIMA: Tell me that you will never doubt my actions, however moral or playful.

That your lips will feel me even in the sandy desert of ancient times.

Tell me, I want to hear it, that my offspring will equal you even if they go astray.

BIGORO: *(Silence.)*

BIZIMA: Tell me!

BIGORO: My beloved must not embarrass me in public.

BIZIMA: Promise!

BIGORO: If luck smiles on the blessed kingdom, your home will bless my nights.

BIZIMA: Promise that my feet will never leave the top of the tree.[2]

BIGORO: Sacred tree, beware. If you, my Queen, disobey and break the *ibanga*,[3] I will cook your bones for my dinner!

SCENE 2

(At dawn, light gradually comes back on stage. An upstage corner remains dark, however, until the end of the play. In the lit part, BIZIMA is seen nearly naked. Her legs spread, she sits in the middle of an exaggeratedly long sofa made of bamboo stems. As if telling a story, she speaks directly to the audience about her marriage to Bigoro.)

BIZIMA: Year: 1880. Season: Agatasi.[4] Family: Munyakarama.[5]

A time when the rains defy the gods, conniving sages sneakily reveal to the kings the sources of their misery and the magic potions capable of melting the clouds into rain.

A time when fertile mothers, anxious to multiply, consult witchdoctors, hoping to harm the ovaries of their native rival to stop them from having babies.

---

2. This metaphor refers to the throne.

3. A secret.

4. The rainy season.

5. One of the clans which has many queens in historical Burundi monarchies. It is the clan of Ririkumutima, the preferred queen of Mwezi Gisabo, King of Burundi (from 1850–1908).

The fate of Nyamuragura, the sage, thus fell upon me. It happened quietly in the fields of the chief, my father Sekabonyi, while he cared for his people.

A cohort from the horizon took shape, meandering through the furrows of the sorghum trees, coming to retrieve the chosen one, chosen by the moon, the one who was going to bring back the rains to the hills and mountains.

Me?

I?

(Four men lift her up and put her on a royal portable bed and carry her from her bedroom to the courtyard. BIZIMA, continuing to speak to the audience, now expresses herself in a poetic tone.)

BIZIMA: Jewe?
Ndi umunyerezi anyereza imbuto z'
    impeshi zikagwiza umwimbu
Jewe ndi mukaminka akamira ibirezi
    n'abagesera
Sinavuze nti ndi uyu canke ndi uriya
Ariko ndi umwe muri ba Nyagutegeka
    ibiteme bikaba ibiraro
Ndi Gendangaruke, Ingonigire,
    Mwenyurandayamene,
Ndi umwe mu bicishije inyota abagenzi

Nkambura ababanyi
Ndi uwutihanganira abihangiye akabi
Ndi bivumuvumu
Nyambaranguhande
Vyumventuhore
Nyambaranguhande
Vyumventuhore
Ndi . . .

BIZIMA: I?
I'm a massager massaging the winter
    seeds and they multiply
I'm the milker milking for homes and
    the outsiders
I didn't say I'm this or that
But I'm one of the heroes, with powers
    to turn meadows into bridges
I'm Gendangaruke, Ingonigire,
    Mwenyurandayamene,
I'm among the ones who made friends
    starve
I can tell you
I never give in before the evil ones
I'm the elegant tall bride
Nyambaranguhande
Vyumventuhore
Nyambaranguhande
Vyumventuhore
I'm . . .

(BIZIMA softly sings "Ngoma ya Ruhinda,"[6] slowly, grandly, and elegantly.)

Ngoma ya Ruhinda kanyoni karitse
    kw'ibenga
Ngoma ya Ruhinda umuyaga uraza
    urakaruza

Lovely bride, a bird nested over deep
    waters
Lovely bride, wind came and
    destroyed its nest

---

6. A folk song for weddings, composed and sung by Giramahoro, one of the traditional cultural troupes in Burundi. To listen to it, follow the link: https:www.youtube.com/watch?v=q7mYHQ4UdqY

Ngoma ya Ruhinda nzopfa nzokira sindabizi ma	Lovely bride, will I die?[7] Will I live? I don't know.
Ngoma ya Ruhinda	Lovely bride,
Nta mukobwa atagira ingorane	Every girl has worries
Yabonye ko koko buca agenda ma	The bride saw that she is leaving her family
Asimbira kw'isoko agura umutaka	Rushed to the market and bought an umbrella
Agura ubudede bumwe bwo mu nda ma	And bought belly beads
Agur'amavuta intake n'agahama	Bought body lotion, perfume, and makeup powder
Agura inyerere agura n'akagufu	Bought inyerere and akagufu[8]
Amahera ahera ataguze ibirezi.	She spent all the money without buying ibirezi.[9]
Ararira maz'ashaka gusaba ma	And she wept endlessly.

(The four men put BIZIMA on the royal sofa. She stops singing to continue telling her story in a smooth, poetic tone.)
I had offered my blood and soul to Bigoro, this damned master
And did so against my will.
Well . . . at the beginning, before I fell under the spell of his blind, sexy eye,
His other eye, the functional one, caught *my* eye, for God's sake!
His greatness . . . his melodious voice
Majestic!
Mythological!
His sweetness . . .
His walk and his long nails
His fingers
His haircut
With a small ihumvyo[10] in the middle of his head.
Bigoro was handsome!
(Suddenly, BIZIMA changes her smooth, poetic tone to a violent, aggressive tone.)
But, I wouldn't let my sons languish on small lands that were not worth the weight of a plot of sorghum field.
I would never do that.

---

7. Note the difference in the punctuation marks. In Kirundi, like in other languages, there are sentences which are not really questions grammatically but by intonation and context, they sound like questions.

8. Leg jewelry (inyerere) and neck jewelry (akagufu).

9. A precious neck jewelry that features a flat, white shell.

10. A traditional Burundian medicinal amulet.

SPEAKING OUR SELVES

Either them or me—someone had to access the damn throne of . . . throne of . . .

(She sings the chorus of "Ngoma ya Ruhinda" again.)

Ngoma ya Ruhinda kanyoni karitse kw'ibenga	Lovely bride, a bird nested over deep waters
Ngoma ya Ruhinda umuyaga uraza urakaruza	Lovely bride, wind came and destroyed its nest
Ngoma ya Ruhinda nzopfa nzokira sindabizi ma	Lovely bride, will I die? Will I live? I don't know.
Ngoma ya Ruhinda.	Ngoma ya Ruhinda.

(She suddenly stops her singing. In a poetic tone, she starts to speak about how terrible she is, which recalls an earlier feeling within herself.)

BIZIMA: Si jewe nazanye umwibutsa.	I'm not the girl in the song.
Ndi bivumuvumu	I'm the elegant tall bride
Nyambaranguhande	Nyambaranguhande
Vyumventuhore	Vyumventuhore
Jewe?	I?
Ndi umunyerezi anyereza imbuto z'impeshi zikagwiza umwimbu	I'm a massager massaging the winter seeds and they multiply
Jewe ndi mukaminka akamira ibirezi n'abagesera	I'm the milker milking for homes and the outsiders
Sinavuze nti ndi uyu canke ndi uriya	I didn't say I'm this or that
Ariko ndi umwe muri ba	But I'm one of the heroes
Gendangaruke,	Gendangaruke,
Ingonigire, Mwenyurandayamene.	Ingonigire, Mwenyurandayamene.

(BIZIMA continues her story with confidence.)

BIZIMA: As a person but also as a mother, I had to fight.

To fight, to fight against the weakness of the . . . *(Interrupted by the sound of a warning bell.)*

To fight to teach these small and great women from my land and elsewhere that at least they may know one thing:

They, too, were capable of killing, lying, saving, pleading, betraying, loving, and all the other evils of the century.

The mountains trembled as I passed.

I had decided to lead a rebellion.

(Silence.)

(BIZIMA continues to address the audience.)

BIZIMA: So what?
You, passive and lost sheep,
Rot and weaken under the yoke and spit of the German beast!
(*BIZIMA puts on a skirt of military colors and a red beret, which can be replaced by a Santa Claus cap. She carries a spear. She is in her military outfit. She sits, legs spread, in the middle of an exaggeratedly long sofa made of bamboo stem.*)

SCENE 3
(*Suddenly, BIZIMA, wearing her military outfit, stands up and approaches the audience. Full light on stage. She is recruiting soldiers. In front of her, a manicure-pedicure salon.*)

BIZIMA: Paint your faces, bastards!
THE CLIENTS: (*In unison.*) Long live dearest Bizima, who defies monsters.
BIZIMA: Where are you from?
THE CLIENTS: From Mugambarara, at Bumbeho.[11] Our homeland is cursed; children die young. We're sorry, but carrying a spear is against our beliefs.
(*BIZIMA brandishes her spear in their direction.*)
BIZIMA: You, join my army!
(*BIZIMA slowly turns her head to address the audience. She continues her story.*)
BIZIMA: My recruitment was not ordinary.
I recruited the weakest, the sowbugs,
In order to strengthen my army.
The fight that awaited us was spiritual
It was the spirit that we would forge.
Thus, with the weak, I was sure I would not be betrayed once in power.
(*Blackout. Light then gradually comes on stage. In front of BIZIMA, there is a nightclub. Seal's "It's a Man's, Man's World" is playing. Three young couples dance without moving their bodies to the rhythm of the song. Yes, we can dance without moving.*)
BIZIMA: Let's go to give voice to those who've lost it!
A COUPLE: (*In unison.*) Long live Bizi-love!
BIZIMA: The war will befit those who are young. Come, join my army!

---

11. Names of imaginary places.

ANOTHER COUPLE: Please, go recruit at church . . . or on social media! We'd do it, but we're too busy having fun here.

(*BIZIMA throws her spear in their direction. Darkness. Then suddenly, lights on stage. BIZIMA is alone at the salon. There are four big mirrors on the walls. The room is now perfumed with the incense that is used during the Kiranga worship sessions.*[12] *Wearing her military outfit, BIZIMA is looking at herself and talking to herself. She then turns to the audience to continue telling her story.*)

BIZIMA: Then my army grew in numbers and became strong. It was filled with living corpses: women abandoned in ubuhundwe,[13] those thrown into imanga,[14] the chosen young man over whom cows walked until he died as a sacrifice during the annual sowing festival . . . and my sons . . . and the Hima chief.[15] But I was missing one person: Mujawibwami, the pisser.[16]

(*Blackout. Suddenly, lights on stage. In the King's palace courtyard. BIZIMA, in a bikini, sunglasses on her head, sits, her legs spread, in the middle of an exaggeratedly long sofa made of bamboo stems. She sips juice through a drinking straw. In front of her, MUJAWIBWAMI (MUJA), is crouching, holding a dog on a leash.*)

MUJA: I've just been chosen.

BIZIMA: Are you happy about it?

MUJA: I'm not allowed to say a word.

BIZIMA: (*Emphatically.*) Are you happy about it?

MUJA: Mothers are honored, but all daughters are grinding their teeth.

BIZIMA: Then run away!

MUJA: They would find me.

BIZIMA: Fear.

MUJA: That's not true.

BIZIMA: Yes, you are afraid.

MUJA: Of what?

BIZIMA: Everything a pisser would be afraid of.

---

12. Burundian traditional masses. Kiranga is a Priest, who is an intermediary between Imana (God) and humans.

13. An abandoned hut given to a divorced or a barren woman.

14. Also called "Igisumanyenzi," a deep hole in which any girl with an unwanted pregnancy was supposed to be thrown.

15. One of the clans in the kingdom of Burundi who were not allowed to assist the Umuganuro festival.

16. One of the women in charge of a singular practice, urinating in public, as part of the crowning celebration of a King, as well as at the end of the annual sowing festival celebration. These women never married, since it was forbidden by tradition.

MUJA: I'm not a pisser!

BIZIMA: Yes, you are.

MUJA: Totally wrong!

BIZIMA: How many liters are you able to piss? After all, you were not chosen for . . .

MUJA: *(Interrupting.)* Stop!

BIZIMA: If you are not brave enough, no one will be brave enough to replace you.

MUJA: In my place? In my place, mothers are honored while daughters grind their teeth in anger and humiliation. This damn festival wouldn't happen if . . .

BIZIMA: *(Interrupting.)* If there wasn't a pissing girl taking part in it? Trust me, dear Muja. The sowing festival doesn't need you!

MUJA: It's a ritual. Its strength lies in the completeness of its acts.

BIZIMA: It's a ritual. Its strength lies in its uniqueness and respect.

MUJA: Respect for what? For a mortal body?

BIZIMA: *(Emphatically.)* For a woman's body.

A woman with curves on which children lean.

A woman with legs, feet, which go, each dawn, towards the field.

A woman with breasts that feed the child . . . I mean can breastfeed . . . you know,

It depends.

And the womb which carries life, and her lips smiling with its passage.

If you want to end up pissing for a so-called ritual of . . .

MUJA: *(Interrupting.)* Ritual of what? Go ahead, say the word dear Queen of many powers.

BIZIMA: Don't you dare speak to me in that macabre tone. I'll kill you . . .

MUJA: *(Interrupting.)* Murderer.

BIZIMA: Pisser.

MUJA: I am not a pisser.

BIZIMA: Pisser pisser pisser.

Pisser.

Pisser.

Pisser.

Pisser.

Pissing girl.

PISSING MACHINE!

(Calmly.) Join my army, Muja. I will cover you with the dignity you deserve.

I will protect you from struggles. And you will chase ghosts and wars with dignity. Listen Muja, on the day of the great feast, piss on the sacred fire. It will be a sign that you can't take it anymore.

MUJA: It is a sacred ritual, Bizima. It is a sacred ritual with a sacred fire . . . for a sacred feast with sacred people, a sacred country, our country. What is my body worth in front of all this?

BIZIMA: It is a festival with a thousand sacred rituals and some of them are twisted. Your degrading role can easily be abolished, and then . . . these sacred people, as you said . . . wait until they embrace the eroticism from elsewhere. This festival will be a legend that will not be told anymore. Stop, Muja! Open your eyes! Get up!

MUJA: What a dreamer! And my family?

BIZIMA: Your family can't curse a pissing girl.

MUJA: No, they will kill me.

BIZIMA: So what? One day or another we will all die of something. Come with me, Muja, I will protect you.

MUJA: What do you want in return?

BIZIMA: You will help me strangle the fucking Queen Ntibanyiha, pretending to be a mugabekazi, the mother of a King.

(BIZIMA turns her head to the audience and directly speaks to them.)

BIZIMA: Muja was the most difficult person to convince. She was the one who had to piss in the middle of the courtyard to chase away the guests.

At the end of the festivities, Muja appeared naked,

And spread her legs and pissssssss . . . (Imitating the sound of streaming urine.)

(BIZIMA invites the audience to spread their legs and imitate the sound of streaming urine.)

SCENE 4

(It's around 5 p.m. BIZIMA, wearing the Burundian Queen's outfit, is massaging BIGORO. He is in the bedroom, lying in the middle of an exaggeratedly long sofa made of bamboo stems.)

BIGORO: Rumor has it that you're plotting against me.

BIZIMA: Let the rumor fly.

BIGORO: Is it true?

BIZIMA: Truth never dies.

BIGORO: Rumor has it that you are plotting, forming a rebellion to kill the King and rule with your sons.

BIZIMA: My sons are your sons!

BIGORO: And are my sons your sons?

BIZIMA: It depends.

BIGORO: You know very well that they cannot succeed me, Bizima.

BIZIMA: And yet, against all odds, you have succeeded your father.

BIGORO: Rumor has it that you are also plotting to end the big feast.[17]

BIZIMA: A monarch does not listen to rumors.

BIGORO: But he can hear them.

BIZIMA: I give you advice day and night. How could I plot against my King?

BIGORO: Greed and envy.

BIZIMA: What do you mean by that?

BIGORO: Your sons are already chiefs, but you dream for more.

BIZIMA: Let me dream.

BIGORO: Bizima, don't do the irreparable. The soothsayers . . .

BIZIMA: *(Interrupting.)* Soothsayers, often lie, you know?

BIGORO: The same soothsayers predicted that by marrying you, the famine would end.

BIZIMA: The famine has stopped, but the wars have increased.

BIGORO: The wars have increased, but I've kept you. You, the only one I sing about when my fingers strum the Inanga.[18]

BIZIMA: Naivete doesn't look good on Kings.

BIGORO: Except when the King feigns it. I'm watching you, Bizima. I don't know what trick you are up to, but know that I'm watching you.

BIZIMA: And me? I care for you, O King, with a thousand ornaments, and I watch over you like a God who is watching over the eye of His creatures. I watch and sleep only when you are safe.
(Pause.) There is a rumor that the German invaders have invited you to Usumbura, the forbidden city, and that you agreed.[19]
Be careful, Bigoro. It's a trap.

BIGORO: If I don't get there, my people will die. Don't you remember the Germans' guns, their fire-breathing beasts?[20]

BIZIMA: Strengthen your army! A people who fight for identity and freedom will never perish.

BIGORO: Yes, it can. In war, there is always a loser.

---

17. Referring to Umuganuro.

18. A traditional wooden instrument with strings made of cows' veins.

19. It was believed that a Burundian King should not see Lake Tanganyika, which is located in the city of Bujumbura (later known as Usumbura during colonialism).

20. During their first battle with the Germans, some of Mwezi's (Bigoro's) troops encountered guns as a weapon for the first time.

158   SPEAKING OUR SELVES

BIZIMA: And a winner. We have to win!

BIGORO: Victory isn't certain. Would you prefer that we all die because we convinced ourselves that we will win? You can't argue with death. Their arsenal is more powerful than our bows. If we resist the invaders once again, my people and I will be a distant memory.

BIZIMA: *(Revolted.)* We will be an indelible memory! Untouchable. The survivors will learn from us and will no longer bow down to an oppressive order.

BIGORO: *(Ironically.)* You are dreaming! When you die, no one will remember you.

BIZIMA: Speak for yourself!

SCENE 5

(It's 7 p.m. BIZIMA, in her military outfit with its visible stain, enters— without knocking—the office of BIRENGE, the new Commander of Rwanda-Urundi.)

BIRENGE: The rules of good manners require that you knock before entering an office.

BIZIMA: Here in Burundi or in your country?

BIRENGE: Here or elsewhere. I see that we still have a lot of work to do. We have to . . .

BIZIMA: *(Interrupting.)* Civilize us? I came to warn you for the first and last time: We don't need your civilization. Leave our land right now!

BIRENGE: Otherwise, what? We have signed a treaty with the Muesi.[21] What am I meddling with anyway?

BIZIMA: You and your people forced the King of Burundi to sign a treaty. You also forced him to pay a fine.

BIRENGE: And so, you come to complain? As who?

BIZIMA: As the King's advisor.

BIRENGE: He should have listened to you before signing.

BIZIMA: I don't have time to waste. Tell me whether or not you are going to leave us alone!

BIRENGE: First of all, you enter my office without knocking, then you call me by my first name, and to top it all, you threaten me! Who are you Madam? Seriously, who are you? The audacity . . .

---

21. Referring to the historical Mwezi (who is named Bigoro in the play). The Germans could not accurately pronounce his name.

BIZIMA: *(Interrupting.)* Your office? On our land? An office built by my people: forced to build it, free of charge. Sometimes under a hot sun. Sometimes under a violent rain. Free of charge, without being paid at all. And you call it your office?

The King, the King of this country, respectful and worthy to be honored. Even the poorest people in the country simply call him King of Burundi. You, little foreigner and invader, would like me to list all your titles for the sake of being polite to you? And you dare to ask me who *I* am?

I

I'm the elegant tall bride

Nyambaranguhande

Vyumventuhore

I

I'm a massager massaging the winter seed and they multiply

I'm the milker milking for homes and the outsiders

I didn't say I'm this or that

But I'm one of the heroes, with powers to turn meadows into bridges

I'm Gendangaruke, Ingonigire, Mwenyurandayamene.

I'm Bizima who never misleads Bigoro.

BIRENGE: I see. The King's favorite Queen. I've heard a lot about you.

BIZIMA: Leave our land!

BIRENGE: I hear that none of your sons will succeed the King . . .

BIZIMA: *(Interrupts.)* The internal affairs of our country don't concern you.

BIRENGE: You are mistaken. The King has specifically asked me to quell a nascent rebellion led by one of his Queens. Nice to meet you, Madam! However, I'd like to suggest something because I'm amazed by your tenacity.

BIZIMA: Uhmm?

BIRENGE: Bigoro expects me to track your rebellion. But I can make sure that you are stronger. Instead of dissolving your troops, you and I, together, will dissolve the royal troops. And then, why not deal with the King . . . his successor . . . so one of your sons . . .

BIZIMA: *(Interrupting.)* Divide and rule. I get it. The same strategy! You want to divide us. I'm leaving by the front door. I warn you, Birenge! If you don't want to leave my country voluntarily, you'll leave it by walking on all fours, tongue hanging out, sweating, without a savior or any hope

160 SPEAKING OUR SELVES

of salvation. I don't want your European civilization. Ours is enough for us!

BIRENGE: We offer you a true God, education, roads, money, and a modern administration . . . *(Pondering.)* . . . and what do we get in return? Nothing!

(BIZIMA bursts out laughing. She leaves the office laughing, clinging to the wall, unable to walk straight. BIRENGE'S "Nothing" makes her laugh uncontrollably.)

SCENE 6

(It's around 11 p.m. We hear sounds of grasshoppers. In his bedroom, BIG-ORO, lying on the same sofa, is in his King's outfit. He is very ill. BIZIMA, in her Queen's outfit, fans him with a traditional fan.)
(Long silence.)

BIGORO: Say it. Let it go.

BIZIMA: I have nothing to say.

BIGORO: You're dying for it, I know.

BIZIMA: No, I won't say anything at all. That I warned you? No! I won't say that.

BIGORO: And yet you warned me.

BIZIMA: *(Neutral and calm.)* How do you prefer to be buried?

BIGORO: You are already planning my funeral.

BIZIMA: How do you want to be buried?

BIGORO: I don't know. Like my ancestors. Like we usually do.

BIZIMA: Except that for you, we'll cut off your ears.

BIGORO: Why?

BIZIMA: They have been useless to you.

BIGORO: Your viper's tongue . . .

BIZIMA: My truthful tongue!

BIGORO: I'm protecting my people, Bizima, and I'll say it again and again. I want to protect us.

BIZIMA: Who asked you to?

BIGORO: A King doesn't wait for his people to demand action.

BIZIMA: Your people are abandoning the sacred practice you value so much. Germans are now taking explicit photographs of your people during sacred cults and Kiranga worship services. Some of your people are helping the invaders expose these pictures in their missions. The sacred feast of sowing, which discriminates against the Hima clan, is losing its sense of the sacred. And look at the way you treat women! Muja and her humiliating duties at your palace, young girls who get pregnant and then are thrown alone in the Imanga, igisumanyenzi, yet the man who is responsible for the pregnancy remains free. The kingdom is tired, Bigoro. Look! Some of the chiefs are being baptized and adopting names from elsewhere. Please, look at the clothes your country's sons adopt, and the forced labor, and the usurpations, and the rapes, and the thefts, and the lies . . .

BIGORO: *(Interrupting.)* Shhhh! Let me die in peace, Madam!

BIZIMA: Madam? Now you call me Madam? No, I have absolutely nothing to say.

BIGORO: And yet you said everything.

BIZIMA: Listen to me, Bigoro. You've protected your people by selling them to colonizers. And now, look at yourself. Sold to the Germans and dying.

BIGORO: The King is dying and you, scheming girl, are dancing on my corpse. I have done my best for my people. Perhaps Imana will reward me for that.

BIZIMA: Certainly, you did your best. But Bigoro, a King does not only do his best; he exceeds his best by going beyond it.

BIGORO: *(Insisting.)* The wisdom, Bizima, the royal wisdom.

BIZIMA: The royal wisdom, you say? Look at the country you leave behind. Who are you leaving it to?

BIGORO: Imana and my son who . . . *(Starts coughing.)*

BIZIMA: Let me be Mbikije's tutor.

BIGORO: He has Ntibanyiha, his mother.

BIZIMA: I raised him.

BIGORO: The tradition, Bizima.

BIZIMA: He will need my advice. Please, let me lead the country.

BIGORO: You are a woman, Bizima.

(While massaging BIGORO, she starts to strangle him with her hands.)

BIZIMA: This country needs me.

BIGORO: *(Breathless.)* I know, but you can't take over from me today.

BIZIMA: They believe in a little boy more than in me?

BIGORO: It is the tradition, Bizima. One day, the little boy will grow up.

BIZIMA: It will be too late to straighten out this country.

BIGORO: It is never too late . . .
(*BIGORO dies of asphyxiation due to strangulation.*)

SCENE 7
(*It's midnight. A green light on stage suggests the outdoors. BIZIMA is in the bush near the King's palace. She is with one hundred young women and men ready to attack the palace. Addressing the audience, BIZIMA starts to describe this meeting with her troops.*)

BIZIMA: That night, the meeting with the recruited girls and boys lasted only a short time. I assigned roles to each of them. They knew in detail what to do and when to do it. Everything was so precise that I could even recite the steps of the revolt in my head. (*And then, she motivates her troops, energetically, with war slogans in Kirundi to which the troops respond in Kirundi: "Ji, Ji, Ji!!"[22]*)
BIZIMA: (*Shouting.*) Abajigijigi.[23]
THE TROOPS: Ji ji ji.[24]
(*BIZIMA starts a riddle game.*)

BIZIMA: Abajigijigi!
BIZIMA: Sokwe[25] . . .
THE TROOPS: Niruze![26]
BIZIMA: Sokwe . . .
THE TROOPS: Soma!
BIZIMA: Agacumu kanje runyurabisaka.
THE TROOPS: Turaguhaye
BIZIMA: Umuravyo!

BIZIMA: Abajigijigi!
BIZIMA: Ready for a riddle?
THE TROOPS: Yeees!
BIZIMA: Ready for a riddle?
THE TROOPS: Tell us!
BIZIMA: My spear scans the ambush.
THE TROOPS: We give up.
BIZIMA: A lightning bolt!

[25](*She motivates the troops again.*)
BIZIMA: Abajigijigi!
THE TROOPS: Ji ji ji!
BIZIMA: Abajigijigi!
THE TROOPS: Ji ji ji!
BIZIMA: Where are you from?
THE TROOPS: The very place from which you come.
BIZIMA: Where are you going?

---

22. This response implies "We're ready," "We're strong," "We must win."
23. The name of the troops created by Bizima.
24. This is the responsive slogan used by the troops.
25. In Kirundi, the introduction to a riddle.
26. In Kirundi, an acknowledgement that one wants to try to answer a riddle.

THE TROOPS: We go where you go.

(BIZIMA continues her narration as she addresses the audience.)

BIZIMA: Everyone was ready—ready to change the course of history!

Ready to overthrow, dominate, break the chain of oppression.

Ready for a new era.

This festival wasn't going to happen like it used to! At least not in my
lifetime.

We were going to liberate the oppressed.

Oh what a wonderful night!

A night of grace

A night of victory

I was ready

For fire and blood

At any cost

No matter what

This revolt was going to happen.

(BIZIMA goes back to motivate the troops.)

BIZIMA: *(Energetically.)* Abajigijigi!

THE TROOPS: Ji ji ji!

BIZIMA: *(Pointing at one warrior.)* Who lied to you? Who lied so that if
chosen, you, alone, would sacrifice yourself for us by letting the King's
cows crush you? *(To another warrior.)* And you woman, who told you
that living in this agahundwe[27] is what you deserve for not getting
married? *(To MUJA.)* Tell me, Muja, who made you believe that pissing
in the middle of a crowd of people was an honor. Who made you believe
that the Himas cannot assist the Umuganuro festival rituals? That
igisumanyenzi is made for unwanted pregnancies?

Who?

Tell me who!

Let's change the course of history!

Let's take possession of this country. Let's make it paradise. A country of
justice and law!

*(Now, BIZIMA, filled with confidence, leads the troops to the King's palace,
shouting.)*

BIZIMA: Abajigijigi!

THE TROOPS: Ji ji ji!

---

27. In Burundian tradition, this is a small hut where unmarried girls were believed to be left to die.

BIZIMA: Abajigijigi!

THE TROOPS: Ji ji ji!

BIZIMA: Abajigijigi!

THE TROOPS: Ji ji ji!

(The volume of the sound gets louder and louder.)

BIZIMA: Where are you from?

THE TROOPS: The very place you come from.

BIZIMA: Where are you going to fight?

THE TROOPS: The place you're going to fight.

BIZIMA: Long live the Queen! Long live the Queen!

(BIZIMA is running around to mobilize her troops, but one by one, they leave the King's palace until she remains alone.)

BIZIMA: Abajigijigi!

(Silence.)

Abajigijigi!

(Silence.)

Abajigijigi!

(Silence.)

Abajigijigi!

(BIZIMA is left alone in the middle of the King's courtyard, standing firmly with confidence and looking at the King's palace. Then, she sees King Bigoro's INTORE, who advance slowly with arrows pointed in her direction. She shouts without fear, with a smile of accomplishment on her lips.)

BIZIMA: Long live the Queen!

Long live the Queen!

Long live the Queen!

(INTORE slowly advance with arrows pointed in BIZIMA'S direction and make a semicircle. BIZIMA moves toward the part of the stage that has been dark since the beginning of Scene 2; it is now lit. She climbs on a rock, above which a rope is hanging on a tree. Knowing the punishment that awaits her, BIZIMA proudly stands upright, looking at INTORE with a smile of victory on her lips. As INTORE approach to catch her, the lights gradually fade on BIZIMA, holding the rope, which is not around her neck.)

BIZIMA: *(Shouting with all her strength.)* The King is dead, Long live the Queen!

(Blackout.)

(THE END.)

The author reserves all serialization and dramatization rights. Request for any of these rights or the translation into languages other than English should be addressed to Claudia Munyengabe at munyengabeclaudiacoco@gmail.com or munyengabec@yahoo.com. Rivardo Niyónīzígiye can be reached at vadoniz23@gmail.com or mbanya.rivardo@gmail.com.

Sudanese playwright Alaa Taha, author of *Green Chili*.

Green Chilli

Alaa Taha

Alaa Taha is a Sudanese actress and playwright based in London, UK and Berlin, Germany. She was born in Taif, Saudi Arabia, to a psychiatrist father and housewife mother, raised in Saudi Arabia and Sudan, before immigrating to the UK.

This transformative backdrop defined her artistic identity. Taha's work encompasses experimental live performance, marked by a profound commitment to deconstructing prevailing narratives within postcolonial storytelling. Continuously exploring through her acting and writing what it means to be an Afro-Arab Muslim woman, Taha, who was raised in Africa and the Middle East and, since, living in the West, is celebrated for her ability to create layered and empowered characters who are never "victims" of their circumstance.

One of her notable achievements, *Green Chilli* (2019), featured in this anthology, was produced at the Uganda National Cultural Centre-National Theatre (UNCC) in Kampala, Uganda, and ran in July 2019. The play was commissioned and written in residence in Kampala, Uganda, supported by the UNCC, 32° East Artists' Foundation and Ugandan Arts Trust. The play was directed by the renowned director and actor, Philip Luswata, produced by lead producer of the UNCC-National Theatre, Edwin Mukalazi, and performed by Uganda's two most celebrated actors and media personalities, Roger Mugisha and Malaika Nnyanzi. The play was further enriched by the musical direction of Ugandan composer and percussionist, Giovanni Kiyingi; movement design by Ugandan dancers and choreographers, Prisca Atite and Shafique Walusimbi; and set design by, Michael Wawuyo Sr.

The play's success led it to be documented for TV by Al Jazeera in 2019, which focused on Taha's comedy as a form of storytelling, accompanied by a social media mini-documentary.

168 SPEAKING OUR SELVES

Taha's creative repertoire includes several other notable plays and performances. *Two* (2021) was winner of the Montez Press Writers Award Shortlist, New York, and published online by renowned New York publisher, Montez Press. *Museum of Innocence II* (2022) was a groundbreaking performance installation held at Ronan McKenzie's Home Gallery in London, UK, presented as a 20-minute song or "tarab" about the Sudan revolution. *Museum of Innocence I* (2019), premiered at NWT House Gallery in Cairo, Egypt, marking the first in Taha's "Museum of Innocence" series, delving into the Sudan revolution of 2018–19.

Other plays of note include *Meat Market* (2013), Soho Theatre Writers Award, London, UK, a dark comedy exploring the margins of nightlife, and a battle against being consumed by the night. And "Neener Neener" (2011), which was performed at Tristan Bates Theatre in London, exploring the gradual process of Westernization of children of the diaspora, and examining how parents hold on to their traditions while their children assimilate and mold inter-identities.

As an actress, Alaa Taha is signed to the prestigious IAG Talent agency. She has brought leading roles to life in numerous productions, earning critical acclaim for her performances. Notable credits include lead role of Faiza in *How to Break Out of a Detention Centre* (2023) at Riverside Studios, London, where *The Guardian* newspaper lauded the acting as "universally compelling." She also captivated audiences as lead role of Jennifer in *Talking About a Revolution: Changing Rooms* (2022) at Lyric Hammersmith and Bristol Old Vic, and as lead role Farah in the Sudanese film, *Do Not Dream of A Wonderful World* (2022). Other cinematic contributions include her role in the film *Shams* (2020), set in Cairo, Egypt.

To connect with Alaa Taha's acting agent, contact Ikki El-Amriti at ikki@iagtalent.com. To connect with Alaa Taha's writing work, she can be engaged directly on social media via Instagram @alaasdiary or through email at alaaplaywright@gmail.com, links: https://www.spotlight.com/7257-5649-7865, https://www.imdb.com/name/nm11349020/, https://www.instagram.com/alaasdiary/

An interview with Alaa Taha is available at https://doi.org/10.3998/mpub.12827650.cmp.1.

ALAA TAHA ON *GREEN CHILLI*:

My journey with *Green Chilli* began in January 2019, when I arrived in Kampala, Uganda, from Berlin, Germany, to create a production commissioned by the Uganda National Cultural Centre-National Theatre. The initial intention was to create a piece that would reflect the context in which it was written, but what unfolded became a profound reflection of my own psyche.

In my very first week in Kampala, I encountered a scenario that left a lasting mark on my creative process. It was a 4 a.m. wake-up call from my host family's maid, who held my phone with an expression I'd never seen before, a mix of shock, concern and care. On inspecting the phone's history, I uncovered a disturbing revelation: the 11-year-old daughter of the military leader who was my host, instead of watching the dance choreography videos she'd explained she wanted to borrow my phone for, had spent hours watching the most graphic and violent depictions of intimacy I had ever encountered. It was shocking and heartbreaking. In just the few days leading up to this, a big sister dynamic began to evolve over a shared passion for acting and dance. This disturbing discovery set me on a journey of months trying to offer a "secret" care (as on seeking professional advice, I wasn't to inform her what I'd discovered unless she were to talk about it herself) and also fathom the motivations behind her behavior. Was it driven by pure curiosity or the scars of deep trauma? And how much of my own judgments were at play here, as a Sudanese Muslim woman, born in Saudi Arabia and now raised, since her age, in the West? How much could I protect her? Two weeks later, I had moved out.

In response to these questions, I created this work to challenge dialogue about how young girls become sexualized and how we judge them, and to finally offer the care I felt I hadn't been able to give. Given that this topic remains shrouded in societal secrecy, I chose to veil this exploration in a comedy play.

The name "Green Chilli" take its inspiration from the *Redpepper*, a tabloid Ugandan newspaper with particular portrayals of sex and gender roles. Rather than focus on its origin, I created a TV show called "The Green Chilli," which allowed me to explore the theatricality of having a TV show within a play—the masks people wear when "onstage" versus "backstage," and scoring the drama with a live onstage band. The actors switch age, sexbodied, and gender roles. In production, an exploration of contrast lighting serves as a further complement to the play's themes.

The purpose of the play is to re-evaluate the societal constructs that shape our understanding of young girls and their evolving identities. Collaborating with a dedicated team of theater makers in Kampala, I embarked on a journey to challenge audience assumptions and beliefs about this topic, whilst challenging my own. May this continue to be the case for others upon the play's publication.

As *Green Chilli* sees publication, my hope is that it continues to serve as a catalyst for critical extrospection and exploration for all, especially that young girl. I wrote it for her.

170 SPEAKING OUR SELVES

Green Chilli
A Comedy Play by Alaa Taha

CHARACTERS

Isaac: Male, 36 (also plays **Abbo**). TV host. High-profile. He is deeply invested in keeping up appearances but is in shambles underneath.

Brown: Female, 31, (also plays **Boy**). TV host. On the rise. Externally, she is trying to make up for her background. Internally she is put together, morally.

Abbo: Female, 15. TV show guest. She thinks she is in control of her decisions though, in actuality, they are being led by others. She is looking for a female role model.

Boy: Male, 18. TV show guest. He doesn't know the show is live. He wants to be the norm among his peers yet be the exception in his legacy.

House band: Live musicians, mostly African drums, on or offstage throughout the live TV show scenes. They play intro, outro, and background music.

Isaac's manager: A voice on the phone.

TV show producer: Appears side stage throughout and prescribes the audience's "judgments" or reactions. This can be done through set design, lighting, or sound.

> **Note on casting:**
> It is essential that the same performers play both the role of the interviewer and interviewee on the TV show (cast of 2 playing cast of 4, playing reversed gender roles). As Isaac is becoming Abbo, he is learning more about himself and is forced to admit his immoral behavior; his body language is used to show the artifice behind his whole charade. On the other hand, as Brown is playing Boy, she does not become more aware but instead more adamant.

> **Note on dialogue:**
> In the dialogue of the play, the symbol "/" is used throughout the script to suggest that a character is interrupted by another speaker. The "—" is used to indicate an unfinished sentence or thought due to being interrupted.

SETTING

The onstage set and backstage area of a television show, *Green Chilli*. TV studios in Kampala, Uganda.

Spring 2018.

Throughout the live TV show, the audience has "judgments" presented to them, on monitors, surtitles, or through lighting effects, which indicate

GREEN CHILLI 171

"how to react." The director and cast can have creative license with these—they can be juxtapositions to the true intent, for example.

Act One

SCENE 1

(ISAAC is enroute to the TV show set. He is sitting in the middle of the audience. A phone rings. It continues to ring for a long time. ISAAC fiddles around, stands up and answers it as he walks through the audience to the stage.)

ISAAC: *(Talking to manager on the phone.)* Eh, eh. Slow down.
(Pause.)
What's the rush? Eh eh, why are you talking to me like that now?
(Pause.)
Don't Isaac me? Why you say my name like that?
(Pause.)
Eh eh. You jajja me now. What is the *Red Pepper*?[1] You know they be cooking tales./ No listen. Making a stew of random things. Nonsense here. Nonsense there. Ah, they say what now? See. They be cooking.
(Pause.)
Whatever they're saying about me, it's just . . . stew.
(Pause.)
Easy.
(Pause.)
Eh eh please, you're hurting my God-given ears.
(Pause.)
Eh what are you talking about, career? My career is fine, that's your job go make it fine.
(Pause.)
Eh eh. All I can hear is nonsense, loud and clear. Loud and clear. Don't forget before this, all this, I jammed the strings, remember? This I think/
(Pause.)
Easy, easy. I'm not late to my own show. I'm just . . .
(Pause.)
. . . not on time eh.
(Pause.)
I'll be there soon there's just a lot of traffic. You know Entebbe Road is a jam in the evening now.

---

1. The *Red Pepper* is a daily tabloid newspaper in Uganda that began publication in 2001.

(Pause.)

Hurry, hurry is not motion. Bugu bugu si muliro.[2] Rushing only slows you down. No one went fast anywhere in a rush. You hear?

(Pause.)

My friend, OK. Whatever it is friend, we can talk about it later, it's probably just . . . bush telegraph.

(Pause.)

Yes I'm coming, just coming through this, there's so many people.

(Pause.)

I cannot have all this nonsense right now. Please, just tell them to have my Johnnie Walker ready on set, yes. And chips, please, don't forget chips. Do not forget the chips.

(Pause.)

I'll deal with the rest later, you know I'm sharper when I've eaten.

(Pause.)

Sharp sharp.

(Pause.)

You're right, true true. I shine after a sip or two.

(Pause.)

Gwe asinga you are the Ah. The Best.

(ISAAC arrives onstage. He finds a plate of chips and a bottle of Johnnie Walker awaiting him. ISAAC rushes to collect them. Picking up chips with one hand, checking the label of the bottle with the other. Noticing it's Red Label, he takes a generous hit. ISAAC prays.)

Eh eh. Up there, my buddy, I need some backup here. Swing by, will you?

SCENE 2

(Live TV show set. BAND already onstage, playing Green Chilli TV show theme tune; most of the scene is a music piece.
Isaac enters, late.)

ISAAC: *(Sings and plays guitar, depending on casting. Enters singing, starts from midway through first chorus of the theme tune, filling in the gaps where Brown's voice should be in her tone.)*

(ISAAC chants over heavy drums.)

"*Green Chilli, Green Chilli*
Green Chilli, Green Chilli
Green Chilli, Green Chilli
Green Chilli, Green Chilli

---

2. Luganda: *warm, warm, is not fire.*

Green Chilli, Green Chilli
(ISAAC sings Verse 1.)
Green Chilli, Green Chilli, the TV show with the spice,
Love life's a mess? We'll set you straight on your path. *(Normally Brown's
    line.)*
Come to us, no where friends and family judge,
Fear not, my friend, we're here to discuss.
With a little of our fine counsel, all of your problems will be handled.
Green Chilli, Green Chilli, we're here to stay.
Live on your boxes, every single day." *(Normally sung together.)*
*(ISAAC looks for Brown. On no sign of her arrival, he continues singing Verse
2, usually sung by Brown.)*
"You're in a pickle, your love life's a mess.
Don't you worry, we'll help you out eh, no stress.
Pick up the phone, friend don't be shy.
With our advice, your love life will be hot pepe spice.
We've got the hosts and the audience too.
They'll dig deep and uncover what's true.
No more guessing, no more lies.
We'll help you bring your secrets to light."
(ISAAC sings the chorus alone.)
"*Green Chilli, Green Chilli*, it's the show with the spice.
Green Chilli, Green Chilli, we'll help you get it right. *(Normally Brown's line.)*
Green Chilli, Green Chilli, no need for WhatsApp advice.
On the airwaves, by your side." *(Normally sung together.)*
(Verse 3, normally Brown's verse, but sung by ISAAC):
"If your love life's been a bit of a *beat skip* gamble.
Don't worry, nothing we can't handle.
Just give us a call, we'll make it right.
Green Chilli, it's the show with the spice."
(At end of song prays privately . . .)
I ask for your help. Help me, help me.
(Back to high tone for audience as BAND continues playing.)
Welcome welcome, friends. Welcome studio audience. We are live on
    national television, ready to catch your cheaters and misleaders, air out
    their laundry and hang it out to dry. This is the show where you be the
    judge and we be the audience. You judge, we discuss. You judge, we
    listen. Everything is opposite around here. Welcome to *The Green Chilli.*
    Who do we have on this week's show?

(BROWN enters. She rushes onstage wiping remnant of dinner from her mouth. On seeing ISAAC, she prepares to sing the intro song.)
BROWN: *"Green Chilli, Green Chilli*, it's the show with the spice.
Da da da da lala la la la.
Green Chilli, Green Chilli.
Laaaa lala la la."
(Into mic.) Testing Hallo One Two.
(Pause.)
Testing Hallo One Two.
(BROWN looks to side stage to the TV SHOW PRODUCER. She notices ISAAC looking confused and realizes they're already on air. Proceeds on as if nothing has happened.)
We are live on national television ready to catch your . . . It's hot in here is it just me or is it hot?
ISAAC: Brown.
BROWN: Isaac. Hmpf Brown-ing me?
ISSAC: *(ISAAC nudges to her that they've already done that part and to wipe her mouth as there's a visible food stain.)*
BROWN: Oh. *(BROWN springs into action, appears to be reading from telecom script or card.)* Welcome I am your host Brown, but you all know me already of course.
ISAAC: *(Mutters).* Many for the wrong reasons.
BROWN: *(Mutters.)* All judgments are good judgments if you ask me.
ISAAC: *(Mutters.)* I didn't ask, Brown.
BROWN: I didn't answer.
ISAAC: Brown.
BROWN: Shall we just see who we're helping today, Isaac.
ISAAC: Only if you've finished your La Cabana[3] that is, Brown.
BROWN: I have, thanks. La Cabana is my favorite, thanks for asking, Isaac.
(Both ISAAC and BROWN appear to react to TV PRODUCER offstage who's nudging them to stop quarrelling and start the show. Their dialogue begins to overlap, marked by /)
ISAAC: Are you lost?
BROWN: /Do you need advice?
ISAAC: /Need a new start?
BROWN: / Leave that WhatsApp Group alone.
ISAAC: /Come to us.
BROWN: /Welcome here to *The Green Chilli.*

---

3. An upscale restaurant in Kampala, Uganda.

ISAAC: /The show where you bring your issues to us and let us tackle them for you.

BROWN: /Instead of people you know who, with the best intentions, can mislead you.

ISAAC: /Try turning to people who you don't, who without judgment, can lead you.

BROWN: /Instead of the blind leading the blind.

ISAAC: /Though sometimes wise if you ask me.

BROWN: /It's a saying.

BROWN: /That's what I was saying, blind people are wise not just blind.

BROWN: /Oh boy.

(Both turn to side stage to the TV PRODUCER who's nudging them once again.)

BROWN: Like I was saying.

ISAAC: Let's just start the show shall we.

BROWN: /I thought you just started it. *(Mutters.)* Without me, may I add.

(Both look to TV PRODUCER offstage who's nudging them to get back to the monitor and focus on the show. BAND steps in and plays intro music again.)

BROWN: Welcome to *The Green Chilli.* Instead of the blind

ISAAC: /or the wise

BROWN: /leading the blind, let's all come together and assess what makes a sound judgment. What is advice if not sound judgment?

ISAAC: Judgment?

BROWN: No, advice.

ISAAC: **OK,** let's see what cases have made their way here this evening.

BROWN: Yes, let's see what we have.

ISAAC: Yes, let's see what cases have made their way all the way here.

BROWN: Yes.

ISAAC: Yes, thanks for repeating me. *Quieter* Mwattu.[4] *[Please in Luganda.]*

BROWN: Eh.

ISAAC: Eh eh.

BROWN: Eh eh eh.

ISAAC: Ehhhhh.

BROWN: Eh. Eh.

ISAAC: *(Pause.)*

BROWN: Eh.

ISAAC: *(Pause.)*

BROWN: Eh. *(Pause.)* Eh.

---

4. *Please* in Luganda.

176 SPEAKING OUR SELVES

ISAAC: How much longer?

(Offstage, the TV PRODUCER cuts to commercial break because of the quarrelling onstage between the hosts.)

BROWN: Let's just get back to the show shall we.

ISAAC: After a quick break. For my lovely co-host Brown here.

(TV PRODUCER offstage or with lighting/set design shows signs, signs that are on stage directing audience's reactions, their judgments.
Blackout—commercial break. Music piece can play. ISAAC and BROWN exit "onstage" and go to "backstage.")

SCENE 3

(ISAAC and BROWN are now backstage. A small, cramped space that ISAAC and BROWN must share together.)

ISAAC: *(Pouring himself a drink, he performs a prayer.)* Back to my own show, please.

BROWN: Wangi[5] [*Pardon me in Luganda*], I'm the only thing propping you up right now. And that. *(Points to his drink.)*

ISAAC: This, this is with ice, doesn't count. Just like your tea is not real tea.

BROWN: Its is' it's good for you.

ISAAC: If it has a label dangling in it and it's as clear as water, it's not real tea.

BROWN: Try it. *(She offers him some. Gets uncomfortably close.)*

ISAAC: Tastes like hot vase water. Mm. *(Offers her a sip of his drink.)*

BROWN: Uh, tastes like petrol. With ice in.

ISAAC: To you. Kale[6]. *(Tops up his drink to back where it was before BROWN drank some.)* It's just, years and years of the same, the same, the same this, the same that.

BROWN: *(Takes bottle from him.)* That's what's changed.

ISAAC: Yimirira[7] [*Stop in Luganda*].

BROWN: I've never seen you drink *this* much.

ISAAC: I'm thirsty.

BROWN: You, you can tell me.

ISAAC: Sitegeera[8].

BROWN: *(Pause.)* I read something.

ISAAC: Like?

BROWN: Like, something like, what you leave onstage stays onstage, it goes away. We're here now, we can make it go away. But, like, what goes on

---

5. *Pardon me* in Luganda.
6. *OK* in Luganda.
7. *Stop* in Luganda.
8. *I don't understand* in Luganda.

screen remains on screen, that never goes. That screen *(Points to any example of a screen around the room and in his hand/pocket.)* Just leave it here. *(Pause.)* Come on, we're here now.

ISAAC: *(Thinks about it.)* I, it's.

BROWN: It's?

ISAAC: I'll tell you after, at Bubbles O'Learys[9]?

BROWN: Oh no no not tonight. Too many Mzungus.

ISAAC: Why, where will you be?

BROWN: I'm . . . Sure you don't want to just leave it here now?

ISAAC: *(Pause.)* Do you think we have any influence now?

BROWN: Who cares about influence. We've got a responsibility.

ISAAC: Maybe at the start, all those years ago. Now, I don't know. Even, I can't even tell my 2-year-old what to do, even. What kind of a man can't get their own child to listen to yes and no?

BROWN: Maybe that's the problem, you're telling.

ISAAC: What are you supposed to do?

BROWN: You know, my mother always says never tell a toddler no. But I think you should never tell anyone no. Not "no, but" just "yes, and". We're all just big toddlers really.

ISAAC: Thanks Oprah.

BROWN: We've got to show, not tell people, we've got to "yes, and. . . ." We've got the show to show them. I still can't believe it.

ISAAC: You'll get used to it. Trust me, it wears off.

BROWN: Well, I'm here for the long haul. *(Holds his hand.)*

ISAAC: *(Eyes distracted, spots someone offstage.)* Ah ah, look . . .

BROWN: *(Follows his eyes offstage.)* What?

ISAAC: *(Shouts offstage.)* Boy? Boy come in. *(Shakes bottle).*

(ISAAC exits quickly. BROWN remains onstage and moves her stuff over to ISAAC'S "side," his territory. After a short while, ISAAC returns visibly more drunk, not noticing what BROWN has done.)

BROWN: But you're not supposed to meet the interviewees before the show.

ISAAC: Well, if you won't drink with me, who will?

BROWN: That's what you want, a drinking partner?

ISAAC: Well. Only old people drink alone.

BROWN: Why are you here then?

ISAAC: Well, I was having a young day today. But now I feel old, thanks.

BROWN: You're not supposed to be drinking with the guests, especially when they are clearly underage.

ISAAC: No, he's an adult.

---

9. Upscale social gathering in Kampala, Uganda.

BROWN: He looked 18.

ISAAC: I mean, what the hell they're drinking at their age already. Seems like a good kid. A good egg. Like a mini-me.

BROWN: How is that a good thing?

ISAAC: I want to help him. He was telling me all about all his huge plans.

BROWN: He was?

ISAAC: Big big plans that kid, business, land, money, he wants it all. I want to help him.

BROWN: He told you all of that?

ISAAC: Yes. He has so many plans, so many plans this man is a real, real MAN.

BROWN: Watch out, when you have money, everyone wants a piece of it.

ISAAC: No, it's like, he needs me.

BROWN: He's just a boy.

ISAAC: Exactly. *(Pause.)* There's no space between a man and a boy. All of a sudden, you're supposed to be, something. With all this, this . . . stuff. Where's all that money supposed to come from? Land doesn't just buy itself. And then everyone expects you to have so much without realizing the struggle for it or wanting to be there with the struggle guy, oh no. You only get things when you've already made it, when you're "a man."

BROWN: Inheritance, that's what.

ISAAC: What if you don't have inheritance?

BROWN: What if you're a woman with only your dad's last name?

ISAAC: Eh?

BROWN: Eh, if you're a woman who's not married. Where's that land if you don't have a claim to it eh.

ISAAC: *(Looking for phone, realizes it's in his pocket.)* Eh eh. *(Laughs.)* Not this again.

(ISAAC and BROWN receive a cue from the TV PRODUCER to go back on set. They rush back to "onstage.")

BROWN: *(Laughs.)*

ISAAC: We got this Let's, let's just do what we always do.

BROWN: Always.

ISAAC: Together.

BROWN: *(Pause.)* Together. Eh eh. *(As she exits, she notices chips left on his plate and helps herself to the remainder.)* Ooh yes. La Cabana chips are better though.

GREEN CHILLI 179

SCENE 4

(Interlude between "backstage" and "onstage." ISAAC and BROWN are "onstage" but off-camera. Upon seeing that the interview guest onstage is a teenage girl):

ISAAC: *(Nudges to BROWN. Smiles.)* Your mouth, something there.
BROWN: *(Smiles.)* Oh, thanks.
ISAAC: I've got you.
BROWN: *(Nudges to ISAAC.)* So, then you interview her?
ISAAC: *(Nudges to BROWN.)* It says you. I mean please, you're a woman.
BROWN: You're a man who knows a lot about women in your time.
ISAAC: But Brown you're a woman, you understand her.
BROWN: You've had enough women to understand them. You should try stepping in our shoes for a change.
ISAAC: Brown, you know you have a way about you eh. You know you're out there, always always out there. With these wild wild thoughts.
BROWN: So, you interview her?
ISAAC: *(Pause.)*
BROWN: OK Isaac I'll do it.
(BAND plays music introducing audience back to live TV show. ISAAC and BROWN are now on camera.)
ISAAC: Welcome, welcome.
BROWN: Welcome.
ISAAC: Wel, come.
(Meanwhile during the following lines ISAAC is transitioning into ABBO.)
BROWN: *(Reading from card or teleprompter.)* Meet our young guest today, Abbo.
Abbo meets Boy at a local bar.
Boy likes Abbo.
Abbo likes Boy.
Boy meets Abbo at said bar every week.
After many more meetings at said bar weekly, and after much deliberation, Abbo eventually gives in to his weekly struggles for her attention.
Turns out attention is not all he was after.
Let's find out what happened and why she needs our help.
So, welcome Abbo, why are you here today?
(BAND plays music piece introducing ABBO to audience.)
ABBO: I wanted to meet you in person Lady Brown, I've heard all about you.

BROWN: Oh, really now, wow.

ABBO: Everyone, everyone's heard about you.

BROWN: I don't know who's everyone, Abbo. This city is small but—

ABBO: Eh even in the village even back there, I looked up to you. Everyone, everyone.

BROWN: Abbo, stop with the compliments. *(Pause.)* But continue.

ABBO: *(Pause.)* I feel like I already know you.

BROWN: I'm not sure about that Abbo. But tell me, why are you here today?

ABBO: I'm—

BROWN: You're—

ABBO: I'm, phew, Madame, it's it's hot in here. All these lights eh.

BROWN: What has he done?

ABBO: *(Pause.)* He—

BROWN: Abbo, what are you looking for?

ABBO: *(Pause.)*

BROWN: *(To ISAAC, who could be offstage, for example.)* Any help here? *(Pause.)* I guess not.

ABBO: You seem old and wise.

BROWN: I'm wise not old.

ABBO: You, you seem wise.

BROWN: Probably not so much older than you.

ABBO: You're, you're just a lot more, more woman in person.

BROWN: Well, I'm the same thing you see almost every day, on or off the screen. Listen Abbo, you came on here today, in front of all these people. What do you want to tell them?

ABBO: I, he, I just want him to apologize. I gave everything, he just put his phone out one day to take picture one day.

BROWN: What do you mean, a picture?

ABBO: A picture.

BROWN: As a couple?

ABBO: Eh we are not a couple.

BROWN: Then what?

ABBO: It was one time I came out the shower and he had his phone and he asked me to come say hi to his friend on the phone on the video and . . . I was not ready. I thought it was strange.

BROWN: Of course, it's strange.

ABBO: Eh. And the worst part is, he was angling the phone camera on himself.

BROWN: On himself?

ABBO: Eh. I didn't even know until my friend saw the video and sent it to me. I looked awful.

BROWN: He took a picture of you and him?

ABBO: Yes.

BROWN: Abbo, he sent it to your friend?

ABBO: Eh. Well, I guess by accident.

BROWN: And is that what was going through your mind Abbo?

ABBO: Ay.

BROWN: The way you looked?

ABBO: Ay.

BROWN: Listen, Abbo, if it were me, I would have not taken part in any of this nonsense.

ABBO: Eh you can judge me but *(Pause).* I just want him to apologize eh.

BROWN: You don't mind that he—

ABBO: *(Pause.)*

BROWN: That he angled the camera on himself?

ABBO: I told him off so much for that, catching me off guard with wig half on half off. I told him to be patient. He's always telling me be patient, be patient, when things are better, he says we have land and we live on it, and you know. But he just pushed me there, so I thought oh. Maybe I am impatient, I guess. I, I just want to make it.

BROWN: How? You know being someone having something is a task, not a hand me down? It doesn't come on a plate you know.

ABBO: But eh Madame I looked terrible in this last one.

BROWN: I'm no Madame. Listen, Abbo, I, we, we have your back.

ABBO: Thank you, I always wanted to meet you.

BROWN: But you know how it always is?

ABBO: No.

BROWN: With these kinds of things, it's easier to get permission than forgiveness.

ABBO: Eh I thought out of anyone you would understand.

(TV PRODUCER shows sign, cut to commercial.)

BROWN: We only have 3 minutes left to commercial, remember we are live on air, airing out your issues.

ABBO: He's a good guy eh.

BROWN: How is he a good guy if he misleads you into filming your time together, Abbo? Let's be the judge of that—and he continues to do that?

ABBO: I didn't even see the phone there, we're not allowed it in P6 only from P7.

BROWN: P what? How old are you, Abbo?

ABBO: 15.

(Offstage): Cut.

(BROWN and ISAAC, as ABBO, exit in a rush. Cut to commercial: music and movement piece—parody of commercials that are sexualizing young women.)

SCENE 5

(ISAAC [as ISAAC] and BROWN are now backstage—out of "character" and visibly worried about events onstage that just happened—that ABBO, their guest, is underage.)

ISAAC: *(Pacing.)* Eh, I didn't know we were letting in children to our show now.

BROWN: *(Following him around.)* She looks 25 not 15.

ISAAC: With all that . . . Pat Pat. *(Pat pats his face to imply makeup.)*

BROWN: YouTube.

ISAAC: Yes, YouTube tutorial this "Welcome to my channel" that. What is this, children, children?

BROWN: /She's a brave little woman.

ISAAC: /Children. Here? Who brought her here?

BROWN: *(Stops following Isaac.)* *(Pause.)* She brought herself.

ISAAC: Eh?

BROWN: Where else could she go?

ISAAC: Her friends, classmates, mother. *(Pause, waits for BROWN to answer.)*

BROWN: *(Silent.)*

ISAAC: *(Continues.)* I'm no better than if she'd consulted her own psyche at this point. She needs the man upstairs.

BROWN: She needs us. Her friends, classmates, mother. What could all those people do? To them, they see her as a certain way. To us, she's a clean slate. A guest. An in-and-then-out again guest. In the home of the coward they laugh while in the home of the brave they cry.[10]

ISAAC: Home? She should be at her home. She's a child.

BROWN: Yes and she's . . . It's hard to have a confidante as a female, a black female, without having someone judge. I mean look at us.

ISAAC: *(Checks skin.)* Same.

BROWN: What?

ISAAC: Same.

---

10. Ugandan proverb.

BROWN: Yes, but you're not a young woman navigating all of this—intimacy—on your own.

ISAAC: Takes two to Tango.

BROWN: I mean, come on.

ISAAC: Brown, you know this is nonsense.

BROWN: Are there opportunities to talk about this stuff meaningfully? If not here, then where?

ISAAC: Come on this is not a meaningful show.

BROWN: It pays for your two wives.

ISAAC: I don't have two—*(Gets distracted starts counting them on one hand—)* one is a partner.

BROWN: It's still one too many.

ISAAC: You can judge. Weren't you carrying around a small collection last year?

BROWN: Who said that?

ISAAC: Everyone.

BROWN: Said who, the *RedPepper*?[11]

ISAAC: *(Remembers Manager's conversation from the start. Starts to fumble for phone and gets visibly agitated.)* But she's a minor.

BROWN: But you're a man?

ISAAC: Eh, but doesn't she have parents?

BROWN: What are they supposed to do? You just said you don't even know what to do with your 2-year-old.

ISAAC: *(Pacing up and down.)* I don't know, give them, give them, you know.

BROWN: Advice?

ISAAC: No, not the other things, you know—you know—the little square packets.

BROWN: And that will help them how?

ISAAC: I don't know, slow them down a bit, you know.

BROWN: It didn't work on you.

ISAAC: If her parents can't help, how can I?

BROWN: You're a parent.

ISAAC: Oh yeah. But what am I supposed to do?

BROWN: Fix it, you're a man.

ISAAC: If her parents can't help—

BROWN: And where are they? She clearly is not afraid of what they think if she comes and parades around, showing herself, devaluing herself, in public like this.

---

11. A Ugandan tabloid newspaper.

ISAAC: If her parents don't know, what are we supposed to do?

BROWN: Isn't it our job, our duty, collectively? To protect girls like her.

ISAAC: Eh. I don't know. *(Pause.)* She does have sharp breasts though.

BROWN: *(Doesn't hear it.)* These young girls—

ISAAC: Sharp sharp.

BROWN: Yes, sharp sharp, we have to fix it sharp. We're going to get fired in about twenty minutes unless you find a way to fix it.

ISAAC: They grow fast these days, up and out.

BROWN: *(Pause.)* You like her?

ISAAC: She looks like a nice young lady.

BROWN: So that makes her a nice young lady?

ISAAC: *(Shouts to side stage.)* Please. Where's my chicken? I asked for a chicken drumstick on the side and what I have received is a thigh. This. Is. An Outrage.

BROWN: Is that all you care about right now?

(Chicken drumstick arrives onstage, elaborately presented.)

ISAAC: Ah that's better, now I can think.

BROWN: You're so predictable. We're about to get fired and all you can think about is a stupid chicken drumstick.

ISAAC: *(ISAAC takes a bite of chicken drumstick and is now more willing to take on the challenge.)* I know what we'll do *(takes another bite)* we'll *(takes another bite)* we'll think about it. Later.

BROWN: Genius.

ISAAC: Pretend like none of this ever happened. Right now, we've got about 2 minutes before we have to go back on set and-

BROWN: And this *(indicates drumstick)* brought about this moment of clarity? To do nothing?

ISAAC: *(Pulling bone through teeth.)* What's your smart plan Brown?

BROWN: I have one.

ISAAC: Mmhmm.

BROWN: Just not right now.

ISAAC: "We're supposed to be smarter than the guys" . . . isn't that what you're always saying to these poor girls?

BROWN: I am smart. I just need, I need . . .

ISAAC: You need some of this.

BROWN: No, did you know about this? From before?

ISAAC: No of course not. You're just hungry, here eat woman.

BROWN: Are you a part of it?

ISAAC: Eh?

BROWN: Are you a part of it?

ISAAC: Eh? Of course not.

BROWN: Well for now we just have to protect her.

ISAAC: She's old enough to know what she wants. I mean she seems like she knows it already. *(Finishes up even though he's already finished everything visible there is of his food).*

BROWN: I didn't know you were like that. I mean 15, 15.

ISAAC: And to be targeted by . . .

BROWN: *(Sarcastic.)* Now?

ISAAC: By . . .

BROWN: By men like you?

ISAAC: By boys, young boys, they need to be men.

BROWN: Like you?

ISAAC: *(Faux formality.)* Like, like unscrupulous *(mispronounces it and tries again)* people who get hold of and share unscrupulous things, just like that. These, these immoral, non-God-fearing people. *(ISAAC frantically tries to find his phone to call his manager and is eating at the same time.)*

BROWN: *(Pause.)*

ISAAC: For manipulation. Eh is that what we've become now? Unscrupulous. And 15? *(ISAAC finds his phone and places it down neglectfully.)*

BROWN: *(Pause.)*

ISAAC: Like it's a status symbol, just another makeup video.

BROWN: You can't just judge like that.

ISAAC: But you didn't know she was 15?

BROWN: No. Did you?

ISAAC: No. *(Pause.)* Jeez. *(Pause.)* I mean how's that going to make us look.

(BROWN is following him around. This is visibly annoying him.)

ISAAC: Do you have to follow me around everywhere?

(BROWN stops, over pours a shot of Johnnie Walker in a glass instead of a shot glass and hands him the "shot." He downs it neglectfully.)

ISAAC: OK I know what we'll do. We'll pretend we got it wrong, and everything will be fine.

BROWN: As usual. *(BROWN prepares another overpoured shot.)* I'll help you with anything you need, you just look after it. One thing.

ISAAC: Yes?

BROWN: Do you think I'm, you know, sharp?

ISAAC: Ummm . . .

(BROWN hands ISAAC yet another overpoured shot, he downs it. ISAAC exits. BROWN stays onstage and goes through his phone. She seems shocked by what she finds there—audience is not aware of what it is yet but it's a message from his manager talking about a picture found of ISAAC dropping

off a girl at school—BROWN puts it away upon hearing ISAAC return.
ISAAC returns. Live BAND plays last part of parody commercial to indicate
return to onstage scene. Both actors return to "onstage.")

Act Two

SCENE 1

(Act Two is the climax of the play—continual flipping between onstage and
offstage presence and dialogue. As the presenters are talking to the young
guests, they realize those problems are the exact ones mirrored in their own
lives currently, leading them to confront their own realities.)
(Onstage, live TV show. ISAAC and BROWN run back on set and they are
back "in character" now. Live BAND is playing the intro song.)

ISAAC: Welcome back to *The Green Chilli*, we're here to *(little stumble as he*
     has had too much to drink)—sorry, sorry—on national TV.
(BAND skips beat.)
BROWN: *(Concerned).* Well, let's meet *(reading from teleprompter)* "Boy"?
ISAAC: Yes. Let's meet the other . . . *(Isaac frantically tries to search for*
     phone, panic on realizing it's not there) . . . the other side of this story.
     (Pause.) There are two sides to everything.
BROWN: Three. Their words, our judgment and God's truth.
ISAAC: Sitegeera.[12] [*I don't understand in Luganda.*] Boy is here, the second-
BROWN: First-
ISAAC: Part in all this, so let's bring him out shall we.
(This introduction to BOY can be a music piece. ISAAC reading lyrics from
teleprompter but adapting them to his own meanings. Meanwhile BROWN is
transitioning into BOY.)
ISAAC: Boy is a Boy who knows what he wants. He saw it, went for it,
     recorded it. He did what any man would do. Get a prize and photograph
     it, anything new? Boy is just a man who met someone. He's learnt of
     Abbo's accusations backstage. Let's see what he has to say about all this.
     "Boy?"
BOY: Sir. Ssebo.[13] [*Sir in Luganda.*]
ISSAC: Boy? What kind of a name is that?
BOY: It's my real name Sir.
ISAAC: Where in earth's name did you get a name like that?
BOY: My maama named me that.

---

12. *I don't understand* in Luganda.
13. *Sir* in Luganda.

ISAAC: I mean where was your father in all of this? What's his name, "Man"?

BOY: My dad gave me a real name, but I don't, I don't know it Sir.

ISAAC: Man gave you a name you don't know?

BOY: *(Pause.)* I just stick with Boy.

ISAAC: But I mean eh where was your mum in all of this? Woman? She had so many boys she ran out of names?

BOY: She had too many girls. After number 4, my dad left. Then. I came as number 5, I think she was so shocked when she saw a boy she just called me Boy. It's been really a curse really.

ISAAC: Boy, you're here. And it's a blessing.

BOY: A curse. Because I mean, why would she bring me here? In front of all these people?

ISAAC: Boy, you've got dirty laundry to air out.

BOY: My conscience is clean.

ISAAC: Well, let's get to the bottom of it. How did you meet Abbo?

BOY: She sent me a message.

ISAAC: She said she met you at a bar.

BOY: A good place to start.

ISAAC: Boy, you shouldn't be drinking unless *(Stumbles because of how much he himself has had.)*—Excuse me. Unless—

BOY: Me? Everyone has their things.

ISAAC: Unless-Yes everyone has their vices but unless you have good reason now.

BOY: It was only supposed to be one. Now I love her.

ISAAC: Love her? Now Boy, you say one thing she says another but— *(Quietly to boy.)*—It's just protocol we have to ask these questions.

BOY: She got my number. She sent me message. She looked nice on the picture. I started calling her Dear.

ISAAC: Dear?

BOY: She's my Dear. Me? What's the big problem? I gave her money for boda boda[14] [motorcycle taxis in East Africa] everything. Everything she want.

ISAAC: Yes Boy but, but you see there's this filming on the phone thing. Yada yada.

BOY: Why all the way here? Me? That's what a man does. Keep everything together. Keep everything private. What a man does, everything private should never be public.

ISAAC: Listen to me, women love to talk.

---

14. Motorcycle taxis in East Africa.

BOY: Listen me I swear I didn't send anything to any of her friends I swear. I just kept them there for you know, sometimes, but someone took them. I took her for one drink and it ended up being 5. And I paid for all of them. And let's not forget—

transport,

data,

airtime,

mobile money,

boda boda.

ISAAC: Boy, you had no say in this whatsoever?

BOY: Maybe a little.

ISAAC: *(To audience.)*—Right we got it, there. *(To BOY.)*—Listen Boy women just like an apology. It's not permission, it's an apology. It's for your sake.

BOY: It's for hers.

(Can be a music piece. Meanwhile BROWN is transitioning back from BOY to BROWN.)

ISAAC: Boy, from what we've seen earlier you like being on camera. There are only 2 types of people, those who like being on camera, and those who like being in camera. Those that like being public, and those that like being private. Those that like spice in their food, and those that don't. There's no in between. This isn't a game of halves.

(BROWN returns as BROWN, not BOY.)

BROWN: Do you know how much it costs eh before all of this? Do you know?

hair,

edge of hair,

nails,

lotion,

elbow cream,

weave,

left elbow cream-

ISAAC: *(To BOY, can be to camera for example)/* You see.

BROWN: Why put her out there?

ISAAC: That girl. She. She slandered him. He's just naive.

BROWN: Please. Or stupid.

ISAAC: He should have called it quits at beer number 3. Everybody, everybody knows that.

BROWN: *(To ISAAC.)* Boy—

GREEN CHILLI   189

ISAAC: /Boy listen, I, we, stand by you.

BROWN: /Boy even though I would love to stay and dig in your shoes it's—

ISAAC: /It's time for a break.

BROWN: Yes, let's—

ISAAC: /Return.

BROWN: /Recover.

(ISAAC and BROWN exit "onstage." Cut to commercial—music/movement piece that is a parody of ads sexualizing young women and men.)

SCENE 2

(Backstage. ISAAC and BROWN are on different ends of the stage now— they've fallen out. ISAAC takes a shot.)

BROWN: You?

ISAAC: Were you looking at my phone? *(Cautious.)* What happened to dream team?

BROWN: *(Purposefully ignores his first question.)* I don't want to be one of your 2, 3, 4—shall I continue?—or worst still, a "partner".

ISAAC: You know Brown Dear; you are a sharp breasted woman aren't you. I had a chance to think about it onstage and I thought yes. You are.

BROWN: Even for you, I'm shocked.

ISAAC: Brown Dear.

BROWN: Dear? We're supposed to be upholding morals and here you are.

ISAAC: And you look younger than, what's her name, Abbo. Yes, you look much younger in my humble opinion.

BROWN: Really? I mean even for you that's—

ISAAC: Yes, much more more more more pert.

BROWN: I know you have your vices but this.

ISAAC: Brown you're even better than her. Like a spicier version. Everyone knows that's better Dear.

BROWN: I don't think there's any getting out of this one.

ISAAC: It's just, just you know how it is, yada yada, someone took that picture by accident.

BROWN: An accident? It's a fact. There's nowhere to hide behind that.

ISAAC: Everyone's on top of it, it will never ever come out.

BROWN: You're on your own.

ISAAC: It's just a picture. It's not a fact.

BROWN: When it comes out everyone will know.

ISAAC: Let's just finish the show, together.

BROWN: Together?

ISAAC: You have this way about you making everything easy.

BROWN: You have a way of making everything hard.

(Phone rings. It's ISAAC'S manager.)

ISAAC: *(To manager on the phone.)* One second. *(To BROWN.)* It's not true dear. Dear, just hold on one second. *(Back to manager on the phone.)* Eh eh what do you mean there have been over 100 complaints to the show already? *(Manager—implied—it's really bad.)* Eh. But how was I to know that? *(Manager—implied—because I sent you a message earlier and you didn't respond.)* I handled it well no, you think I did, OK? What should I do? I know what. *(ISAAC paces around as manager—implied—gives long speech about how ISAAC should've handled it and how he should handle it now.)*

(ISAAC puts phone down. Picks up the Red Pepper newspaper and shows it to BROWN.)

Look at this, it said you went for a boy in his twenties. And you're what, 31?

BROWN: You need to be careful, with this *(drinking)* with that *(women).*

ISAAC: He probably rides a boda boda.

BROWN: He has a car.

ISAAC: He's short.

BROWN: You're drunk dear.

ISAAC: Dear, I've only had 3 shots today—

(BROWN exits to take message. BROWN returns onstage.)

BROWN: We're getting over 50 complaints to the show a minute, can you just—

ISAAC: Me? I'm sober Dear.

BROWN: Just make it to the end without becoming drunk at least. We'll deal with the rest later.

ISAAC: We're running a show of a show here eh.

BROWN: You. You're on your own this time.

(ISAAC answers phone—it's his manager.)

ISAAC: Again? Just tell me how to fix this show I'll do it. I'll do it. I'll show you I can do it.

BROWN: *(Pause.)* But you did do it didn't you.

ISAAC: *(To BROWN.)* I don't know what you're talking about.

BROWN: It's been following you around hasn't it.

ISAAC: The only thing that's been following me around is you.

(From TV PRODUCER/Teleprompter—Audience starts to find out one by one about ISAAC'S picture that's leaked. Showing him picking up a schoolgirl from school in his car.)

BROWN: You've done a lot of things but This. *(Pause.)* Is she a nice young lady?

ISAAC: She's nice. Big everything for a young girl. *(Backtracks.)* But you know I was just helping her here and there. *(ISAAC downs 2 shots in a row.)*

BROWN: Wow slow down.

ISAAC: It's nothing new.

BROWN: Ok let's just invite more disaster, shall we?

ISAAC: My name is clean.

BROWN: We only have everything to lose.

(Audience finds out about the leak of ISAAC'S picture of his dropping off a girl at school, can be a music piece.)

BROWN: That picture shows you were dropping her off. At School.

ISAAC: Well, everyone needs a lift.

BROWN: You don't have a daughter, or do you?

ISAAC: Me?

BROWN: Typical.

ISAAC: Brown Dear I was just helping her with fees here and there.

BROWN: Nothing more?

ISAAC: Nothing. Like I said, everyone needs a lift.

BROWN: I know the *Red Pepper* can be cruel but.

ISAAC: I don't know how they got the picture. Do you?

BROWN: You know how they are.

ISAAC: You, see? These immoral non-God-fearing people. They see a picture and think it's a fact. Everyone does. It's a photo, you can't read anymore into it than that. You can't judge character from a picture or video. It's not a fact. It's an impression.

BROWN: But you can do that with Abbo?

ISAAC: You know I know everything about you Brown. You're just loose. Sloppy. I can make a few calls. Just a few calls here and there. Then let's see how your career goes.

BROWN: You wouldn't do that.

ISAAC: This is my house now get out of it.

BROWN: This time it's not. Have you even tried putting yourself in that girl's shoes?

ISAAC: I'm a size 12. They won't fit.

BROWN: You can't even put yourself in someone else's shoes, can you?

(ISAAC picks up his phone. It's his manager calling again.)

ISAAC: *(To manager on phone.)* Just make this pass through the backdoor not the front, OK?

(BROWN exits to transition as BOY.)

ISAAC: *(On phone still.)* I'll get another show. Just make it go away.

What do you mean you're not sure you can? It's not up to me, it's up to you
to fix it.

Fix it, just fix it. *(ISAAC puts phone down.)* No no no no no no.

*(ISAAC exits stage and returns with BOY (BROWN), who's carrying a bottle
of alcohol.)*

BOY: You. *(Pause.)* Uncle, are you OK?

ISAAC: Uncle? Uncle! Listen Boy I am not your uncle.

BOY: Did you mean what you said earlier? *(Pause.)* You can help me?
(Pause.)

With money?

ISAAC: Maybe with some contacts, I know some people who can help you.

BOY: But you said you want to, how you say it, "invest."

ISAAC: Well, yes. Well no. Well.

BOY: Me I want to look after her. I just don't have money. Me I have no help.
It's hard. I have big, big dreams. I told her we'll buy land, build a house.
We go on holiday. Be patient be patient. She doesn't believe me. Abbo,
she knows she's nice. Everybody wants her but she wants everything and
nobody. She wants too much.

ISAAC: OK OK I—*(Masks drunkenness.)*—meant what I said, Boy.

BOY: Uncle are you sure?

ISAAC: I am not your Uncle Boy.

BOY: OK. But you are sure?

ISAAC: But I see something in you Boy.

BOY: Me, eh?

ISAAC: Yes. You have something.

BOY: Like you?

ISAAC: No no no no. You, you're the opposite of me.

BOY: Me? I don't know, I'm just trying Uncle.

ISAAC: No Uncle! Trying is better than being handed it.

BOY: I do not understand what you mean Sir.

ISAAC: Boy, I'm not Sir, I'm not Uncle. OK?

BOY: Yes Uncle.

ISAAC: I'm not—never mind. We'll sort it out after the show, OK?

BOY: You will help me?

ISAAC: Just, just don't tell Brown or Abbo or any woman.

BOY: But why?

ISAAC: She won't understand. These are man to man "investments" eh. OK?

BOY: OK. Wow, you do that for me.

ISAAC: One million shillings.

GREEN CHILLI 193

BOY: One million shillings?

ISAAC: But you have to invest it, yes? In what you are telling me? Don't just waste it on beer or what or what.

BOY: It's OK. All I want is a house. Then I can be man of the house.

ISAAC: Yes, this is a little investment for you to start to be a man. *(ISAAC fumbles in pocket and takes out 50k note then hands it to BOY.)* Yes, that's it, the note with a gorilla, you see?

BOY: Thank you Sir—I mean thank you Uncle—I mean thank you.

(BOY doesn't realize he's only been given 50k and starts to walk offstage, ISAAC calls him back.)

ISAAC: BOY. Just one thing.

(BOY returns to onstage.)

BOY: Yes.

ISAAC: You can tell everyone else. In fact, here let's take a picture.

(ISAAC takes the 50k note from BOY and swaps it for a 5k note; they take a picture together.)

Great, now share that where you like, OK?

BOY: OK.

ISAAC: Great, now go, go.

BOY: Thank you so much so so much Sir.

ISAAC: Everyone everyone knows now.

(BOY exits stage. ISAAC goes to take a celebratory shot, overpours it and downs the drink, then exits stage.

Isaac transitions into ABBO.)

SCENE 3

(On set, live TV show. ISAAC and BROWN return as ABBO and BOY. They're onstage but not on air yet. Music playing that's not the live band.)

ABBO: You think I'm stupid?

BOY: Abbo Abbo you are not stupid Dear.

ABBO: You think I'm stupid, eh?

BOY: Abbo.

ABBO: I do everything, everything and you don't even give me two minutes of FaceTime?

BOY: Eh? Abbo Dear why all of this eh? Why all of these people?

ABBO: You want to go and make me look stupid. You even sent it to my friend.

BOY: Abbo Dear. You looked nice in it, I made sure.

194   SPEAKING OUR SELVES

ABBO: Boy I just wanted you to go and go and make money, you say you
were supposed to be a doctor, then you say you want to have business,
then you say you want to buy a land, you say you say you say, then you
say let me take a picture.

BOY: /Abbo.

ABBO: /then you say let me take a video -

BOY: Abbo.

ABBO: /then you send it to my friend?

BOY: Abbo Dear, what do you want eh?

ABBO: Nah ah.

BOY: More money?

ABBO: Eh *(ABBO says "yes" as eh throughout.)*

BOY: More transport money?

ABBO: Eh.

BOY: More mobile money?

ABBO: Eh.

BOY: Airtime?

ABBO: Eh.

BOY: Data?

ABBO: Eh.

BOY: What do you want?

ABBO: Me, I just want few things, it is not much.

BOY: *(Pause.)*

ABBO: You are a Boy, Boy. You should go and be a Boy and not pretend to
be this big man when you are just a small boy.

BOY: You? You just take take from me, take take everything.

ABBO: Eh? You take from me, you don't think I can take something from
you?

BOY: Abbo even if we are poor we can live a good life.

ABBO: I can go and get others eh you are not the only one eh.

BOY: What?

ABBO: Me I am a nice looking lady I can go to other men eh.

BOY: Abbo, Abbo you're too young. Just let me look after you   -

ABBO: / Nah ah.

BOY: / and not let you become spoiled like all these other girls.

ABBO: Me I am not spoiled. You cannot even buy me small pair of shoes. I
want more shoes, you know I like shoes.

BOY: I buy you shoes I buy you school shoes. *(BOY goes to pull out the 50k
ISAAC gave him earlier from his pocket.)* I saw you backstage talking to
that man like a man now you come to me and talk to me like I'm just a
small child.

(ABBO storms off like a small child.)
BOY: Abbo.
(ABBO returns.)
ABBO: Nah ah. I can just go and go and be with someone who can buy me
    shoes.
BOY: Every Friday I pick you up, no?
ABBO: Me anything? Nah ah.
BOY: Abbo.
ABBO: It's all these women who raised you into a Boy, you'll always be just a
    Boy.
BOY: You don't know what you want.
ABBO: I just want to look nice, like Lady Brown, and you say "You do this
    and I bring you this" then you bring nothing.
BOY: You want shoes?
ABBO: Me? Yes.
BOY: I bring you designer shoes.
ABBO: And two pairs.
BOY: I know you've been asking for them for a long time.
ABBO: Yes, you see Lady Brown? Just like Lady Brown.
BOY: You want to be like that woman, eh?
ABBO: Eh.
BOY: You want to be like that woman, eh? She is old and not even married,
    you want to be like that eh?
ABBO: She seems like a nice young lady. She looks nice.
BOY: That does not make her a nice young lady. You you've only been with
    me you're not spoiled yet, she, everyone has seen her, all the pictures of
    her coming out of all those places, dressed in a provocative outfit. That.
    You want to be like that? Maama said "Her who keeps losing children
    doesn't invent names anymore." That's her, No names.
ABBO: Me? Yes, she is always looking nice.
BOY: Abbo you know I've been saving money for you for some time.
ABBO: I know you don't have money eh. I have the eye to see it. You think I
    have no eyes? I'm blind eh?
BOY: Every little I have Abbo I was saving. But for you, you just come and
    ask.
ABBO: No you ask for things, I don't want to give and then I give them and
    then I don't receive? I don't want to be disrespected like that. Nah ah.
    You want me to miss out on those shoes?
BOY: Abbo.
ABBO: Nah ah. I will not be disrespected like that, you will get ideas.
BOY: Abbo Dear no.

ABBO: I saw you onstage with that man saying this and that, big talk acting like you're a big man.

BOY: Sorry Dear.

ABBO: Eh? Do not say sorry. Do not say things that will be against you in the future. Because if you say you are sorry, be sorry. It will be a different story.

BOY: Sorry Dear. He was just telling me things, he was saying he can help, because I remind him of him.

ABBO: How can he help us when he is drunk?

BOY: He is a man.

ABBO: And now you are drunk.

BOY: No. Abbo I am sorry, for not giving you such things.

ABBO: Exactly. See. *(Points to her shoes.)*

BOY: I know now why you came on here dear, you just want to be seen.

ABBO: Eh.

BOY: To feel important eh?

ABBO: All of this and you don't want me to be seen?

BOY: Of course I do. I just don't want you to be spoiled. You stay how you are. You stay in school. And then we can talk.

ABBO: This "Be patient, be patient," again. I am so tired of this eh. I want everything now. Now now.

BOY: Dear I will give you everything now now, you just wait.

ABBO: Eh? You say now, then you say wait. Eh? Me? I have options you know.

(Abbo puts the 5k she received from BOY back in his pocket.)

BOY: But you have a choice. You can come with me and never have to make money—or you can grow and worry and grow and make money alone.

ABBO: Me I can start young like Brown.

BOY: Abbo, don't be like her, old and spoiled. Everyone has seen her pictures coming out of where and where in provocative outfits. You you want to be like her eh?

ABBO: Eh? You said you have seen all her pictures?

BOY: No. Abbo, me, I can forget about this small small thing.

ABBO: You made me look stupid eh.

BOY: You made me look like a small small boy.

ABBO: You are.

BOY: You might not care because your maama is too busy making money for you and everyone to notice but me. Everyone everyone in the village will be talking about this. But you know talk in the village dies down. Talk here stays.

GREEN CHILLI   197

ABBO: *(Pause.)* Eh.

BOY: But we can move on from this eh. You know I can have money now. That is what that man was saying. There's a way. You just, just choose. You have a choice now. So my Dear?

ABBO: Eh.

BOY: What do you want?

ABBO: I choose, the money.

BOY: Yes.

ABBO: But not from you.

BOY: Eh?

ABBO: Me? I choose the money.

BOY: Dear, please. I have not understood everything you have said. You want me to try and go and find someone else who is not spoiled? I do not want all of that. You want me to go out there and go around with this and that? No, I do not want that.

ABBO: Then you should be careful what you do with the new things eh before they become old things.

(TV PRODUCER signals to ABBO and BOY to exit.)

Act Three

SCENE 1

(Backstage. ISAAC and BROWN, back "out of character." ISAAC is now drunk, slurring words. BROWN is serving herself from catering that has now arrived backstage for the show's crew. ISAAC hands out an empty glass to BROWN.)

ISAAC: Bring me juice.

BROWN: Juice? No I will not bring you juice.

ISAAC: But Dear.

BROWN: You think I am here to come and serve you juice? Nah ah.

ISAAC: You changed your tune.

BROWN: Eh.

ISAAC: Who are you to judge? They are just kids.

BROWN: I thought you were calling him a man before.

ISAAC: I thought he was. You hear this shoes shoes talk? He is a kid. They are KIDS.

BROWN: *(Sarcastic.)* Well yes.

ISAAC: Before I was worried for me. Now I am worried for them.

BROWN: You've changed sharp. Sharp sharp.

ISAAC: I didn't know what it was like for them.

BROWN: Because you are the one defiling them.

ISAAC: No no no no no.

BROWN: No?

ISAAC: No Brown. No. The girl in the photo asked me to help her, to buy her some things.

BROWN: She asked you? I'm sure it was you that approached her.

ISAAC: I swear Brown she asked me for help, her father is my friend, way way back, and he has not been as fortunate as me and me when I see someone who needs help I just give it to them. It's my God. Given. Duty.

BROWN: And nothing more happened?

ISAAC: I swear.

BROWN: You swear? But you're always swearing. How do I know that you are real swearing?

ISAAC: I swear. On *(swears on his chest, searches for other things to swear on)*. I swear Brown. I mean—

BROWN: You helped me to get this job, when I had only met you once?

ISAAC: You see. I saw something in you and I thought why not? Eh. Why? If I can help, then why let you just sit like that.

BROWN: Sit?

ISAAC: You know what I mean.

BROWN: You swear that you swear?

ISAAC: Yes. The same with that girl I was dropping off at school. I was just helping.

BROWN: You help, but you never help yourself.

ISAAC: And then it's always at a cost to me. No-one can tell these things. Especially not what a picture in the *Red Pepper* can tell you.

BROWN: Who helps you?

ISAAC: Who helps these young men? They are just expected to make it and have money and then provide and then—

BROWN: But that BOY, you don't even know him.

ISAAC: I know he needs help.

BROWN: I know you have your personal vices, beer, food, women . . . *(Takes a breath to continue.)*

ISAAC: /I do love some nice sharp breasts and some nice cold cold beer.

BROWN: /but even for you, defilement?

ISAAC: I do fear God.

BROWN: Then you need to stop swearing.

ISAAC: It's just a lot of pressure, all of this money stuff.

BROWN: All this is about money?

ISAAC: This this this whole financial burden is a . . . heavy load. Everyone sees me, they smell money and they want some.

BROWN: You're more than your "role." Make a new one.

ISAAC: *(Pause.)* Alright, I'll make an effort to cut down on the swearing, but Brown? You hear me right? You see me right?

(BROWN caves in and brings him some food and juice on noticing his vulnerability.)

BROWN: Here.

ISAAC: *(Pushes food away.)* I don't want it.

BROWN: Just eat? You need to sober up fast before we go back on set.

ISAAC: *(Pushes food away.)* I don't need it.

BROWN: Eh? This is the most drunk I have ever seen you.

(ISAAC absentmindedly takes the food and juice and places it down next to him, ignores it—does not touch it for the remainder of the scene.)

ISAAC: Thanks but I don't need anymore. That chicken made me feel sick. Look.

BROWN: What?

ISAAC: Does my belly look bigger than usual? It's that chicken I swear.

BROWN: Wow you really are the most drunk and delusional I have ever seen you.

ISAAC: That Boy he doesn't even have a belly yet, and he drinks beer, and he does not even expand one bit. They're, they're just, school kids.

BROWN: That's what I was saying.

ISAAC: School kids.

BROWN: OK just sober up now.

ISAAC: School KIDS.

BROWN: *(To herself.)* It is true what they say, when you see someone at their most childlike, that's when you see them at their most true.

ISAAC: It's easy for us when we are sitting in these open glass houses. But for them they are sitting in these dorms, these closed houses together.

BROWN: *(Ignoring ISAAC, thinking he's just drunk, tucking into food.)* Yes.

ISAAC: It's always the same. When they are young and in the house, we show them affection, open.

BROWN: *(Tucking into food.)* Yes.

ISAAC: When they leave for school, those closed spaces? That is when the tough love begins.

BROWN: *(Tucking into food.)* Yes.

ISAAC: They go from the open space to the closed one.

BROWN: *(Tucking into food.)* Yes.

ISAAC: And then they return home.

BROWN: *(Tucking into food.)* Yes.

ISAAC: And then we rear them more tough at home. And then we rear them tough at school. That's the best way we say.

BROWN: *(Tucking into food.)* Yes.

ISAAC: And then, and there, they can go and be more open to each other.

BROWN: *(Tucking into food.)* Yes.

ISAAC: Then they are just going to go and find that affection elsewhere.

BROWN: *(Tucking into food.)* Yes.

ISAAC: And then that's how it is until they leave that home, and we expect them to know how to be, like us.

BROWN: *(Tucking into food.)* Yes.

ISAAC: These school kids.

BROWN: *(Tucking into food.)* Yes.

ISAAC: Teaching each other.

BROWN: *(Tucking into food.)* Yes.

ISAAC: The blind leading the blind.

BROWN: *(Tucking into food.)* Yes.

ISAAC: You've been blindly consuming that.

BROWN: *(Tucking into food.)* Yes. *(Brown looks up and realizes what ISAAC has just said.)* No. *(BROWN doesn't hear or pay attention to most of his speech, thinking he's just having another drunken rant.)* No, boys will be boys and men will be men.

ISAAC: And girls will be women.

BROWN: You're just drunk.

ISAAC: I'm sober now. Watching all that that nonsense.

BROWN: They're just kids.

ISAAC: Did you see them there, talking about this and that, shoes and mobile money. Is that all there is to it?

BROWN: They're just kids, kids will be kids.

ISAAC: Is that what my son will be, Boy?

BROWN: You need to actually step in their shoes to know what it is like for them.

ISAAC: You can't just sit in your glasshouse and judge from up there and take a moral high ground and think whatever you want to think.

BROWN: They're just kids being kids.

ISAAC: You, you have not had kids Brown you cannot understand it in the same way.

BROWN: *(Pause.)* Does that make me spoiled?

ISAAC: No that does not make you spoiled who said anything about you? I was talking about them.

BROWN: Am I old and barren and spoiled?

ISAAC: No, you are just childless.

BROWN: Because that's the way it turned out.

ISAAC: Because you go for these young young immature men.

BROWN: That's all there is now.

ISAAC: No that just makes you not understand it. You won't be with little ones calling you "Mama." You're not even with the big ones who call you "Dear."

BROWN: That's an old-fashioned word anyway I prefer babe. Or just being called by God given name.

ISAAC: It's OK, you don't have to take things so personal. It's not so personal.

BROWN: You make them sound like they are good when they are used and bad when they are spoiled. And these judged people grow old and maybe then barren.

ISAAC: It's not personal.

BROWN: Eat up?

ISAAC: I don't need it now. I've got bigger things to focus my attention on, instead of just blindly eating eating drinking drinking.

BROWN: Are you sure?

(ISAAC exits backstage and returns onstage for final segment of the show. BROWN remains backstage.)

SCENE 2

(On set, live TV show. ISAAC enters. He is now drunk, slurring words. BAND already onstage. They start playing intro tune when ISAAC comes onstage. They are confused why he is without BROWN.)

ISAAC: *(Sings outro.)*

OUTRO: Thanks for tuning in, we've had a blast.

Hope our advice has helped, and the laughs will last.

Join us next time, for more spicy fun.

Green Chilli, the show that's number one!

(At end of song mutters). . . . Welcome back to the third segment of the show. Now, my host is not here because I want to address something you may have heard. Eh eh. I had a speech prepared for me. EVERYTHING IS ALWAYS PREPARED FOR ME. WHERE IS IT. WHERE IS IT? *(Pause.)* All I can remember is, is . . . She, she was just a schoolgirl I was helping with fees. That is all. You can think what you want, but, but that's all there was to it.

Sometimes you can hear something, see something, take it and make it fact. That is not a verified fact, as my co-host says. That way you just throw mud on someone's name. And it's hard to get mud off your skin let alone your name. We are ordinary people here, and here we are thinking we are not. We are. Me? I am.

(BROWN is backstage, starts to tell from reactions backstage that something unusual is happening with ISAAC.)

To have a show like this, for what? For bickering and judging who did what to who, who deserves what? It's all just . . . show. Not tell. No-one knows. It's all just the blind leading the blind.

(BROWN enters "onstage" finishing mouth full.)

BROWN: A crap show?

ISAAC: Crap crap crap crap crap crap.

(ISAAC pushes BROWN to a camera spot much further away from him.)

BROWN: What, what are you doing?

ISAAC: *(To BROWN.)* Two seconds Dear.

BROWN: *(Not realizing what is happening, insincere.)* Wow I'm full. And it's hot in here, no?

(ISAAC nudges to BROWN that she has remnants of her dinner she's just had backstage in between her teeth.)

BROWN: Oh.

(BROWN springs into action singing outro tune.)

BROWN: Welcome back to the third segment of the show.

ISAAC: *(Mouthing to BROWN.)* We have already done that part.

BROWN: *(Mouthing to ISAAC, enjoying that he is drunk.)* You have done it and you are wasted.

ISAAC: *(Mouthing back to BROWN.)* Sobered up.

BROWN: *(Mouthing to ISAAC.)* You are wasted.

ISAAC: *(Mouthing back to BROWN.)* I am sober. *(Back to audience.)* Now I know you have been following me for 7 years, yada yada, but I never intended to be in that high position.

BROWN: What position is that? On top of a bar stool.

ISAAC: Everyone knows that I do not like to sit up so high it makes me nauseous. And it is not right to put a drinking person up so high.

BROWN: *(Sarcastic.)* What a sound judgment.

ISAAC: *(Imitating BROWN'S line from earlier.)* "All judgments are good judgments if you ask me."

BROWN: *(Imitating ISAAC'S line from earlier.)* "I didn't ask."

ISAAC: Let's just get back to the show shall we.

BROWN: Yes, let's see what we've learnt today.

ISAAC: Yes, let's see what cases made their way all the way here.

BROWN: Yes, yes, thanks for repeating me eh.

ISAAC: Eh.

BROWN: Eh eh eh.

ISAAC: Ehhhhh.

BROWN: Eh. Eh.

ISAAC: *(Pause.)*

BROWN: Eh.

ISAAC: *(Pause.)*

BROWN: Eh. *(Pause.)* Eh.

ISAAC: How much longer?

BROWN: Are you ready that is?

ISAAC: *(Imitating BROWN'S line from earlier.)* "I'm always on, ask yourself." *(Both ISAAC and BROWN look to TV PRODUCER offstage nudging them to get back to the monitor and focus on the show.)*

BROWN: *(Frustrated, looking to cameraman.)* OK well. *(Looks to teleprompter, realizes its empty . . . improvises.)* So, what did we catch today?

ISAAC: To check how old someone is before you bring them onstage? Sharp sharp breasts or otherwise.

BROWN: / To stop swearing.

ISAAC: /To stop belittling.

BROWN: /To stop give give giving mindless handouts,

money,

advice,

shots,

otherwise.

ISAAC: /To offer a helping hand, if you've been dealt a stronger one,

money,

advice,

shots,

or otherwise.

BROWN: /Some drunkards never change their ways.

ISAAC: /And some cloudy skies will never cry rain.

(TV PRODUCER hurriedly directs BAND to start playing outro music.)

BROWN: *(Overlap.)* We'll see you next time. Bring your issues to us. Instead of the blind leading the blind.

ISAAC: /Or the wise.

BROWN: /Eh?

(Both turn to side stage—implied producer offstage who's nudging them once again.)

Like I was saying.

ISAAC: *(To BROWN.)* You want the show? Have it. Have you not even been slightly affected by Boy?

BROWN: He's such a sweet young boy.

ISAAC: Brown?

BROWN: He is-

ISAAC: -Well, I do not want to see another Abbo-

BROWN: -You will not. And here you are, back to your usual, interrupting me again.

ISAAC: I *(dragged out I)* am a changed man.

BROWN: That's what all men say.

ISAAC: I am.

BROWN: Instead of this—*(Mouths.)*—drunken—*(Back to normal.)*—host, let's just bring Abbo and Boy shall we before you start again with your speech. *(Mouthing to ISAAC.)* You do love your speeches.

ISAAC: *(To audience.)* We don't need to bring them onstage again, we've already heard enough.

BROWN: *(To audience.)* Welcome Abbo and–

ISAAC: *(To audience.)* Time to end the show. Goodbye Abbo and—*(To BROWN.)* Brown Dear—

BROWN: Eh.

ISAAC: Eh. You want the show? Here, have it.

BROWN: Eh eh.

ISAAC: EH. I'm done with this show.

BROWN: Eh eh eh.

(ISAAC starts walking from stage past audience towards exit door, stops to

say the following line then continues walking towards the door.)
ISAAC: I can still hear you you know.
BROWN: Eh eh eh eh eh.
(ISAAC exits.)
(Off stage: Cut.)
(BROWN exits.)
(Final audience judgment signage is presented as surtitles or lighting: "This show will no longer be aired due to breaching Ugandan national broadcasting guidelines and for featuring underage unaccompanied minors, drinking, profanity, amongst a host of other issues.")
(Blackout.)

The author reserves all translation, serialization, and dramatization rights. Requests for any of these rights should be addressed to Alaa Taha at alaaplaywright@gmail.com, instagram.com/alaasdiary.

Ethiopian playwright Meaza Worku, author of *Desperate to Fight*.

Desperate to Fight

Meaza Worku

Meaza Worku, Ethiopian dramatist born in 1978, is best known for her drama writing for stage, radio, television, and comic books with the main focuses on justice, humanity, and environment. She studied Theatre Arts at Addis Ababa University (2000) and received her diploma in "Intercultural Adult Pedagogy" from Sweden University of West (2006). Meaza went on to launch a career in acting and directing. *Aquarachu (The Short Cut,* 2002) was her directorial debut, here a mini-serial television drama followed by *Yekirbruk* (*Short-sighted*, 2003), her first television play as author. She also worked as a radio journalist and entertainment program producer. In her career, she has written more than 20 short radio plays.

Zinegnochu /Celebrities (2012), Meaza's first theater play, was staged at the Addis Ababa Culture & Theatre Hall in 2012. In 2011, she wrote her second play (her first play in English), *Desperate to Fight,* which was selected for development by the Sundance Institute East Africa, an initiative of the Sundance Institute Theatre Program. The play was read at the Theatre Lab venue on Manda Island, Kenya (2011) and at New York's Baryshnikov Arts Center (2012). *Desperate to Fight* was also selected for the WPIC (Women Playwrights' International Conference), held in Stockholm (August 2012). The play was performed at the Kwani? Litfest in Nairobi in December 2012, as well as at the Ubumuntu Arts Festival in Kigali, Rwanda (June 2015). The Rwandan production was first staged at the Uganda National Theatre as part of the Kampala International Theatre Festival (November 2014), and then in Bujumbura, Burundi (March 2016). *Desperate to Fight* is translated into Amharic by the playwright herself, and it has been produced and staged in Addis Ababa in unconventional theater spaces for more than two years. *Desperate to Fight* was also translated into German by theatralize.company, as well as in Arabic, published by the Egyptian Culture Minister for the 29th

Cairo International Festival for Contemporary and Experimental Theater (September 2022). Meaza's latest staged play, *Shakespeare Is Ethiopian*, premiered in Addis Ababa at the Grand Celebration of Ethiopian Modern Theater Centenary (2020).

Meaza Worku's short plays on climate change, *Cross Roads* (2017) and *By the River* (2019) for Climate Change Theatre Action have also been performed, translated, and published. *By the River* appears in *Lighting the Way: An Anthology of Short Plays about the Climate Crisis* (2020), which was subsequently translated into Italian by Emilia Romagna Teatro Fondazione for "Planet B Project," and staged in Cesena, Bologna, and Modena, Italy in 2021.

In Ethiopia, Meaza Worku is best known for her radio and television serial drama writing and directing. She also writes comic books. A 44-episode television serial *Derso Mels* (Round Trip) was voted by viewers as the best television drama in 2010. Her other creative works include *Alehu* (*I am Here*), a 16-episode television anthology drama (2012); and multiple radio series, which she wrote and directed (commissioned by Johns Hopkins Center for Communication Programs, John Snow, Inc., and/or BBC Media Action), including *Alga balga* (*Easy*, 34 episodes, 2009); *Hiwot Mesenado* (24 episodes, 2010); *Wefe komech* (*The First Walk*, 40 episodes, 2015); *Sefere Tsidu* (26 episodes, 2016); *Erkab* (24 episodes, 2018), and *Nigat* (*Dawn*, 12 episodes, 2022).

Meaza worked as the Program Director for the *Crossing Boundaries International Performing Arts Festival and Conference* (Addis Ababa, 2015) and organized the first and the second edition of Ethiopian Human Rights Film Festival (2021, 2022). She's the founder and manager of Meaza Film Production and Arts Consultancy. She is also founding member and Board Chair of Sile-Theater Theater Society, an arts movement founded during the Covid-19 pandemic, dedicated to lifting theater both during and after the pandemic. It continues as a civil society organization that works through the performing arts as agents of peace, reconciliation, humanity, as well as the cultivation of youth talent.

Meaza is active on Facebook, Instagram, X Space, Twitter, and YouTube. She can also be reached via email at lemeazaworku@gmail.com and website www.siletheater.com

An interview with Meaza Worku is available at https://doi.org/10.3998/mpub.12827650.cmp.11.

[*Editors' Note*: Final arrangements having been delayed by complications from Covid-19, the publication here of *Desperate to Fight* was to have been Meaza Worku's first play script published in English. Rather, it is the short play, *By the River* (2020), as cited in her biography. *Desperate to Fight* is Meaza's second play to be published in English.]

MEAZA WORKU ON *DESPERATE TO FIGHT*:

Desperate to Fight is a paradoxical story of love, relationships, and marriage. It forces each of us to question the ground on which we stand. Through the lens of uniquely women's stories, I try, here, to reflect upon an individual's behavior, interpersonal relationships, and social norms, within the political context of my home country, Ethiopia. Yet, it is an uncommon story due to the woman's insistence upon her own decision-making in her life. Her voice says NO and liberates a soul from any form of oppressions and norms.

Desperate to Fight was conceived as a sign of an independent theater maker's rebellion against the conventional, male-dominated, state-controlled and corrupt art system. The play was created to showcase that theater can happen in unconventional alternative spaces and still impact the art scene and its audience. When reading my play, please also consider that marriage is institutionalized as a singular opportunity, or chance, in a woman's lifetime. It's highly unusual for an Ethiopian woman to have multiple divorces and still to be treated as "normal"—that is, not to be stigmatized, not to be judged, and not to be valued as "less than" other human beings.

210   SPEAKING OUR SELVES

Desperate to Fight
Meaza Worku

CHARACTERS
Marta: An independent, working, single woman between ages 35–40.
Shibiru: A 30-year-old aggressive and emotional man.
Yohannis: A gentle man in his early thirties; a reserved and cold person.
Million: A 47-year-old, well organized and strict man.
All male roles can be played by one actor.
Place: A condominium house in the city of Addis Ababa.
Time: The present.
(Evening. MARTA'S studio apartment. Everything is there, i.e., bed, a dressing table very near to a bed, the kitchen and small chairs; typical Ethiopian single lady's home, tidy and everything is under control. The only messy thing in the room seems to be the woman's hair. She is sitting in front of the dressing table mirror, very depressed and annoyed. She is in a bathrobe and barefoot, but in the course of the play, she will dress to go out.)

MARTA: *(Hurriedly stands and goes to the nearest wall and listens.)* Can you hear them? Can't you hear them? Come on? An old deaf man can hear them from 10 km away. I am not sure if this condominium is made out of stone or paper. You know what?—It is like sitting in bus with your neighbors. You can feel their breath. And they can hear you thinking. It is always like this. I can hear them kissing, touching each other, making love—and I wonder if they can hear me thinking. Everything is transparent. Transparent as water!
(Irritated. She gets back to her seat.)
MARTA: Transparent and visible as—as seeing yourself in the mirror— alone, single, divorced, aged—Oh! I hate them!!
(Walks from one side of the room to the other.)
MARTA: My neighbors—they are noisy as hell!! I don't know about hell, but I know whatever they do is loud as hell, and it is driving me crazy! They are loud when they eat, they are loud when they talk, and they are loud when they pee—all the furniture they have has a squeaking sound— they are even loud when they love each other.—You hear? They have started it already. That is how it is! It sounds like an argument. I don't know why but it starts when she stops talking to him—he begs, begs and begs. Then she continues to blame him and he carries on begging. She warns him not to touch her, he begs, she provokes him—he begs, she

cries—he begs. He always begs. They are always like this. The nagging and the begging activity slowly grow, and grow and—ends up with their stupid squeaking bed sound. After that, all I can hear is their noisy bed and her begging. I don't understand them. I don't understand myself! But I understand there is a little, little devil in me who pushes me to pray for this couple to fight for real. Yes! I want them to slap and knock each other's head off, scream, throw things at each other, smash that earsplitting bed, and blow up this building.

(She hits, pushes, throws things around in her tidy room. The room gets messy. She finally feels relieved and lies down on her bed.)

MARTA: Yeeeeeees! I want this world to blooooooooooow up and to change into small ashes! And from that particular ash I want my man to grow as fresh as I always dream. The man I can stick to—to the end of my life, as every woman can be able to attach their body and soul with the same, same, same one man to her entire womanhood. Like my neighbor.—I want to get wedded to that newly ash- grown man. I want to get married again—for the fourth time!

(MARTA gets up from the bed goes to the dressing table to organize herself, to comb her hair and so on.)

(Mimicking her mother.)

"Listen to me Marta! You are not a child anymore! Three divorces are not an honor for woman. People are talking about you! They say you are 'allergic' to marriage, relationship, men—whatever is normal. You better get a husband and start thinking about children and settling down. You have to prove them wrong."

Whenever my mama said that to me, my answer was "NO." But this time I said

"Oh! That is a blessed idea, will you pleeeeeeeeeeese find me one?"

"What? A husband? Are you serious? Would you really accept a husband who I will bring for you?"

"Why not? I brought myself three headaches and it didn't work out. Let's give it a try."

"There is nothing to try. After all, you are not Elizabeth Taylor. Do you know Elizabeth Taylor got married and divorced eight times?"

"I can't see a problem with marrying and divorcing eight men. If she can love them she can definitely hate them.—If she can marry them she can definitely divorce them. Who is this Elizabeth by the way?"

"Marriage is a serious and continuous relationship! It is not a bus stop where you can get on and off whenever you want to."

I knew my mother wouldn't let me go until I say: "I surrender!" So, I let her search a lifetime husband for me. After all I am tired of searching. I have searched three times and found three men whom I was blindly in love with. My problem is—my problem, as much as I can love them madly I can also hate them extremely. Like the bus stop—I have reached my destination so fast. With men? Oh! I reach the end very quick. I can't wait lifelong. I love them for real. I hate them for real. When I hate, I fight. A real fight! Not the calculated fight like my neighbors have had which usually ends up with love and bed squeaking. When I fight, I fight to the end of the world—to divorce!

(She puts on some lipstick.)

My mother is a very desperate woman. After we had that discussion on the searching of my new husband, yesterday she called me to announce that she found the perfect man.

"Perfect?"

"Yes! I have a background check on this man. He is rich."

"He is a father of six children from two marriages."

"Rich eh?"

"Have No worry! Both of the mothers of his children are dead. The children are grown-ups. The most interesting part is that—all the children are male."

"So who do you want me to marry the children or the father?"

"Of course the father! It is your fourth marriage for God's sake? There is nothing to choose."

"Well—thank you for helping me find my perfect man, mama—let me think about it."

"What is there to think about?—My daughter, remember this is your last chance. Time is not as plenty as men. This is your last night to think. This man is doing you a favor Marta, do yourself a favor and meet him."

(She puts her dress in order.)

MARTA: So this is my last night to think! The father of six will be waiting for me at 8:00 o'clock.

(She goes to the window and gazes and abruptly starts to talk.)

MARTA—Are you kidding me a father of six? *(Laughs.)* Hahahahahahahah—marry a father of six boys? And live together with seven boys?—Oh! The earth will have to smash into hell first—a two times widower? The world must change into ash before that could practically happen to Marta—and perhaps this building must blow up. *(Pause.)* At the very least, this stupid couple must fight a real fight like World War II.

(SHIBIRU appears in a light.)

MARTA: Shibiru! *(She looks at the audience and says)* My first husband.

(Time shift: This is a memory scene.)

SHIBIRU: *(Suspicious and drunk.)* Where have you been?

MARTA: I should ask you the same question! Shibiru, you come home late at mid-night and you ask me where I have been? I have been here the whole day and night waiting for you. Where have you been?—Do you want something to eat?

SHIBIRU: Don't change the subject! You just came in. Didn't you?—Just few minutes before I did.

MARTA: Please don't start!

SHIBIRU: Tell me! Did you go to that son of a bitch? Did you tell him that you miss him?

MARTA: Who?

SHIBIRU: Your first choice?

MARTA: *(Exasperated.)* My first choice?

SHIBIRU: Come on! You told me that I was not your first choice.

MARTA: I have already got married to you. Does it really matter?

SHIBIRU: Yes! It matters! It matters when the woman you love—the woman you call your wife tells you, You are not her first choice. It hurts!

MARTA: I chose to marry you.

SHIBIRU: But I was not the first choice.

MARTA: It doesn't matter to me.

SHIBIRU: Do not keep telling me that. It matters to me.

MARTA: What do you want me to do then?

SHIBIRU: Nothing!

MARTA: Thank you! Can I bring the dinner now?

SHIBIRU: I have already eaten and drunk.

MARTA: I can see that you're drunk.

SHIBIRU: I drank because I am angry at your first choice.

MARTA: You can drink in the name of all men in the world. But don't blame me that I have something to do with them.

SHIBIRU: You have something to do with your first choice.

MARTA: Yes! He was my first boyfriend.

SHIBIRU: You see? You still think he is the first.

MARTA: Because that is the truth.

SHIBIRU: Tell me one true thing.

MARTA: What?

SHIBIRU: Do you still love him?

MARTA: I know my answer will give you a very good reason to drink for the coming hundred years. Forget my first choice! He is married. Just go to your bed!

SHIBIRU: How do you know he is married?

MARTA: I heard. He got married three weeks ago.

SHIBIRU: Who told you?

MARTA: That also matters eh?

SHIBIRU: When did you see him last?

MARTA: When we got separated, two years ago.

SHIBIRU: Then how do you know he got married?

MARTA: I know.

SHIBIRU: How the hell do you know, if you are not seeing him? Or are you asking people around how he is doing?

MARTA: No! He sent me an invitation card.

SHIBIRU: Why?

MARTA: To ask me to attend.

SHIBIRU: And?

MARTA: I did not go?

SHIBIRU: Why?

MARTA: Why? Because I cannot stand seeing him getting married.

SHIBIRU: You see?—You still have feelings for him.

MARTA: I don't know.

SHIBIRU: Of course you know! I want to know.

MARTA: I can't tell you more. The more you know the more you go jealous. The more you get jealous, the more I get headaches.

SHIBIRU: I am not jealous.

MARTA: Then why do you insist to know?

SHIBIRU: Because—because I think communication is important for our marriage. Transparency is important.

MARTA: Transparency is what puts me in to an interrogation. If I kept my mouth shut, I could have saved energy. Or should I tell you a lie?

SHIBIRU: Transparency is truth.

MARTA: Truth is that—You are not my first choice.

SHIBIRU: Do you also know where he lives?

MARTA: Who?

SHIBIRU: Your first choice for God's sake.

MARTA: You can find his address on the invitation card.

SHIBIRU: Give me the card!

MARTA: I threw it away.

SHIBIRU: Where did you throw it?

MARTA: In the garbage bin. Why?

SHIBIRU: I will go and visit him.

MARTA: What? Are you going to fight?

SHIBIRU: Why should I fight? I don't need to fight as long as he is honest with me. But I am going just to ask him.

MARTA: Ask him what?

SHIBIRU: I will ask his name.

MARTA: I told you a hundred times his name is Yohannis!

SHIBIRU: Don't say his name!!

MARTA: This is the end of our discussion and your visit plan.

SHIBIRU: Are you his first choice too? That is what I want to know.

MARTA: What if I am?

SHIBIRU: Then why would he marry that woman?

MARTA: For the same reason I married you.

SHIBIRU: And why in the name of St. Marriage was that?

MARTA: I am sick and tired of your suspicions. How long do we have to live like this?

SHIBIRU: A hundred and a thousand questions are out there, hanging on the air. All my questions must get answers before I go to bed. I can't go to sleep uncertain.

MARTA: Then I will write an FAQ for you.

SHIBIRU: Who is he?

MARTA: FAQ? *(Laughs.)* You can find frequently asked questions about me in every discussion we have had for the last one and half years.

SHIBIRU: I don't understand.

MARTA: *(Furiously.)* And I don't understand you!—You are not that sweet and cheerful Shibiru anymore. What happened to you? Oh! I am lost—Good night. *(She goes to her bed and he walks towards the door.)* What are you doing? Where do you think you are going?

SHIBIRU: To that garbage bin.

MARTA: Are you out of your mind?—My first choice is in the middle of his honeymoon sleep and I am in the middle of my nightmare! *(SHIBIRU vanishes.)* Ohhhh!

(She walks to the dressing table and starts to talk.)

MARTA: Life with Shibiru was an example of torment. Living with him was like living in World War II. He was always in ambush. I couldn't stand it any longer. I threw Shibiru out of my life. Divorce! What a relief! Ohffffff!

(Returns to the dressing table to fix her hair, then, she gets up and curiously walks to the wall and listens.)

MARTA: Did she say it is over? I wish it was true, she has said it a thousand times. She is a liar. She just wants him to beg. She knows he will. I know he will. She has to complain first and pretend that she will leave him, and then he will beg. That is the calculation.

(She gets back from the wall and continues to narrate.)

MARTA: Any ways, after I got separated with Shibiru, I made up with Yohannis.— Yohannis was a very handsome man, the man I once dearly, madly and blindly loved. We had broken up after I got married. Actually, I got married to make him angry. And he was the one and main reason for my first divorce and he owed me. After Shibiru he and I made up. His marriage had not gone well either. He was alone and I was alone. After all we were each other's first choice. I proposed to him. Can you believe this? I didn't tell this to anyone, but I did. I convinced him to marry me.—Let me put it this way—I begged him to marry me. Surprisingly, he said "OKay!" He was sad that his wife left him; he needed someone to comfort him. "OKay!" "OKay?" "OKaaaaay!" Elellelelelellelele! We got married! He became my second husband. My first choice, but my second husband.

(*YOHANNIS appears. A memory scene:*)

MARTA: Are you not going to kiss me hello?

YOHANNIS: I am tired.

MARTA: Are you too tired to kiss?

YOHANNIS: I am tired of everything.

MARTA: Tired of everything? Did you have a long day?

YOHANNIS: It was not my day. It is my life I am concerned about.

MARTA: What about your life?

YOHANNIS: I want to end it.

MARTA: What? You want to end it? You want to end your life?

YOHANNIS: No! It is not my life I want to end.

MARTA: I don't understand what you—

YOHANNIS: It is us.

MARTA: Us?

YOHANNIS: Yes! We need to end this . . . this . . . What we call marriage.

MARTA: You mean . . .

YOHANNIS: I have a confession to make.

MARTA: Confession?

YOHANNIS: Okay—Forget the confession, I want a divorce.

MARTA: Why?

YOHANNIS: You will get mad if I tell you the truth.

MARTA: I won't get mad. Tell me the truth! Is there another woman? Are you going back to your ex-wife?

YOHANNIS: No!

MARTA: Then why do you want to leave me?

YOHANNIS: I don't want to leave you. I just don't want to be married to you.

MARTA: Why? What did I do to you?

YOHANNIS: I don't love you Marta.

MARTA: You don't—what?

DESPERATE TO FIGHT **217**

YOHANNIS: I don't even like you.

MARTA: You don't like me?

YOHANNIS:—No.

MARTA: Not even a little?

YOHANNIS: No.

MARTA: Have you tried your best?

YOHANNIS: Yes! But I can't. Before I got you I practically worshipped you. But the woman I saw in the hands of another man isn't the one I see here before me now.

MARTA: I don't even know why I married you. You depress me. You are as cold as the stone which spent the night outside.

YOHANNIS: Then go. I'm not stopping you. There are lots of stay-at-home stones out there and you're free.

MARTA: Fine. I'll go. But you'll regret this. You'll never have a chance to be with someone like me ever again.

YOHANNIS: We will see.

MARTA: *(Breaks down crying.)* You're the wicked one now. How can you be so hurtful?

YOHANNIS: You think I was not hurt when you married another man?

MARTA: Is this supposed to be payback? Is that why you said "okay" to marry me? Revenge?

YOHANNIS: You know I am not that type of person. I did forgive you, but I do not forget that you left me for another man.

MARTA: What? You forgive but not forget? What type of person does that make you look like?

YOHANNIS: Loving, caring, forgiving—

MARTA: And heart breaking! Ohahahaha *(she cries out)* . . .

YOHANNIS: *(Trying not to give in.)* Those fake or real tears?

MARTA: What do you care?

YOHANNIS: I'm sorry. Please, don't be mad. I'm just trying to help.

MARTA: The best way to help me is to leave me alone.

YOHANNIS: Fine, Marta forgive me for trying to be nice.

MARTA: "Nice?" Is that your definition of nice? Rejecting me? Telling me I'm a traitor?

YOHANNIS: That's not what I'm saying.

MARTA: Then what are you saying?

YOHANNIS: I am saying that you can find someone who likes you better.

MARTA: What if no one likes me that way?

YOHANNIS: Don't be Sorry. I believe we all have someone waiting for us.

MARTA: I hope you're right.

218   SPEAKING OUR SELVES

YOHANNIS: I know I'm right.

MARTA: Yohannis? Are you sure you couldn't be that someone?

YOHANNIS: I don't know, Marta. Let's give it some time. Right now, I'm
tired, hungry, and confused.

MARTA: Would you like something to eat?

YOHANNIS: If it is okay with you.

MARTA: What would you like to eat?

YOHANNIS: Can I have my last bowl of porridge? I love it when you do it.

MARTA: *(Burst into tears.)* Hahahahahaha!

YOHANNIS: What? Did I say something bad?

MARTA: No!

YOHANNIS: Then why are you crying? Please stop!

MARTA: Would you like me to stop crying?

YOHANNIS: Yes! Of course.

MARTA: Can I get a hug?

YOHANNIS: Of course! Why not? You still are my wife. One last goodbye
hug!

(He hugs her warmly.)

MARTA: *(Still hugging.)* Is it okay if I look you up sometime?

YOHANNIS: I don't know. I don't know anything right now. But one thing's
for sure.

MARTA: *(Still in an embrace.)* What is that Yohannis?

YOHANNIS: You can keep the house.

MARTA: The house? This is my uncle's house? *(Slowly releases him and goes
to the door and opens it.)* Please leave!

YOHANNIS: What about my porridge?

MARTA: Out!

YOHANNIS: I will come tomorrow. To discuss the divorce!

(He tries to give a goodbye kiss, but she refuses.
Marta forcefully closes the door and sits on the bed.)

MARTA: That is how my second marriage ended. I was ashamed to have two
divorces and I thought I would die without Yohannis, but I moved on.
Moved on and kept living in this same house with this noisy couple.
(She goes to the wall and listens; we hear the woman next door crying.)
Why is he quiet today? When she cries he always begs, that's how it's
supposed to work. Yes—She keeps on crying—And he—he—wait a
minute! No! He is not home. She is crying, but I can't hear him. Did he
leave her? No! He was home a few minutes ago. Why is he silent? I hate
it when men go silent. Something is not normal when men shut up! He

DESPERATE TO FIGHT   219

has to speak! He has to beg before she starts to cry. He must say something. There must be something—something—a word or two—an utter.
(Gets back from the wall and thinks.)

MARTA: When I asked Yohannis to say something, he said it all. He said he had never loved me. He said he could not forget the past. So, the best I could do was to let him live with his past. After that—he kept on recalling his past and I kept on marrying. I was 30. I could not live single, divorced or widowed—there must be someone in my life. I met that someone. I married that someone because he was better than my two ex-husbands. He did not care about my past. My ex-husbands could live neither today nor the future. On the contrary my third husband could not live the past. I thought he was a very visionary man.

(MILLION gets into the house and sits on the chair surrounded by pieces of paper.)

MILLION: Okay! Think, think, and think. There must be something else you bought.

MARTA: No Million.

MILLION: I gave you a ten thousand birr and you brought me an 8000 and 530 birr and 80 cents receipt.[1] Something is missing here.

MARTA: Yes! I think I bought something and forgot to ask for a receipt.

MILLION: Most shops have a cash register machine. You agreed to shop from those stores. It is very important that we get receipts honey. Otherwise we go bankrupt.

MARTA: I don't really remember where and why—

MILLION: You should remember. Relax now, honey—think!—Think of the cosmetics shops that you went through.

MARTA: I didn't go to the cosmetics shop today. I went straight to the supermarket and bought some food.

MILLION: Where did you go after that?

MARTA: I took a taxi and came home directly.

MILLION: We agreed to use buses. Okay—good. You took a taxi and paid for your transportation—are you sure you got your balance?

MARTA: I did not pay. I came with our neighbor Meseret. She paid for all of us.

MILLION: That is very good. Then where did you spend the one thousand 460 birr and 20 cents?

MARTA: I don't know Million.

---

1. The birr is the basic monetary unit in Ethiopia.

MILLION: You must know! I could have shopped myself, if I knew you are unable to manage your finances correctly. We should set up a proper bookkeeping system in this house.

MARTA: Everything is getting expensive. Maybe that is why—

MILLION: The receipt does not show you've paid extra, but lost money honey.

MARTA: All I know is—I spent all the money on food.

MILLION: We are only two, honey. We cannot eat more than ten-thousand-birr worth of food in a month.

MARTA: Why not?

MILLION: Why not? Because that is what we planned. That is why. And it is all in the paper.

MARTA: What if we eat thousands? What if we eat millions? What if we eat you!?

MILLION: Calm down honey! We can eat the whole world in the future, but for the time being we cannot afford to spend more than ten thousand birr for something that only changes into waste.

MARTA: Everything is a waste. You are a waste of my time.

MILLION: Easy Mar! You are getting edgy honey. Let us calm down first—take a deep breath!

MARTA: Ohffffffffffffffff!

MILLION: Ohffffffffff!—very good!—Now we can discuss everything like grown-ups. I know the topic of money makes you crazy, but can you at least try? Just think of the future.

MARTA: How?

MILLION: I know you are fond of spending money on useless luxuries. It's okay. That is a human's feeble nature. I am here to help. I am coaching you to concentrate on your affordable needs. I have to cleanse you with the spirit of prioritizing. You can call it saving.

MARTA: I call it torture!

MILLION: Come on! A little bit sacrifice won't hurt. You deserve better than this entire artificial world honey.

MARTA: Money is artificial!

MILLION: But it can buy you non-artificial things.

MARTA: For instance?

MILLION: For instance? Hmmmm—land, people—I mean you can buy human resources.

MARTA: You can buy the universe, but don't ask me for the receipt. I don't have the receipts; I don't have the money! So what? What do you want me to do? Hang myself!?

MILLION: I need a financial report on your shopping!

MARTA: What is this? An accountant's office or something? All I bought was a stupid wall clock and I am sentenced to inspection death. Get off Million!

MILLION: You bought a wall clock?

MARTA: Yes! You see that on that wall?

MILLION: Why? Was it in our plan?

MARTA: NO! And I don't care.

MILLION: You should have told me earlier. All our discussion was a waste of time. Time is money for God's sake! How many times should I have to tell you that Marta?

MARTA: You told me money is everything a million times.

MILLION: Do we really need that clock?

MARTA: Yes!

MILLION: Why?

MARTA: Because it is that clock which tells me time is up.

MILLION: What time?

MARTA: The time to break-up!

MILLION: Which break-up is this? Is it in our plan?

MARTA: I can't take this anymore Million. I want a divorce!

MILLION: How much will it cost?—Think twice before you mention things like that. It may backfire on you.

MARTA: Why?

MILLION: Because you won't get a penny out of me. I know you like to earn a living by divorcing.

MARTA: What?

MILLION: Last time you got a house. Now you want my money?

MARTA: I want you and your money out of my life!

MILLION: Don't say I didn't warn you!

MARTA: Don't say I didn't warn you!!

MILLION: Think about it, Marta! Getting a divorce is costly these days. How can you pay for a lawyer? You spent all your money on a wall clock.

MARTA: (Screaming at him.) Out!

MILLION: (Stands and walks towards the door.) I will still need the receipt for the wall clock by the way.

(He goes out.)

MARTA: "May God give you a husband who does not know mathematics" was one of my grandmother's blessings. His name was Million because his parents wanted to see him a millionaire. And he worked very hard to meet his parents' dream. He made me believe that we will have a bright future together. I admired him for that. I admired when he convinced me that a marriage ceremony is nothing but a waste of resource. I admired him when he persuaded me that children are nothing but a waste of money. So, I agreed not to have a child until the right time would come. I waited two years. God knows how long I can still wait. I am 35. Even the new wall clock does not work forever.

(MARTA goes to the wall and listens. The woman is crying.)

MARTA: Is she still crying? He is so cruel. Shouldn't he at least console her as he used to do? Will you please beg her? She has never cried this long. *(A loud crash.)* Wow! They broke something. It was ear piercing! Horrible! I think they are in a real fight! Sometimes it is good to fight for real! *(Another crash is heard, and she covers her ear.)* Wow! What was that? What an earthquake! It feels like they blew up the building!—I think this time it is for real. I should call my mama.

(She puts on her shoes hurriedly, picks up her cell phone, and calls while reacting to the disturbing sound coming from next door.)

MARTA: Hi Mama! *(Slap and scream from next door.)* Ouch!—He is going to kill her! —What? Yes, I am okay! I know it is late. Did I wake you up?—There is a war here—The third world war maybe. I think we have reached Judgment Day. I am not asleep—I said I am okay Mama! *(Another slap.)* I think so—it is my neighbors.

(The fighting grows more violent.)

MARTA: Oh! They are fighting. I think he is beating her. *(A woman's cry.)*—Yes! She is screaming. Can you hear? *(Scream.)* No! I did not call to tell you this—I called to ask you something—Is the man still available?—The man with two dead wives. Mama—Yes! The widower. The man you said has six sons. You gave me an assignment to meet him, remember?—Yes! I am ready—Yes of course! I will marry him—I am serious. I will marry him—But on two conditions—Yes! First, I want you to check on him—Check how his wives died. Was it a natural death or suspicious?—Yes! I am going to live with him Mama. I am going to stay under the same roof and sleep in the same bed with him. *(The husband yells.)* I am not asking you to psychoanalyze the man. It is just a simple investigation. Is he a lover or a killer? I should know that—Oh My God! He is going to kill her. She is screaming like hell—Which second condition? Okay! Yes—Is he willing to have another child?—Of course I want to have a child. Please Mama! Ask him and let me know. I don't care if the marriage does work or not. But I have to gain something out of it this time—Yes! Yes! Yes!—She is calling for help!—Call me after you check this Mama—I can't talk to you right now! I have to extinguish the fire!—Call you. Love you.

(She runs out of the house.)

THE END

The author reserves all translation, serialization, and dramatization rights. Requests for any of these rights should be addressed to Meaza Worku at lemeazaworku@gmail.com.

Beninese playwright Nathalie Hounvo Yekpe, author of *Course Aux Noces*.

Course Aux Noces

Nathalie Hounvo Yekpe

Bidossessi Nathalie Hounvo Yekpe is a Beninese author, actress, and director. She studied acting and directing and obtained a professional degree in theater at the International Theater School of Benin (EITB) in Cotonou. As actress, Hounvo Yekpe has performed in Benin in numerous Francophone African plays as well as in French works and international classics. She has held roles, for example, in *Madame Paradji* by José Pliya, directed by Xavier Pinon (2004); in *Kondo, le Requin* [Kondo, the Shark] by Jean Pliya, directed by Tola Koukoui (2007–2017); in *Le Cid* by Pierre Corneille, directed by Isidore Dokpa (2008); in *Les Nègres* [The Blacks] by Jean Genet, directed by Emmanuel Daumas (2011); in *Black Beauty*, written and directed by Nina de la Chevalerie (2013); in *Wave* by Guillaume Poix, directed by Jean-Michel Coulon (2014); in *Africa Democratik Room*, written and directed by Bérangère Janelle (2016); in *Doguicimi* [Doguicimi, A Wife] by Paul Hazoumé, directed by Nicolas de Dravo (2017); in *25 Décembre* [December 25], written and directed by Didier Nassegande (2018); in *Dans l'ombre qui s'éclaire* [In the Lightening Shadow], written and directed by Sarah Mouline (2020); in *Shameless*, written and directed by Meïmouna Coffi (2020); in *Tassi Hangbé: la reine interdite* [Tassi Hangbé; The Forbidden Queen] by Florent Couao-Zotti, directed by Ousmane Aledji (2021); in *Faustine d'Agla: effet doppler* [Faustine from Agla: the Doppler Effect], written and directed by Hurcyle Gnonhoue (2022–2023); and in *La Maison de poupée* [*A Doll's House*] by Henrik Ibsen, directed by Tella Kpomahou (2022). She has also performed at international festivals, such as Les Nuits de Fourvière (Lyon, France); Made in Germany (Stuttgart, Germany); MASA (Abidjan, Côte d'Ivoire); FITHEB (Benin); The Improvisation Championship (Brussels, Quebec, Luxembourg); and PANAF (Algiers, Algeria).

As director, Hounvo Yekpe has successfully staged a number of Francophone African and French plays. She has also worked, often internationally, as assistant director. In Benin, she has staged *La Fuite* [The Flight] by Gao Xingjian in 2006; *Certifié Sincère* [Certified Sincere] by Florent Couao-Zotti in 2010; *L'Oeuf et la Poule* [The Egg and the Chicken] by Catherine Verlaguet in 2017; *Au paradis, les femmes ne pètent pas* [In Paradise, Women Don't Fart] by Michel Beretti in 2018; *Nous étions assis sur le rivage du monde* [We Were Sitting on the Shores of the World] by José Pliya in 2022; and, also in 2022, *Impulsion* by Faustine Noguès. She also assisted Djamel Abdelli in the staging of *Gogohoun* [The Rump Dance] in El Jadida, Morocco (2010); Patrice Toton in the staging of *Jenana*, a production of the International Theatre Festival of Benin (2012); Marielle Pinsard in the staging of *On va tout dallasser Pamela* [We'll Strut Our Stuff Like They Do on Dallas], at the Vidy-Lausanne Theatre in Switzerland (2016); and Alougbine Dine in the staging of *Renaissance* in Porto-Novo, Benin (2019–2020).

As writer, Hounvo Yekpe began by writing short stories, monologues, and a television series. In 2016, she co-wrote with Michel Beretti *Trop de diables sous leurs jupes* [Too Many Devils Under their Skirts] (Plurielles editions, 2016). In 2021, she was awarded a place in the Discoveries residency sponsored by The Francophone Program for New Theatrical Writing, a program that offers writing residencies especially to Francophone women in Limoges, France and mentors them as they fashion their theater work. It was during this residency that she wrote *Course aux noces* [The Race to Get Married], which launched her career in France. In 2022, the play was read as part of the Zébrures du Printemps Festival in Limoges and by the Radio France Internationale team during the Avignon festival. It was also featured as a reading at the Théâtre les 3T in Châtellerault, France. In October 2023, three different Beninese cultural centers produced readings of *The Race to Get Married* in preparation for a full production during the 2024–2025 season. Nathalie Hounvo Yekpe has also benefited from two residency programs in 2023, the first at the Comédie de Valence, France, during which she wrote her play *Plus être* [Being No More]. That same year, she wrote *Les faiseuses d'ange* [The Abortionists] at the CCRI [Centre Culturel de rencontre International] John Smith in Ouidah, Benin. In addition, she also gives theater workshops in Cotonou.

An interview with Nathalie Hounvo Yekpe is available at https://doi.org/10.3998/mpub.12827650.cmp.12.

NATHALIE HOUNVO YEKPE ON *COURSE AUX NOCES*:

In writing this piece, I placed a mirror before my society—a mirror, so that it questions itself. Through *Course Aux Noces* (translated by Judith G. Miller as *The Race to Get Married, 2024)*, I hope to draw people's attention to the pressure that African women are under in their relationship to men and society.

In my country, as we say in a popular proverb, "an unmarried woman is a field where the rain does not fall." She is the laughingstock of the neighborhood, the whole village, or even the entire municipality. She is called all kinds of names. The result is that all women look for the chance to fit into a home or even a semblance of home. They dream of love as portrayed in soap-opera or reality-TV love stories, never missing any episode programmed on both international and national television channels. These stories always end in church and with a luxury wedding. Yet, in reality, when a woman cannot catch the man who will offer her the wedding of her dreams, she must still sit under *some* man's roof—or risk lasting shame.

Traditionally, once in a man's home, the woman can, in fact, be the one who pays the rent at the end of each month. She is under the roof of a man. That is what counts. For women, only through "marriage" can they secure shelter, a social role, and a way to obtain a modicum of respect from others. It does not matter if the man in question is the husband of another woman. The main thing is that he has the power to recognize any given woman as his wife. A couple does not have to go in front of the mayor to legalize a marriage nor do they have to appear before God and men. One man, alone, is granted the power to claim his wife, his woman, as property—regardless of her own will and desires.

Yet, today, at the advent of the twenty-first century—under other skies—one of the fundamental freedoms for women is the freedom to decide whether or not to marry. In other countries, today's women have the social and legal authority, and the power, to decide their own relationship to marriage. A woman can now choose whether or not to be engaged, to become someone's wife, partner, or mother. She has choice.

Course Aux Noces

Nathalie Hounvo Yekpe

Translated from the French by Judith G. Miller as *The Race to Get Married*

(This text was developed in 2022 thanks to the residency program "Découvertes" of the Limoges-based Francophone Theater Festival.)

CHARACTERS

Baké: A woman who knows everything and controls everything.
Oya: A woman who knows nothing and controls nothing.
Madila: A woman who knows everything but controls nothing.
Koffi: The "victim."
Chorus of Neighborhood Gossips
Medical Personnel

SCENE 1

OYA: Every day, on the back of your neck, you feel other people looking at you. Behind your back, they whisper; they murmur. You turn around; you can touch it with your fingers. It grimaces. Laughter breaks out. You turn back; it's so close you can touch it. It shuts up. Other people enjoy doing this. They do it all the time. You, you walk on. You walk and they whisper. You walk and they murmur. You walk and they touch each other with the tips of their fingers. You walk and they make faces. You walk and they burst into laughter. You turn around and they shut up. They shut up when your sisters pass by. Your sisters are worried. Worried about what's being said. They are worried about you. The family is alarmed. The aunties are gossiping. The whole family is complaining. Uncles, aunts, cousins, chickens . . . They're saying, "She's 25 years old, and no fiancé." "She's 30 years old, and not married." "Thirty-five years old and still not married." "Forty years old, what a disgrace!" They organize prayer meetings. They pray to the good Lord to take pity on your soul and give you a man who'll keep you at his side from morning 'til night. You don't give a damn. You don't give a damn? You tell yourself you shouldn't pay attention to what's being said, about you, about your life. All bullshit! Deep inside, you hurt, you hurt a lot. But you keep the pain to yourself. You close your heart's ears so they can't hear what's being whispered around you, what's being murmured about you. But they hear, all the same. They hear and your heart aches; it aches a lot. The pores of your skin absorb the migrating whispers that rush into your tired heart like sperm when it spies an egg. Sometimes your eyes drip, run all by themselves. They can't deal with the "they say" of your heart. They say you're not desirable. They say you're not a feather-weight. They say you're not light enough. They say your charcoal color skin is like a patch of dirt. They say that. They say that every day. Do you hear it? What are you waiting for? Go shop. Go to Dantokpa Market or Adjamé Market. There you'll find the soaps specially made to clean away excessive pigmentation. That's what other women do, those whose brilliant skin intimidates even the sun. They wash it hard; they scrub it hard. Even if the elbows and the knees join the Black Lives Matter movement by refusing to get lighter, they scrub; they put make-up on. As much foundation as they can handle. But you refuse to wash; you refuse to scrub your skin; you only do what you want to. And so, you threw the scale into the garbage, because the needle kept going in the same direction, just like the hands on a watch. It doesn't matter that you follow a diet. A nutritionist prescribed a very expensive supermarket, the only one in the country that imports vegetables and fresh produce from elsewhere. Doctor Diet declared, "Our local dishes contain too much fat and don't work with the diet I've created specially to help you lose weight easily." You subscribed. Nothing changed. What? You've accepted it? You don't want to try to lose weight anymore? You don't care whether you're attractive or not? What? You accept yourself as you are? That's cute! Bravo! Is that why you chucked out all the mirrors in your apartment? That's why you don't allow yourself to be photo-graphed? On social media, you cite the words of a so-called strong woman: "Accept what is, let go of what was, and have confidence in what will be." You repeat it so often, the echo of your inner voice keeps sleep away from your eyes. No, it's not other people's whispering that keeps you from sleeping. But the space that whispering takes up in your life is so enormous, there's no place to sit down and listen to what your heart wants to say, to hear the murmur of your own desires.

Breathe!

(Sound of church bells.)

SONG: *(Like a lullaby.)*

This is my pretty baby.

Don't touch him; don't slap him, I beg you.

Whether he behaves or doesn't,

He's my baby.
Don't cry pretty baby.
Don't cry in the middle of the night.When you cry during the night,
    monsters steal your voice.
Don't cry, my own pretty baby.[1]

SCENE 2

*(The siren of an ambulance. We're in the street, at the entrance to a dwelling.
A crowd of women, men, and children is gathering.)*

CHORUS OF NEIGHBORHOOD GOSSIPS: May her soul rest in peace!
She isn't dead yet.
I swear to you she is.
How do you know?
I never said I knew.
But you swore.
You can swear without knowing.
So, you agree she's not dead.
No.
They say she's still breathing.
Look, she's moving her left hand.
You're saying just anything now. It's an EMT guy who's lifting her hand.
She's not moving.
Her case is critical. Not sure she'll make it.
How do you know?
I'm telling you what I see.
And just what do you see?
An ambulance.
I'm going to recite the prayer to the Virgin who Undoes Knots.
Do you think she was a virgin?
What do I know about it?
But then, why recite a prayer to the Virgin?
I said the Virgin who Undoes Knots. She's a saint I call on in difficult
    situations. That's all.
And she answers you?
Yes, of course.
That's nuts.
Why?

---

1. This first song is in Mina in the original text (a major language of Benin and Togo), translated into French by the author and into English in this version.

Hello?

A virgin who unties knots should worry about virgins, don't you think?

Is she a member of your family?

Who? The virgin?

No, the woman who wants to kill herself.

We're neighbors.

Can you give us the name of a close contact?

Her husband works at the Mayor's office.

Which Mayor's office?

What husband? She doesn't have a husband.

And the guy at the Mayor's office?

That's history.

He dumped her?

Yeah, I think so.

You think so, or you know so?

I don't know, but I believe it could be. That's enough, isn't it?

So, you don't know somebody close we can speak to?

Well, in any case, you never see anybody with her.

And you never see her with anybody either.

Like all the other people in that household. They never go out during the
day. Only at night.

Ah, so you think they work at night?

Who knows.

That's all lies. You're just making things up. What do you know?

We knocked on all the doors. There's nobody else in the house.

I think she has a sister. But I don't know her phone number.

I'm telling you she just got dumped. I'm sure of it. She must have been
desperate.

She's gutsy all the same. I couldn't have done it.

Well, she didn't do it either. She's still breathing.

How could you want to end your life when you're so young?

Well, if she'd really wanted to end her life, she should have jumped off the
bridge. It's simpler . . . and cheaper. Not very ecological, but efficient all
the same.

She could have used a gun. One second and bang!

Yeah, and that's classic. Dirty as well.

Not at all. It's pretty hip to see those stains, those explosions of blood on the
walls, like in the movies! And the policemen who go round and round
in those little rooms, like on T.V. . . . .

She isn't as young as all that.

232 SPEAKING OUR SELVES

Living alone must drive you crazy.

Especially when you're not so young anymore.

To the point of swallowing a whole bottle of meds?

Emptying a whole bottle in hopes it'll turn your stomach inside out isn't very creative.

What are you saying! Of course, it is. A visceral earthquake in your gallbladder and pancreatic tissue.

Genius, then!

Every time I want to commit suicide, I feel I should go to the Himalayas.

You want to kill yourself?

Every day that God made.

Do *you* want to kill yourself?

Yes!

And you?

Yes!

So, what are you waiting for?

I don't know how to find the Himalayas.

She's between life and death. God have pity on her. My God . . .

She's slipping away!

I hope God welcomes her into his holy home.

What nonsense!

Are you afraid?

Who? Me? What of?

That they'll arrest you.

Why?

Because of the drugs.

What? You've started up again?

What are you talking about?

Cut it out! Everybody knows you're selling contaminated drugs again.

Shut your big mouth!

Wow, you posted it on your Facebook page!

Already a ton of views and more than 200 shares.

"A Fatso kills herself in Houéyiho."[2] What a stupid title. Can't you find something better?

Are you kidding? It's the first time I've had a thousand views in less than an hour. The title is raking them in.

It's not cool to create a buzz around other people's misery.

---

2. Houéyiho refers to a recently developed section of Cotonou, the capital of Benin. In the Fon language, the name Houéyiho means "twilight," which signals a bad omen for Beninese people. In this part of the capital, luxurious villas are juxtaposed with improvised dwellings of people without means, who get by as they can.

Killjoy!

Dumb ass!

That'll teach her to try to steal other people's husbands.

That's not it. He broke her heart and then he married someone else.

Sounds normal. Who wants to put *that* under his roof?

All the girls born after her in this neighborhood are already out of the neighborhood and under some husband's roof.

Some of them already have children in high school.

If only she had a husband. He would've stopped her from doing what she did.

She doesn't have a husband. She doesn't have a husband. So what? It's not the end of the world.

Not the world. But the end of her life. And if not, what's the purpose of a dog who doesn't have a master?

How about wandering in the streets and eating shit off piles of garbage.

Hey, look!

What are they doing?

They're getting her to lie down on the stretcher and giving her some oxygen. They're attaching the safety strap. Someone's opening the ambulance doors. She's in the vehicle. The ambulance is taking off. You can hear the siren; you can see the top light circling, as though it were dizzy. The ambulance is making its way between houses and pedestrians. Now it's entering the interstate highway. The highway is packed with vehicles and motor bikes moving as slow as turtles. Stop! A family of giant snails is crossing the road. The ambulance surely doesn't want to squash them on the asphalt. It's scolding the cars and the motor bikes. Some of them give way when it passes. The others are in too much of a hurry. They don't want to give way. The ambulance is screaming even louder. Policemen at the Saint Michel Crossroads force the motor bikes and the vehicles to give way. The ambulance is heading towards the university hospital as fast as it can. Its tires are squealing on the blacktop. You can still hear the ambulance, but its lights have disappeared. It's arriving at the emergency entrance.

MEDICAL PERSONNEL: On three, we turn her on her side. One, two, three . . . We're losing her . . .

SCENE 3

OYA: Too late. Don't close now; it's not the right time. Should have done so when you couldn't tell a cat from its shadow. It's way too late now. What do you expect me to do when you refuse to cover my eyes? Huh? Am I

234 SPEAKING OUR SELVES

supposed to keep them open all night long? All night long I begged you. You did exactly what you wanted. I had to force you to shut. The pharmacist told me two pills . . . and two more if you didn't obey . . . So, it's exactly what I did! It's not my fault if you decided to act like crazies. Every time you resist, I take two. Two plus two plus two times two and two more . . . But now it's daylight, not the time to sleep. Come on, get up now. Quick! Get up, you lazybones! Day has chased the night away. Can't you hear me? Why don't you obey? How long do you intend to stay closed? What's that bell I'm hearing? No more sleep, no more peace. I have to get up. Where are my legs? I have to leave for work. I earn my living by the sweat of my brow. I'm no parasite, not me. Unlock, you dirty eyelids . . . Men love blow jobs. That's what they say. I don't do what they say. If I did, I'd have already self-destructed. But I'm not like that. Ask for taxi money the first time you go out? That's not my style. My phone, my braids, my underwear, my entertainment, my jewelry, my rent—I pay for everything myself. Take money for my family from him? Out of the question. I like my independence. What a load of bull, they say to me. They also say, the quicker he feels you depend on him, the quicker he'll put you under his roof, his protection. Man is a protector by nature; we should pretend to be his grateful dependents. What destroys a couple, they say, is not the *tchiza,* the other woman. No! What destroys a couple is when the wife stops thinking like a *tchiza* and doesn't wheedle any more money out of her husband. He feels useless, impotent. And no man can accept that. For a man, impotency is like joining the opposition to the government. The independent woman is a reflection of his own impotency. When face to face with her, he has to figure out how to set up barriers. A safe distance that gets bigger with time and ends up a border. A woman who doesn't want to belong to somebody finishes her life all alone, with eyelids that only obey pills. Shut up and sleep . . . No, get up! I said up! Up straight! It's day outside. You, shut up, old hag!

MEDICAL PERSONNEL: One, two, three . . . defibrillator . . . pulse . . .

SCENE 4
(BAKÉ and MADILA, OYA'S sisters, are pacing in the hospital corridor.)

MADILA: Do you think she's going to make it?
BAKÉ: We can't know for sure.
MADILA: But it's not the first time she's had her heart broken.
BAKÉ: It's the first time she's tried to kill herself.
MADILA: Which means?

COURSE AUX NOCES 235

BAKÉ: It's more serious than we imagined.

MADILA: I would never have imagined this.

BAKÉ: She isn't made of stone, you know.

MADILA: I never thought she'd take it this far.

BAKÉ: Farther still!

MADILA: Really terrible then?

BAKÉ: She said they were finally taking the big leap this year.

MADILA: Why didn't she call him?

BAKÉ: The bastard doesn't pick up her calls.

MADILA: She must have needed someone to listen, to hear her story.

BAKÉ: We can't be sure.

MADILA: Sure about what?

BAKÉ: That she'll make it.

MADILA: She needs help.

BAKÉ: Only time can help.

MADILA: There's no time to lose. We have to help her.

BAKÉ: A broken heart—you have to let it heal by itself.

MADILA: But who's talking about heart? What counts before everything else is life.

BAKÉ: There's no life without heart, little sister.

MADILA: Don't you think you could try to be more positive? It sounds like you don't want her to be cured.

BAKÉ: Cured of what?

MADILA: Am I hallucinating? She's been in a coma for two days; are you completely unhinged!

BAKÉ: Cut it out!

MADILA: No, I won't. It's too sad.

BAKÉ: Yes, a coma is sad. But what can we do?

MADILA: What's sad is how little you care about your own sister's life.

BAKÉ: Is that what you think?

MADILA: Yes.

BAKÉ: So, Oya suddenly means something to you?

MADILA: How can you doubt it?

BAKÉ: A lot. I can doubt it a lot. Where were you? Where were you these last two days when I was pacing the corridors. Tell me! When I was begging the nurses to give me some news about my sister? Where were you when I tried to get hold of you? You—Madame I know everything— you hardly arrived before you started to lecture me. You think you know more about what people are suffering from than the doctor and the patient herself.

MADILA: That's crazy.

BAKÉ: Where were you when she called you? She called you more than 20 times this week and you never picked up. I read the messages she sent you.

(MADILA scrolls through her cell phone.)

MADILA: Believe me, there's no call from Oya.

BAKÉ: Don't lie to me.

MADILA: I swear.

BAKÉ: Then take a look at this.

(MADILA takes OYA'S phone from BAKÉ and examines it carefully.)

MADILA: I don't understand.

BAKÉ: Me neither. I don't get it. I don't understand how you could do it.

MADILA: Really...

BAKÉ: Ignore her cries for help like that.

MADILA: I didn't get one call from Oya this week.

BAKÉ: I don't believe you.

MADILA: Not one message.

BAKÉ: You've changed, Madila. A lot. You think you're better than us now.

MADILA: That's not true.

BAKÉ: What's true is you now live in the chichi ex-pat neighborhood. Your children go to French school. You ride in super-expensive cars. But you're still my father's daughter. You're not better than anybody.

MADILA: It's not what you think.

BAKÉ: I really fooled myself. I thought your marriage would save our family.

MADILA: We both thought that.

BAKÉ: But you're only saving your own skin.

MADILA: That's not true.

BAKÉ: You've really made it. Gala dinners on the arm of your darling, vacations with the children in Europe. You're not just anybody now. It's normal for you to be ashamed of your sisters.

MADILA: I'm the one I'm ashamed of.

BAKÉ: Normal.

MADILA: And I'm lost.

BAKÉ: We're the ones who lost you. Poor Oya! She couldn't stand losing her little sister. That's why she wanted to kill herself.

MADILA: But it wasn't me who dumped her.

BAKÉ: A guy dumps you, you can get back up on your feet again. It's not the end of the world. If your family dumps you, the world disappears under your feet.

MADILA: Blood only kills those who're slaves to it.

COURSE AUX NOCES **237**

BAKÉ: Is that why you've taken yourself so far away?

(*BAKÉ'S telephone rings. She checks the number a moment and doesn't pick up.*)

MADILA: You're not answering?

BAKÉ: . . .

MADILA: Is it her?

(*BAKÉ shakes her head yes.*)

MADILA: She's still driving you crazy?

BAKÉ: . . .

MADILA: You should get out of that situation.

BAKÉ: Leave my husband? Are you nuts?

MADILA: He's not your husband. He belongs to someone else.

BAKÉ: Not my husband! I live under his roof, and we have a child. Not my husband!

MADILA: You're the one who pays the rent.

BAKÉ: The man is always the head of the family.

MADILA: But you aren't married.

BAKÉ: Don't start that again!

MADILA: I just want you to open your eyes. She thinks she has the right to call you. She threatens you. Why? Because she's the legitimate wife, the one with the title. He isn't your husband.

BAKÉ: You can't help yourself from thinking you're better than everybody. Right? Look! Here is my hand. It has five fingers. They aren't all equal. Our destinies couldn't have had the same shape. We aren't the same; we weren't born under the same stars. Don't forget, if you're married today to a rich man, it's because . . .

MADILA: Fuck you!

MEDICAL PERSONNEL (*Off-stage.*): The family of Oya Mankoussotan?

(*BAKÉ and MADILA exit hurriedly.*)

SCENE 5

KOFFI: I was worried. I've been calling all day.

MADILA: You shouldn't have done it.

KOFFI: What? Worry about you or call?

MADILA: Block my sister's number.

KOFFI: I don't know what you're talking about.

MADILA: Is that so? So, you don't know how the number of my big sister landed on a shitty blacklist in my own telephone?

KOFFI: You know perfectly well what I think about that kind of woman.

238 SPEAKING OUR SELVES

MADILA: That kind of woman is my sister. And, I had no idea you'd forbidden her to enter our house.

KOFFI: My house!

MADILA: You have no right to block contacts on my phone.

KOFFI: Your phone bought with my money.

(MADILA exits and comes back in a moment with a suitcase.)

KOFFI: Just what are you doing?

MADILA: I have to leave.

KOFFI: Where to?

MADILA: Home.

KOFFI: This is your home.

MADILA: No. Yours. You just reminded me.

KOFFI: You're playing with words.

MADILA: I don't have a lot of time. I just came back to pick up a few things.

(KOFFI blocks her way.)

MADILA: Stop it!

KOFFI: . . .

MADILA: It's not the time for this.

KOFFI: . . .

MADILA: Let me pass.

KOFFI: . . .

MADILA: Oya is sick.

KOFFI: . . .

MADILA: She's in critical condition.

KOFFI: You're not a doctor.

MADILA: She needs me.

KOFFI: She needs therapy.

MADILA: I don't want to abandon her at a time like this.

KOFFI: But you're able to abandon your home whenever you're in the mood?

(Pause.)

MADILA: The doctor says she shouldn't be alone.

KOFFI: I've always said that.

MADILA: Somebody needs to take care of her.

KOFFI: Her husband.

MADILA: You know she doesn't need a husband.

KOFFI: I don't understand.

MADILA: What?

KOFFI: Why your sister doesn't want to get married.

MADILA: There isn't a husband market where a woman can pick up what she needs when she wants to.

COURSE AUX NOCES **239**

KOFFI: If she stopped playing at being a man, she'd increase her chances of being spotted by a real one.

MADILA: You tell her that.

KOFFI: What?

MADILA: I'll bring her here when she leaves the hospital.

KOFFI: No way.

MADILA: You'll have to choose. Either I take care of her there or I bring her here.

KOFFI: Out of the question.

KOFFI: My house is not an insane asylum.

MADILA: She isn't insane.

KOFFI: You have to be insane to want to end your own life.

MADILA: She didn't want to kill herself. She just wanted to sleep. She said, "There's too much pressure! Job, colleagues, neighbors . . . the virus!" You should read the messages she sent me these last few days. I never received them because *someone* had blocked her phone number from reaching me.

KOFFI: Is that right?

MADILA: And she misses the children. She adores them.

KOFFI: We've already talked about this, Madila. I don't want my girls to become run-arounds as a result of spending time with your sister.

(MADILA picks up her suitcase and tries to leave. (KOFFI stops her gently.)

KOFFI: I'm sorry.

MADILA: Let me go!

KOFFI: That's not what I wanted to say.

MADILA: Let me go.

KOFFI: You twist everything I say.

MADILA: What you say, however, is very clear and precise.

KOFFI: I'll explain.

MADILA: No need.

KOFFI: Let me explain.

MADILA: You despise my family. Since forever. No need to explain it.

KOFFI: But I have to tell you . . .

MADILA: What?

KOFFI: You don't know what happened to me today. It was awful. Let me tell you.

MADILA: Something terrible happened to you today, really?

KOFFI: No man deserves what happened to me.

MADILA: When? When did it happen? Today? While I was gone?

KOFFI: Let me tell you about it.

MADILA: While I was at the hospital? Oh God! You called. You called me several times. I didn't want to pick up. I was angry. I was mad at you about so little, when you really needed me.

KOFFI: I'm not angry with you, sweetheart.

(KOFFI takes MADILA'S hand and leads her to the sofa.)

MADILA: Are you OK now?

KOFFI: I was having a hard day, too much tension, too much pressure. One of those hot days that chokes you, makes you want to leave your own skin, go somewhere to find some air, away from your problems. Parents on my back, obsessed by their dreams of my making it, personnel who're asking for a raise every morning, banks refusing requests for a loan . . . Nothing's going right—in a word, chaos! I leave the office and jump into my Rover. A little moment to think, just what it takes to come up with a plan, an escape from prison. Get away, escape from myself, even if for just a couple of hours. I drive by the Houéyiho development and all of a sudden, I feel like going in. Yet, that kind of place doesn't usually figure in the craziest dreams of a man of my standing. Most would never want to step into its guts. Maybe it was fate? What a devil fate is, right? So, I put on the turn signal and enter. I wonder how anyone dared give such a name to a development? It makes sense that nobody ever gets out of there.

MADILA: Then what happened?

KOFFI: In the midst of a sordid neighborhood, a little dog crossed my path.

MADILA: Did he bite you?

KOFFI: It was a female.

MADILA: Show me. We should go to the hospital! A dog bites you and you do nothing—that's a death certificate. You need a rabies shot, a shot against tetanus . . . We have to go to the hospital.

KOFFI: She was born in that degenerate neighborhood. The poor thing grew up there. So she wouldn't die of hunger, she wandered, and fed off the slim droppings of the dirty children in that loathsome neighborhood.

MADILA: Darling, we have to get this taken care of.

KOFFI: We stared at each other. I couldn't resist. I have a heart, you know. I gave the little dog something to eat. And like everyone who's poor, she ate everything and asked for more. I gave her something, again. She asked me over and over, and every time, I gave her something. She ate and ate. The bitch got fat. Oh yes, the little flea-bag dog wasn't a sweet little thing. She trapped us, me and my money, with her fat belly. Not nice at all, that little dog. Not nice.

MADILA: Please stop it!

KOFFI: Why? Don't you like my story of the poor little dog? Too sad? Too dirty?

(KOFFI grabs a shopping bag from a corner of the room and takes some fancy lingerie out.)

MADILA: No, not today, please.

KOFFI: Bad girl, Madila. Not nice at all. I pulled you out of that disgusting place. I washed you. Today, you know what shower gel, chocolate, and butter are. You know how to eat properly at table. You discovered what silverware was for. And you refuse to satisfy me? That's the least thing a man expects from his wife. Put these on!

MADILA: Not today.

KOFFI: Why?

MADILA: I have to go to the hospital. Oya's waiting for me.

KOFFI: She can wait a few more hours. Here, the client is king.

(KOFFI holds out a bottle of cognac to MADILA.)

MADILA: I'm your wife, not your slut.

KOFFI: If you're talking about Sylvana, I'd never let another man get near her.

MADILA: Really?

KOFFI: Never.

MADILA: Just why is that?

KOFFI: Because I love her.

MADILA: But I'm your wife.

KOFFI: Thus, my beauty, you have conjugal duties. She has no duties, Sylvana. On the contrary, she's *my* mistress.

MADILA: I hate you.

KOFFI: Put these on!

(MADILA walks over to the bar, pours out two glasses of cognac. She drinks one down immediately and hands the other to KOFFI. She serves herself again. KOFFI puts on some music.)

KOFFI: Get changed before the clients arrive!

(MADILA starts to undress; she unbuttons her blouse. KOFFI empties his glass. MADILA serves him again.)

KOFFI: Tonight, we have high-class clients, the best. They paid a lot to have you, sweetheart. A lot. That's how we are in this country. Always ready to pay a lot to possess what belongs to someone else. I have great business sense. They all want my wife and I make them pay for it. My darling wife, my goose with the golden eggs, my little dog. Not a scruffy, scabby dog, no, not that kind. You're no longer a lost dog from a disgusting neighborhood. You've become very clean, all over. You've changed class. And like my father says, "Water washes, but it's money that makes everything beautiful."

MADILA: Water never changed anybody's nature.

KOFFI: You're not like the other ones. I don't want you to hang out in that filthy neighborhood, OK? Look at me when I speak to you. Never again! OK?

MADILA: You're hurting me.

KOFFI: You belong to me, that's why they're ready to pay the price. Your first name without my name would just make you an ordinary whore. My name changes everything!

MADILA: Watch out or the little dog might just plant her teeth in your skin!

KOFFI: Come on and dance! Move your ass! Let's go!

(MADILA sobs.)

KOFFI: Cut that out. Quit your belly-aching; that just won't do. Didn't you say you wanted to bite me. Didn't you? Go ahead. So, the sweet little dog only knows how to bark; she doesn't bite? Too afraid—the sweet little dog. Too unhappy as well.

MADILA: You're hurting me.

KOFFI: Really? Where?

(He tears her blouse, grabs her breasts.)

KOFFI: Here? Here? Does it hurt here? Ah . . . lower? So, you hurt there? You like it, don't you? You like it? Tell me you like it.

MADILA: . . .

KOFFI: God, you're hot!

MADILA: . . .

KOFFI: Me, too. I'm burning up. I'm dizzy. I can feel my muscles contract.

MADILA: . . .

KOFFI: You're beautiful Madila. You're . . . Why?

MADILA: I'm your wife.

KOFFI: You've put me in prison.

MADILA: I belong to you.

KOFFI: Prisoner of a stinking union, prisoner of my own hormones. God! Treacherous desire—why did I become a victim of the hell I created for her?

MADILA: I'm your wife. It's normal for you to want me.

KOFFI: You wanted the ring. You got it. You won't get anything more. Not a thing.

MADILA: I have my children. They're not nothing.

KOFFI: Your children carry my name. You have nothing.

MADILA: Phone them and call off the entertainment. Let me take care of you. We still have things to say to each other.

KOFFI: We're not changing anything. They've already paid. So, get to work. All the people on this planet deserve the life they get. Do what you're supposed to. And, please, don't try to bare the fangs you don't have.

(KOFFI pulls himself away from MADILA, stumbles, and collapses on the ground. He is writhing in pain.)

KOFFI: What did you do to me?

MADILA: . . .

KOFFI: Bring me some water!

MADILA: . . .

KOFFI: Give me some water; I'm suffocating.

MADILA: . . .

KOFFI: What's happening to me?

MADILA: . . .

KOFFI: Was it the drink?

MADILA: . . .

KOFFI: You didn't put poison in it, did you?

(MADILA cries.)

KOFFI: I'm sick.

MADILA: It won't take long. Not long.

KOFFI: I beg you.

MADILA: People deserve their shitty lives.

(Pause. KOFFI doesn't move. MADILA takes him in her arms.)

MADILA: I've been burning for years. With desire. With desire for you. An eternal fire. My darling, you're irresistible. You're the only author of the volcano I carry inside me. It's true; I did something unimaginable to become your wife. I admit it. Without your knowing, I recognize that too. But can't you see, my darling, in my world, a woman chooses her man, not the opposite. I chose you and it cost me. That choice cost me and will cost even more from now on. Losing you is the worst thing that could have happened to me. Way too costly! But how does one lose what one doesn't have, never had, never possessed? When I hear my girl-friends complain about their husbands—some of them even talk about rape—I think to myself, "You're stinking lucky, my friends." I'd give anything for my man to see me, to touch me . . . desire me." I wouldn't be bothered in the least if he decided to take it out on me when his bank refused a loan. I'd fulfill my conjugal duties with pleasure when his secretary refused to open her legs in order to be promoted. And who cares if he thinks of Sylvana when he's in me? I don't ask for anything more than to fulfill my duty. Nothing is more sacred than a wife's duty. But I'm under embargo. Don't even have the right to my duties. It's awful to hear others complain when you don't even have the right to your responsibilities. It's unfair. Awful to spend ten years under the roof of a man who doesn't see you, doesn't touch you, doesn't desire you . . . I had to go fast, be adaptable and clever. It was a race against the clock and

age. A race to get married. I won the race. I earned the ultimate trophy: Your Name. But I lost my self. By forcing you to marry me, I destroyed my own name. I plunged it in mud. I wrapped my dignity in a papaya's dry leaf and I allowed you to piss on it. I plunged my own honor in shit so I'd have the honor of wearing your name. Every evening, there was always one, or two, or three high class clients. Every evening . . .
And all those rapes perpetrated on me killed my love. My love for you—dead. My love for your name—dead. I'm out of love, no more for me, no more for those women who'll do anything to catch a husband. No love for the aunties, for all those mothers who push girls to marry no matter what the price. No love for the *dadas*,[3] the big sisters who won't let their little sisters live their lives, live their own disappointments and their own broken hearts. No more love. No more love for men who love their own egos too much, those men who think they're truly made in God's image and believe that everything should come to them. I have no more love—none for you, my husband.

(The doorbell rings.)

(MADILA speaks, but KOFFI is unresponsive.)

MADILA: Your friends are here, darling . . . They're growing restless . . . Aren't you going to open the door? . . . They're leaning on the doorbell. They're really impatient. Go open the door, darling. The client is king. You can't leave them like that at the door. They paid a huge amount . . . The doorbell's ringing, my love. It's ringing.

SCENE 6

CHORUS OF NEIGHBORHOOD GOSSIPS: Who would have believed it?
Believed what?
This day would come.
Don't count your chickens before they hatch.
What does that mean?
You still have to wait for the yes.
Really?
As long as he hasn't said yes, nothing is sure.
Don't tell me you think he's going to chicken out.
Did you ever think this would happen?
Think what?
This day would come.
No.

---

3. Madila uses the term "dada" to speak of big sisters. It is a Fon language expression that designates older and more powerful female siblings.

COURSE AUX NOCES   245

What's going on?

She's late.

Not yet. It's still a little early.

I would've come well before it started, if I was her.

Normal! You're a man.

What does that mean?

It's normal for the man to wait for the woman, and not the contrary.

That's bullshit! What law says that?

The law of nature.

What nature? She put a spell on that guy!

Oh yeah? You don't think it's a normal love story?

Who still talks about love in the 21st century?

I'll bet my ass she trapped him with her magic.

Her and her sisters. The whole extended family. They all got caught up in her situation. They washed their dirty linen together until they figured out what to do.

Is that it? Now I understand why there was such a hurry.

They were afraid the spell would wear off and he'd change his mind.

What kind of crap is this? She met him at the hospital. The doctor was totally charmed by his patient.

What charm? What are you seeing? Where?

You mean the doctor?

No, the charm!

A circus!

You can't fool me; this marriage is a joke.

I don't think so. The doctor is an educated man. He would never have accepted such a deal.

They say she did the "yes-yes."[4]

The "yes-yes?"

Yes.

When a woman casts the "yes-yes," you give in to everything she wants. It's the most powerful spell of all times.

And, you know, she's from Banamè.

What? She's really from that village?

Why?

Women from that region are very powerful. A Banamè woman is capable of casting the "yes-yes" spell on God himself—if she sets her sights on him.

---

4. Some of the Neighborhood Gossips accuse the character Oya of casting a spell (*Gbotémi* in the Fon language) on her husband to be. In their eyes, this very powerful spell, called *le oui-oui* (or yes-yes) is exceptionally potent because Oya's family is originally from Banamè, a village in central Benin, where a cult has grown around a woman believed to have powers as great as the Judeo-Christian God.

That poor doctor.

He's not such a sorry fool as that. I even think he's a lucky man.

Lucky? Are you kidding?

Marrying a real virgin. That's not the norm today.

Real virgin! What virgin? An old maid like that!

Well at least she doesn't have a kid. There are plenty of kids around from young ladies who aren't so young anymore.

Isn't that the truth!

So, now you're talking about me?

Who feel victimized . . .

And why shouldn't they feel victimized when they've listened to a seducer who leaves them with a kid?

Seducer! Who? Me?

Yes, you, the father of my daughter—and all those other bastards who run away from their duties as fathers.

I confirm.

You're not a father just because one out of a million of your spermatozoa did the work instead of you.

I confirm.

Being a father means taking on responsibilities, huge responsibilities.

I confirm. I like. I share.

Look!

What!

It's her!

The other one.

What other one?

Don't you see her?

She's hidden behind the door at the back.

She's moving.

Hey, it's the little sister.

Yeah, the youngest.

The killer?

Yeah, the one who murdered her husband.

She's still alive?

You mean, she's not in prison?

In an asylum, instead. It seems she went bonkers.

They're all nuts in that family.

Looks like this celebration will be really something!

What's she doing now?

She's entering her sister's room.

Is she going to kill her?
Should we call the police?
The firemen?
There's no fire here!
But if she's crazy, she could start one. Right?
Quick! Call the fire department!
She's going to burn us all down—you, me, the houses, the street, the capital,
the country . . . Everything! Burned up! Incinerated! The bride, the
family, the guests . . .
What guests?
There aren't any guests. You forget we've been watching everything from
our courtyard.
It's an intimate ceremony, only close family are present.
Fucking virus!
What do we do?
Nothing.
For the moment.
But as soon as we see something weird, we'll call 911.[5]
Yeah.

SCENE 7

(*A bedroom. OYA is in front of her mirror, dressed in a peignoir. Her wedding
dress is on a hanger nearby. MADILA enters. She watches OYA for a long
time. Then she sings.*)

MADILA (*Singing like a griotte or praise-singer in staccato verses.*): They met.
They were drawn to each other.
They stared at each other. They kissed each other.
Who cares if she isn't the last woman he'll bed, you have to get married.
Who cares if this is the last day we see her smile, you have to get married.
You have to get married. You have to get married. You have to get married.
We're in a matrimonial emergency, a matter of life or death.
Married to be accepted by others.
Married to profit from the envious looks of cousins living as concubines.
Married to not die of humiliation.
Married in order to live.
Live according to rules decided by others.
Others who don't give a fuck about what you want.

---

5. The chorus thinks about calling 118 for help, which is the Beninese equivalent of 911, the emergency phone number used in this version because it is familiar to Anglophone readers.

Not a fuck about what you feel.
Nor a fuck about what you desire.
Not a fuck about what you love.
Not a fuck . . .

OYA: Madila?

MADILA: Have you seen what you look like?

OYA: What are you doing here?

MADILA: It's an important day. Did you think I would miss it?

OYA: Did you escape?

MADILA: An important day for you and, so, important for all of us.

OYA: I'm bringing you back to the hospital.

MADILA: You're not going to leave your fiancé in the lurch, are you?

OYA: You're the person who's most important to me.

MADILA: Then let me stay. Let me share this special day with you.

(Pause. OYA takes off her peignoir and puts on her wedding dress. MADILA helps her dress. She sings.)

MADILA *(Still in staccato verses, like a griotte.)*: Today, she will sleep under her husband's roof.
Today and forever, she will sleep under her husband's roof.
She will keep watch when she doesn't sleep and when she sees red under her husband's roof.
Under her husband's roof. Under her husband's roof.
If her husband has no bed to offer,
He will put her to bed on a floor mat. What's most important is not the bed.
If her husband has no bed to offer,
She'll sleep on the ground, even on a dirt floor.
What's most important isn't the mat, isn't the floor.
The most important is to stay under her husband's roof.
The most important is to live under her husband's roof.
Under her husband's roof, under her husband's roof.
If tomorrow she can't find a reason to live under her husband's roof,
The others will find reasons for her to live under his roof.
The most important is not the heart's reason.
It's reason's reason.
The most important is to die under the husband's roof.
Under the husband's roof, under the husband's roof.

OYA: Please, stop it.

MADILA: What do you want me to stop?

OYA: You're ruining the atmosphere. We're not at a funeral, you know.

MADILA: But you look like you're going to one.

(Pause.)

OYA: Your doctor says you're making good progress.

MADILA: I'm not crazy.

OYA: That's not what I said.

MADILA: It's what you think.

OYA: You have to finish the treatment.

MADILA: I was never crazy. It was my lawyer's idea.

OYA: Really?

MADILA: A stroke of genius, I admit!

OYA: From the beginning?

MADILA: From the beginning.

OYA: You were pretending all that time?

MADILA: We all pretend all the time. Everybody pretends.

(Pause.)

OYA: Where will you go, after this?

MADILA: . . .

OYA: You have to continue the treatment. Otherwise, they'll send you back to prison.

MADILA: I'll go away.

OYA: Swear you will!

MADILA: I swear it.

OYA: Should I believe you?

MADILA: Believe me; once you take the big step, my sister, I won't be able to do anything anymore.

OYA: Nothing?

MADILA: Nothing.

OYA: I don't think I understand what you're saying.

MADILA: Why are you doing this?

OYA: I don't know what you're talking about.

MADILA: Why are you getting married like this?

OYA: Like what?

MADILA: As if you were damned.

OYA: I don't understand.

MADILA: You don't love him.

OYA: You know nothing about it.

MADILA: You don't have to.

(BAKÉ enters.)

BAKÉ: We're just waiting for the bride. Good God, Oya, you haven't put on your make-up yet! . . . Madila!?

OYA: She came to attend the ceremony. After that . . .

BAKÉ: Out of the question.

OYA: Why?

BAKÉ: Oya, you're not going to . . . , not you too!

MADILA: What? Go crazy? You don't want her to go crazy like me? And yet you're doing everything so . . .

OYA: Madila!

MADILA: Getting tied to someone for life is an enormous error. You should never mix up law and love. Love has no limits. Love, yes, forbids nothing. But law keeps us from living free.

BAKÉ: Law defends women. It protects us.

MADILA: I know how to defend myself without any help.

BAKÉ: You killed him in cold blood.

MADILA: He killed me every day.

BAKÉ: You've no remorse at all?

MADILA: Yes, some. Having done what you said, followed your scheme.

OYA: I don't understand.

MADILA: If I hadn't listened to you, I'd still be myself.

OYA: Hello?

MADILA *(Locking eyes with BAKÉ.)*: Tell her! Tell her the truth.

OYA: The truth?

BAKÉ *(To OYA.)*: Come on. Sit down and let me do your make-up.

OYA: What's this truth she's talking about?

BAKÉ: Don't listen to her. You know she's . . .

MADILA: Crazy? Maybe. But I will not accept seeing Oya end up like me. Tell her the truth.

BAKÉ: They're waiting for us outside.

OYA: They can wait a little longer.

BAKÉ: They'll hear everything.

MADILA: Who cares?

BAKÉ: Let's go Oya.

MADILA: Tell her.

OYA: Tell me.

MADILA: Tell her, I'll help.

BAKÉ: It's your story.

MADILA: But you're the author. Let's start with the day you spoke to me about Koffi for the first time.

OYA: You knew Koffi before Madila?

BAKÉ: A man like Koffi is an opportunity that won't present itself more than once in a woman's life.

MADILA: That's what you said that day.

BAKÉ: He was handsome . . .

MADILA: . . . And rich. You said . . .

BAKÉ: Sister, a man like Koffi is an opportunity that won't present itself more than once in a woman's life.

MADILA: And if I don't fall in love with him?

BAKÉ: Don't! Really, don't! He's the one who has to fall in love. You have to have him eating out of the palm of your hand.

MADILA: I can't let him touch me if I don't feel anything for him.

BAKÉ: You don't need feelings for that; not the feelings you think, in any case.

MADILA: Really?

BAKÉ: What's your favorite city?

MADILA: Venice.

BAKÉ: Think of Venice when he enters you. Recite the names of all the cities you dream of visiting, for example.

MADILA: Tokyo, Born, Bobo, Nantes, Bombay, Jakarta, Djougou, Bangkok, Istanbul, Cape Town, Takoradi, Luanda, Cairo, Segou, Addis Ababa, Toulouse, Nati, Abomey, Joburg, Bassila, Barcelona, Nopegali, Marrakech, Assini, Dakar, Beijing . . .

BAKÉ: That's it. And think about great food as well.

MADILA *(Moaning with pleasure)*: Peanut sauce!

BAKÉ: No, I'm talking about restaurant meals.

MADILA: Raclette, vinaigrette, white sauce, tomato sauce, butter and lemon sauce, hot sauce, sauce with peas, sauce with mushrooms, bechamel . . .

(Pause.)

BAKÉ: I organized everything to perfection. The night you met you were more beautiful than Cinderella before the clock struck 12.

MADILA: He fell for me the minute he saw me in the foyer of the hotel.

BAKÉ: I'd reserved a room for you specially for that night.

OYA: You slept with him the first time you met?

BAKÉ: We had to go fast. I didn't have enough money to pay for several nights in a five-star hotel.

MADILA: That night was a dream. Beyond anything I could have hoped for.

BAKÉ: You mean, anything except for something unexpected?

(BAKÉ and MADILA laugh.)

OYA: Something unexpected?

MADILA: Four times, and every time he used a condom.

OYA: But that's good, isn't it?

BAKÉ: It put the mission in jeopardy. Luckily, Koffi isn't part of that race of badly brought up guys who throw everything in the toilet. Madila

252 SPEAKING OUR SELVES

discretely shifted through the garbage and recuperated the precious
liquid from the four rubbers—and watered her womb with it.

OYA: But that's horrible!

MADILA: When I told him I was pregnant, he refused to believe it was him.
Baké had the idea of posting a photo of the ultrasound on Koffi's
Facebook page and congratulating him on becoming a father. All of his
family, all of his friends found out that way. He didn't have a choice
except to marry me to avoid a scandal. Poor guy. You should have seen
his face when he saw the results of the paternity test.

(MADILA and BAKÉ laugh. OYA is outraged.)

BAKÉ: I won the jackpot for you.

MADILA: You did it for yourself.

BAKÉ: For us. I did it for us. I thought if one of us hit it big, she would help
the others. But you couldn't even be bothered to introduce Oya to one of
your husband's friends.

MADILA: Fuck you! Fuck you! Seven times seventy-seven times. Fuck you!

BAKÉ: Oya, call the hospital. It's time for her medicine.

MADILA: I'm not crazy. I'm not crazy.

OYA: After the wedding, I'll take her back to the hospital.

BAKÉ: We won't be able to control her.

MADILA: Fuck you!

OYA: Calm down, Madila.

*(BAKÉ searches through her bag, finds her phone. MADILA jumps on her,
grabs the phone and throws it on the ground.)*

MADILA: There won't be a marriage, no marriage, I'm telling you. Let her
stay free. Oya can't end up like the two of us.

BAKÉ *(To Oya.):* Call her doctor.

OYA: Calm down, please! You're not going to spoil the most beautiful day of
my life!

MADILA: The most beautiful day of your life? You're sad! I saw you through
the crack in the door. I wasn't going to enter—just look at you. Share
your happiness from a distance. I stayed there, behind the door; I
watched you for several long minutes. You were crying, Oya. I saw you
cry and your tears drowned my heart.

OYA: We love each other, my doctor and me. Truly. That day at the hospital,
when I finally opened my eyes, he was standing there, right next to the
bed, my hand in his, introducing the catheter. I knew from that moment
he was the one.

MADILA: You're getting married for a catheter?

OYA: I love everything about him. He took care of me. He took care of my heart. Both of us want this marriage. Baké had nothing to do with it . . . I was sad, yes, but because you weren't here for this special day. I miss you. That's all.

(OYA hugs MADILA; and both women cry.)

MADILA: I miss you too, all the time. I miss my children. I can't stand knowing they're with their grandparents. Those people hate me.

BAKÉ: You killed their son.

MADILA: A monster! How could I love him?

OYA: You thought you loved him once.

MADILA: Why do our hearts always betray us? I did love him. I swear it, with time I fell totally in love with him.

BAKÉ: I told you it would happen. "The more you eat, the more you like it!"

OYA: That's not love. It's the Stockholm syndrome. She only thought she loved him.

MADILA: He never made love to me after that night in the hotel. He'd say I was too poor for his jewels. He multiplied the number of mistresses he took. He made fun of me. He humiliated me in every way he could. The more time passed, the more he hated me. I represented the revenge of his ex.

BAKÉ: Shut up!

OYA: His ex?

MADILA: Oh yes, my sister was dumped by the man she considers an opportunity that only comes your way once in a lifetime. She worked out a diabolical plan to keep him in the family.

OYA *(To BAKÉ.):* Koffi was your ex?

BAKÉ: She's sick.

OYA: Answer me!

BAKÉ: She's delirious. It's crazy talk.

MADILA: Koffi was furious when he learned about the ultrasound showing up on Facebook. But his anger then was nothing compared to his fury when he knew I wasn't the rich heiress I'd pretended to be. Just the sister of my sister. You must have known he'd make me pay for it. Ten years of acting the completely fulfilled woman who has everything she could ever desire. Ten years of rape. I couldn't take it anymore.

OYA: Why didn't you plead self-defense?

BAKÉ: A woman must fulfill her conjugal duty.

OYA: Being raped?

BAKÉ: A husband's desire for his wife can never be judged as rape. When the husband calls the wife to his bed and she refuses, the angels curse her all night long.

MADILA: That's what you always said to me when I complained.
(Pause.)
OYA: You knew there was rape?
BAKÉ: Koffi was her husband. It's normal.
MADILA: It wasn't love-making. It was tearing me apart. He cut me into little pieces and scattered them all over the floor. I couldn't ever collect myself. Every night there was another client. Sometimes two or three at the same time. They came from everywhere, very important people. Koffi created a huge network.
OYA: Prostitution!
MADILA: I'm the goose with the golden eggs.
OYA: You should've told us, brought charges.
MADILA: He was too well connected.
OYA: Why didn't you ask for a divorce?
MADILA: He would never have given me custody of the twins. Where are my children? Where are they? Poor little chicks, orphans, exiled, weaned . . . They're only baby girls. I know they're hungry. When my breasts grow hard, I know they're crying from hunger. They're dying of hunger. I feel it. Touch my breasts. Go ahead, feel them. See how hard they are. Touch them. Feel my children's tears flowing from my nipples. Where are my babies? Give them back to me!
BAKÉ: They're not little anymore. Your kids are ten years old. Snap out of it!
MADILA: Shut up, you witch!
(MADILA grows nervous and aggressive. BAKÉ manages to grab her and ties her up, attaching her to the sofa.
Pause.
We hear church bells.)
BAKÉ *(To OYA.)*: We have to go now.
OYA: Are we going to leave her all alone?
BAKÉ: We'll look after her when the wedding's over.
OYA *(To MADILA.)*: Little sister, I'll make sure you're all right.
MADILA: Promise?
OYA: I give you the word of the mouth that tasted our mother's breasts before you did.
(BAKÉ picks up a bouquet of flowers that she gives to OYA. They leave.)
MADILA: Long live the married couple! May they be very happy! Long live the bride; she's so lovely. And since she's attracted to male odor, like honey attracts ants, may that odor constipate her, swell her belly, make her dizzy. May the odor of the male make her vomit and may she excrete the male.

Long live the groom, who will soon be condemned. Condemned to lie for the rest of his life. Condemned . . .

May the heavens rain down on their house all the storms that result from the agreement they're ready to sign. A rain of arguments, a rain of distrust, a rain of betrayals, of secrets, of conflicts, of torments, of disagreements, of enmity. May He who lives high up there and whose power to destroy humanity is infinite, overwhelm them with trials and temptations. May He gift them with a multitude of secret liaisons. May He give the couple a home filled with bastards, for what He has joined together, no man can tear asunder. Since they decided to lock themselves in a ring, may this circle of fire burn without consuming them totally. May the ring shine in order to attract other dreamers to its prison. May the ring shine for centuries and centuries! And if anyone present has any objections, let them close their mouths and keep them shut forever.

(We still hear church bells. They ring louder and louder, and then, abruptly, they stop.
Blackout.)

(END.)

The author reserves all serialization and dramatization rights. Requests for any of these rights or the translation into languages other than English should be addressed to Nathalie Hounvo Yekpe at nathaliey@gmail.com. Judith G. Miller can be reached at judith.miller@nyu.edu.

Other Contributors

Judith G. Miller
Photograph: © Ellen Kolikoff

Judith G. Miller (translator) is Professor Emerita of French Literature (with a specialization in theater) and Collegiate Professor at New York University. She previously taught for some twenty years at the University of Wisconsin-Madison, where she produced plays in French with her students. Miller has also served as Director of New York University in Paris and as Dean of Arts and Humanities at New York University Abu Dhabi. She has published extensively on French and Francophone theater texts and productions and has translated over 40 plays from French to English. Recent works include: the anthology, *Seven Plays by Koffi Kwahulé: In and Out of Africa* (University of Michigan Press, 2017); a study of the major French theater director, *Ariane Mnouchkine* (Routledge, 2018); a translation of Gerty Dambury's novel, *The Restless* (Feminist Press, 2018); a translation of Béatrice Picon-Vallin's history and analysis of France's Théâtre du Soleil, *The Théâtre du Soleil: The First Fifty-Five Years* (Routledge, 2020); and *Contemporary Francophone African Plays: An Anthology* (Bucknell, 2024), which includes translations of plays by Bernard Dadié, Sénouvo Agbota Zinsou, Werewere Liking, Sony Labou Tansi, Koffi Kwahulé, Kangni Alem, José Pliya, Yolande Mukagasana, Gustave Akakpo, Kossi Efoui, and Penda Diouf. Miller is currently working on a translation for Liverpool University Press of *Race et Théâtre* by Sylvie Chalaye, in which Chalaye traces the presence of actors of color and themes of Blackness in French theater.

Interviews with Judith Graves Miller are available at https://doi.org/10.3998/mpub.12827650.cmp.9 (Diama's *Tafé Fanga*) and https://doi.org/10.3998/mpub.12827650.cmp.10 (Yekpe's *The Race to Get Married*).

Rivardo Niyónīzígiye

Born in Kibimba-Gisozi, Burundi, **Rivardo Niyónīzígiye** (translator) is a blogger, playwright, and actor. He graduated from the University of Burundi in Arts and Social Sciences, English Language and Literature department. Author of *Les Retrouvailles*, published in 2014 in Paris, he did several writing workshops since 2011. In 2014, he embraced theater, with acting and staging workshops, respectively, with Benoît Marchand, Olivier Coyette (Théâtre de Poche, Belgium), and Clemens Bechtel (Theater Konstanz).

In 2017, he participated in the Small Citizens project where his original idea was developed to create *The Children of Amazi*, a piece for young audiences that toured in Rwanda, Uganda, Tunisia, Belgium, France, Austria, and Switzerland.

Author of various plays about history, culture, humanity and values, in 2023, he co-authored *The Ingabo—A Night to Fall*, a collaboration between Burundi and Germany focusing on the seven years of resistance of the kingdom of Burundi against the German occupation from 1896–1903.

A devotee of folk music and pastoral poetry, Niyónīzígiye has been coordinating, since 2017, talks called "Ibiteramo vy'icuramayagwa," which are sessions of creations and exchange about Burundian literature in Kirundi with the aim of enhancing it. Two short story collections called *Amata n'Ubuki* (*Milk and Honey*) have been produced during these sessions. He is among the collective authors in *Chroniques des Grands Lacs* (2019), which includes his short story "Iwacu" about the nostalgia of one's home for migrants in captivity. He believes that language and literature are the best tools to unite generations and communities.

An interview with Rivardo Niyónīzígiye is available at https://doi.org/10.3998/mpub.12827650.cmp.14.

Esi Sutherland-Addy

Esi Sutherland-Addy (Foreword) is a retired Associate Professor of African Studies at the University of Ghana and adjunct professor at the Accra Center of New York University. Her main research and teaching interests are written and oral literature, including theater, women's literature, educational and cultural policy. Her current research project, funded by the Andrew Mellon Foundation, is entitled *Oral Traditions and Expressive Diversity,* collection and digitization of Ghanaian Oral Traditions.

Professor Sutherland-Addy's selected publications include "Ama Ata Aidoo in Conversation with Esi Sutherland-Addy" (2017), *Obsidian: Literature and Arts in the African Diaspora* vol. 44, no. 2 (Fall 2018): 124+; Takyiwaa Manuh and Esi Sutherland-Addy, eds., *Africa in Contemporary Perspective* (Accra: Sub Saharan Publishers, 2013); Esi Sutherland-Addy, Ama Ata Aidoo, and Kati Dagadu, *Ghana: Where the Bead Speaks* (Accra: UNESCO/Foundation for Contemporary Art-Ghana, 2011); E. Sutherland-Addy, "Mfantse meets English: Interpretations of Ama Ata Aidoo's Multi-lingual Idiom," in A. Adams, ed., *Essays in Honour of Ama Ata Aidoo at 70—A Reader in African Cultural Studies* (Oxford: Ayebia, 2012), 329–44; Esi Sutherland-Addy and Aminata Diaw, eds., *Women Writing Africa: West Africa and the Sahel* (New York, Feminist Press, CUNY, 2007); Esi Sutherland-Addy, "Creating for and with Children in Ghana. Efua Sutherland: A Retrospective," in Michael Etherton, ed., *African Theatre: Youth* (Oxford: James Currey, 2006), 1–15; Anne V. Adams and Esi Sutherland-Addy, eds., *The Legacy of Efua Sutherland: Pan-African Cultural Activism* (Oxford: Ayebia Clarke, 2005).

Sutherland-Addy was until recently Academic Associate Director of the African Humanities Program of the American Council for Learned Societies. She was Deputy Minister for Tourism and Culture (1986) and Higher Education (1986–1993) in the Republic of Ghana. Sutherland-Addy's civil society activities lie in the areas of higher education, girls' education, children, Pan Africanism, culture, and public space. Sutherland-Addy has served on several national and international boards including the Open Society for West Africa, and The Commonwealth of Learning and the Board of Trustees of the Voluntary Fund for Technical Cooperation of the United Nations High Commission for Human Rights, the Forum of African Women Educationalists (Ghana), Afram Publications Ghana Ltd, and the PANAFEST Foundation. She is also a member of the Board of Mmofra Foundation and the Steering Committee of the Beyond the Return Initiative of the Government of Ghana.

Sutherland-Addy has a number of awards to her credit including Honorary Fellowship of the College of (Preceptors)Teachers, UK, 1998; Award for Meritorious Service, Ghana Civil Service, 2000; Team Award to the Rockefeller Study Centre for Women Writing Africa, 2001/2; Doctor of Letters Honoris Causa (University of Education, Winneba) 2004; Excellence in Distance Education Award (EDE): Honorary Fellowship of the Commonwealth of Learning, 2008, and Tourism Icon—Ghana Tourism Authority, 2021.

An interview with Esi Sutherland-Addy is available at https://doi.org/10.3998/mpub.12827650.cmp.6.

Robert H. Vorlicky

Robert H. Vorlicky (editor), most recently Visiting Professor of Theater, New York University Abu Dhabi, is retired from the Department of Drama, Tisch School of the Arts, NYU. He is the initial Director of the Honors Program and a former Director of Theatre Studies in the Department of Drama. Dr. Vorlicky is also an affiliate faculty member of NYU's Department of English and the Department of Social and Cultural Analysis. Vorlicky is the author of *Act Like a Man: Challenging Masculinities in American Drama* (CHOICE Award for Outstanding Academic Publication); editor of *Tony*

Kushner in Conversation; and editor of *From Inner Worlds to Outer Space: The Multimedia Performances of Dan Kwong* (all published by the University of Michigan Press). With Professor Una Chaudhuri (NYU), he edits the Critical Performances series at Michigan.

Vorlicky is past president of the international American Theatre and Drama Society (1999–2002). On the editorial boards of several academic journals and book series, he publishes widely and speaks nationally and internationally on U.S. drama, performance, and theory, gender and representation, and African theater. Vorlicky has received numerous fellowships, including those from the National Endowment for the Humanities, the Fulbright Foundation (senior professorship at the University of Zagreb, Croatia), Karolyi Foundation in Creative Writing, Wisconsin Arts Board, and numerous research grants from NYU's Tisch School of the Arts and NYU Abu Dhabi's Division of Arts and Humanities. He is a curator and dramaturg for mainstage productions in the Drama Department, as well as in the department's training studios. Professor Vorlicky is a multiple nominee for the Distinguished Teaching Award at NYU. He has been a visiting professor in Theatre Studies at Yale.

An interview with Robert Vorlicky is available at https://doi.org/10.3998/mpub.12827650.cmp.3.

Joshua Williams

Joshua Williams (translator) is a writer, translator, director, theater historian and performance theorist. He is currently a 2023–2024 ACLS Fellow and a Visiting Scholar at Tufts University. His academic research concerns the political figure of the animal in East African theater and performance. His articles, essays, and reviews have appeared in *ASTR Online*, *Theatre Journal*, *The Johannesburg Salon*, *Theatre Survey*, *Performance Research*, *African Theatre*, *Modern Drama*, the *Journal of Dramatic Theory and Criticism*,

Antennae, The Cambridge Companion to Theatre and Science, Theatre After Empire, Africa is a Country, HowlRound, Brittle Paper, and the *Los Angeles Review of Books.* He earned his AB from Princeton University in Comparative Literature with certificates in African Studies and Creative Writing; his MA from the School of Oriental and African Studies at the University of London, also in Comparative Literature; and his PhD in Performance Studies, with a Designated Emphasis in Critical Theory, from the University of California, Berkeley. He has taught at Harvard, NYU, and Brandeis, and is the performance review editor of *Theatre Journal.*

In 2007, *New York Magazine* named him "a star of tomorrow" on the basis of his forthcoming novel, *Bird in Blue.* He's published creative nonfiction essays in *Blunderbuss* and *Hippocampus.* His plays have been produced or developed at Theatre Intime, Princeton University, the Capital Fringe Festival, 1 Shanthi Road, UC Berkeley, CU Boulder, the New York Musical Theatre Festival, CAP 21, Ars Nova's ANT Fest, SUNY Buffalo, the Rhinebeck Writers Retreat, PlayGround San Francisco / Thick House, EST-Sloan, Apples and Oranges' THEatre ACCELERATOR, Goodspeed Musicals Johnny Mercer Foundation Writers Grove, MAP Fund, and TED. As a 2012–2013, 2014–2015, and 2015–2016 member of the PlayGround San Francisco Writing Pool, he had three of his short plays read at Berkeley Repertory Theatre and one published in *The Best of PlayGround.* In 2011, he directed the North American premiere of the Tanzanian dramatist Ebrahim Hussein's *Kinjeketile* at UC Berkeley.

In addition to Penina Muhando's *Nguzo Mama,* he is currently translating Ebrahim Hussein's complete plays from Kiswahili into English.

An interview with Joshua Williams is available at https://doi.org/10.3998/mpub.12827650.cmp.8.

Acknowledgments

This book's journey began in Kampala and, with its publication, it now takes on global reach. As editors, we are grateful to each of the contributors to this anthology; it would not exist without its exceptional playwrights, translators, and essayist. We are honored by your enthusiasm for the project and trust in us to do the right thing with your art. We learned so much from our collaborations, marked by your creativity, discipline, understanding, and professionalism. You are the reason for this book's life; this book is yours.

We profoundly thank LeAnn Fields of the University of Michigan Press, not only for respecting the value of this project from its pre-Covid-19 beginning, but for whole-heartedly and astutely shepherding it through the process from proposal to copyediting. This book is in honor of LeAnn's truly pioneering and life-long professional advocacy for scholarly and practical publications in Theater, Drama, and Performance Studies. She is a consummate believer in the value of art and scholarship as critical components to create meaningful human, societal connections. LeAnn's local to international legacies are grounded in her passion that books can enliven our capacity to imagine and work toward a more humane, compassionate world. How blessed we are, as have been innumerable authors, to have worked with LeAnn.

We'd like to thank the anonymous readers of the manuscript. We appreciate your insightful comments that enriched this text, as well as your generous support for its publication. Our heartfelt appreciation to Sara Cohen (Editorial Director), Marcia LaBrenz (Production Editor), Cheryl Bowman (Copy Editor), and Haley Winkle (Associate Editor), who patiently and expertly guided us through the final stages of the book's preparation for publication. Likewise, much gratitude to Michigan's entire staff who worked tirelessly to bring this book to the public.

Particular thanks to Judith G. Miller, an extraordinary scholar and translator of African theater, for her wise counsel throughout different stages of this project. And thank you, Judy, for bringing to our attention several gifted Francophone African women playwrights, previously unknown to us. Special kudos also to Catherine Coray, Arts Professor, Experimental Theatre Wing, NYU Tisch School of the Arts. Catherine, a true maker of life's magic, introduced us to one another (as she has done for many other artists and scholars throughout the world), knowing that our interests were in conversation with one another. Thank you, Judy and Catherine!

We thank the incredibly generous support of the Senior Research Grants, awarded by the Arts and Humanities Division, New York University Abu Dhabi. Through allocations provided by the Division's competitive funding, all contributors received honoraria for the right to include their work in the initial proposal for the anthology. While publication of the work could not be guaranteed at the initial stage, we wanted the artists and scholars to know that their work was valued from the start, regardless of the outcome. Our manuscript existed because of the contributors' labor and for this, they earned compensatory recognition from the start. We thank NYUAD for its acute foresight in making possible this warranted commitment, as well as for enacting the vision to compensate artists when circulating their work as components of larger, collaborative projects.

Asiimwe:

The journey of this anthology started when the world was looking a lot different from the way it does today. Who knew that there was going to be a time when being one with another in the same physical space, in community, was not only impossible but also very dangerous. The possibility of this anthology not being able to see the light of day glared at us in the face. The uncertainty and fragility that Covid-19 threw at the world left me not just physically separated from family, but also questioning the form or shape theater was going to survive. So, being able to see this anthology to fruition is truly a miracle.

First, in a very special way, I would like to thank Professor Robert H. Vorlicky (Bob), my co-editor, for pouring his heart, intellect, and dedication into this anthology. From our very first conversations about African women playwrights for his syllabus at NYU Abu Dhabi, to his several trips to Uganda, to inviting me to speak at NYUAD, along with Celma Costa (Mozambique) and Dalia Basiouny (Egypt)—during which time the first in-depth discussion between Bob and me about doing this anthology occurred—I never doubted his commitment to making sure that this anthology came to pass. I am deeply grateful for his unwavering support and devotion. Bob, from the bottom of my heart, thank you!

To my former colleagues at the Sundance Institute East Africa, Philip Himberg, Christopher Hibma, and Roberta Levitow, I'm eternally grateful for the opportunity you gave me to lead the Sundance Institute East Africa initiative through which I got to meet many East African theater-makers and theater-makers from other parts of the continent. These connections became very handy as we started reaching out to contacts for any recommendations for this anthology. The Kampala International Theatre Festival, which was born out of the Sundance Institute investment in East African artists, became a springboard from which the conversations about this anthology emerged and where the initial encounters with some contributors in this anthology happened. Without my work at the Sundance, it is possible that my knowledge and understanding of the many African women playwrights would have been limited.

Thank you to my family: my husband, Edmund Kawe, and our son, Ahumuza J. Kawe, for enduring my time away from them, long nights, and working weekends. To my siblings, especially my sister, Phoebe Nankunda Tumwine, thank you for your understanding when occasionally I'd have to leave your hospital bed to respond to an email about this book. I look forward to gifting you with a copy of this anthology!

To my colleague, Ginny Kyokusiima, thank you for stepping into my shoes and responding to any urgent emails during the time I could not be available. Your support allowed my mind to be at ease.

Lastly, I'm grateful to God for life and the amazing experience and journey it has been working on this anthology.

To everyone who stood by my side and contributed to this work, in any way: many beautiful things cannot be seen or touched but they are felt with the heart. What you've done for me is something I'm going to treasure for a very long time, and I thank you from the bottom of my heart!

Bob:

My sincere gratitude to the staff and administration of the Arts and Humanities Division, NYU Abu Dhabi, for their on-going guidance, help, and generosity during the early stages of this project. Among those most directly involved, my appreciation to Tina Galanopoulos, Theresa Dabla, Lily Moinette, Aya El Mir, and besties Abhishek Majumdar and Caitlin Newsom.

From Spring 2015–January 2023, I was teaching between NYU New York's Drama Department and NYUAD's Theater Program and Core Curriculum. During these eight years, I taught NYUAD classes focused on African Drama, African Women Playwrights, and Gender, Representation, and Global Performance. This international experience remains a highlight of my career in higher education; there were no dominant voices in the classrooms since each room was filled with difference, not sameness among pupils and instructor. Within this configuration, we remained committed to keeping the conversations going, no matter how challenging, uncomfortable, or seemingly agreeable. I'm forever grateful to the many students I've taught over a life-time career in teaching. So many of you enriched my professional and personal, intellectual and artistic lives. I have come to truly understand in my gut what it means to feel and think of the global future embodied in the younger generation. I saw it in your faces as you spoke from your hearts and minds during class and on-campus. I saw it in your eyes as you listened, intently, to others. Like the writers in this anthology—some of whose plays you read in my classrooms—you are committed to a world of equity, inclusion, and peace. The world is in good hands.

Infinite gratitude to those who have stood by my side: brother Bill, son Sasha, Esmaeil, Judy, Una, and no less endearingly, my enduringly supportive extended and immediate family—you know who you are. My love to each of you.

And to my beloved co-editor: Asiimwe, our collaboration across time zones and thousands of miles, along with our unwavering belief in this project, have been a dream come true. I can't imagine having undertaken this book with anyone else. Your elegance, creative genius, integrity, intelligence, and kindness have been ever present throughout. I have learned so very much from you, and my life has been enriched beyond words through our interaction. You are family. Thank *you* from the bottom of *my* heart! The book lives!